WILL&GRACe

Fabulously Uncensored

WiLL&

Fabulously Uncensored

GRACe

Written by JIM COLUCCI

Designed by NUMBER SEVENTEEN, NEW YORK

Produced by ROUNDTABLE PRESS, INC.

Time Inc. HOME ENTERTAINMENT

PRESIDENT: Rob Gursha

VICE PRESIDENT, NEW PRODUCT DEVELOPMENT: Richard Fraiman

EXECUTIVE DIRECTOR, MARKETING SERVICES: Carol Pittard

DIRECTOR, RETAIL & SPECIAL SALES: Tom Mifsud

DIRECTOR OF FINANCE: Tricia Griffin

PREPRESS MANAGER: Emily Rabin

BOOK PRODUCTION MANAGER: Jonathan Polsky

ASSOCIATE PRODUCT MANAGER: Victoria Alfonso

SPECIAL THANKS: Bozena Bannett, Alexandra Bliss, Bernadette Corbie, Robert Dente, Gina Di Meglio, Anne-Michelle Gallero, Suzanne Janso, Robert Marasco, Natalie McCrea, Margarita Quiogue, Mary Jane Rigoroso, Steven Sandonato, Grace Sullivan

For Roundtable Press, Inc.

DIRECTORS: Julie Merberg and Marsha Melnick

EDITOR: Michael Robin

ASSOCIATE EDITOR: Sara Newberry

PRODUCTION EDITOR: John Glenn

DESIGN: Number Seventeen, New York

ISBN: 1-932273-40-9

IF YOU WOULD LIKE TO ORDER ANY OF OUR HARDCOVER COLLECTOR'S EDITION BOOKS, PLEASE CALL US AT 1-800-327-6388.
(MONDAY THROUGH FRIDAY, 7:00 A.M.–8:00 P.M. OR SATURDAY, 7:00 A.M.–6:00 P.M. CENTRAL TIME).

CONTENTS

MAX &

DAVID

In the fall of 1997, NBC president Warren Littlefield stunned Max Mutchnick and David Kohan with a most unconventional suggestion. They'd thought they'd heard everything back in 1993 when a Hollywood executive received their adaptation of the children's book *The Cricket in Times Square* with: **"Great–but does it have to be a cricket?"**

But Littlefield's response to Max and David's idea for a new romantic comedy to replace the departing Mad About You *was even more unusual. "The show was set in San Francisco, and there were two straight couples, each of whom had a different set of problems that doomed them," David remembers. "And then there was a third, neighbor couple who seemed to get along best, with the best communication, the most honesty, and the most fun—except they weren't really a couple."*

The NBC execs noticed how Max and David came particularly alive when discussing this last pair—gay "Will," and his live-in, straight, female best friend, "Grace." And so, in a historic move for a network president, Warren Littlefield made his daring choice. "In a stroke of genius, Warren said, 'That's the series,'" Max remembers. "'The neighbors are the series. Go away and make that your show.'"

David (with bandanna) and Max (hanging ten) with the cast of Beverly Hills High School's production of *West Side Story*

WHEN DAVID MET ...
JASON?

When they met while attending Beverly Hills High School, David Kohan and Jason (a.k.a. Max, after a name change in college) Mutchnick already had a lot in common. "Show business was the family business for both of us," Max explains. David's father was a television writer who'd worked on shows like **THE CAROL BURNETT SHOW** and **THE ODD COUPLE**. Max's mother, Brenda, was a marketing executive at Paramount Pictures, where Max often roamed the back lot wonderland. "That's really where I got my education," he says. "I just sat around on the stages of shows like **LAVERNE & SHIRLEY**, **HAPPY DAYS**, and **BLANSKY'S BEAUTIES**, and thought, 'This is what I want to do with my life.'"

Beverly Hills High School is different: its theater department is a cool place to be. That's where David bonded with a girl he had known since childhood, Janet Eisenberg, and her boyfriend, Max. Max's **WILL & GRACE** office holds many photos from those days, including one of himself, Janet, and David in a high school production of **WEST SIDE STORY**. In another, senior prom dates Max and Janet pose with their friend Amy and her date, David, home on a break from his freshman year in college. "So actually, we even ended up going to a prom together," David jokes.

Jason (aka Max) and Janet Eisenberg head off to their senior prom in June, 1983

THE REAL GRACE ADLER

Many fans say they're "so Grace Adler." But Janet Eisenberg really is. "We both love clothes. Grace has big feet like me," she says, "and we would both eat food out of the garbage can. The super-competitive thing—that's me." But mostly, it's about her unique relationship with Max Mutchnick…. "The whole game-playing thing, knowing each other better than anyone else, finishing each other's sentences—that's me and Max."

Janet first met David Kohan in the third grade, when he and his twin brother, Jono, were simply the mean and horrible buddies of a friend's older brother. She met (then Jason) Mutchnick at temple in the eighth grade. "When I tell this story, we sound like such Jewish people—we're not THAT Jewish," Janet says. Nevertheless, they did several shows at their temple together—**JESUS CHRIST SUPERSTAR** among them—with Max always snagging the biggest role. "We were all drama geeks. But you always knew who he was—hilarious, extroverted, everything he is today. He was always the star," she says.

When it came time for the prom, Max couldn't afford to rent a limousine, so instead, he borrowed Janet's father's Oldsmobile Cutlass Supreme and worked some magic. "He decorated it like a Mexican float, with flowers all over it, and hired two underclassmen girls to ride on mopeds ahead of us, like a motorcade, and another girl to be our chauffeur."

The two attended separate liberal arts colleges—Janet at Berkeley, in northern California, Max at Emerson in Boston—but would always reunite on break. After college, in the late '80s, both Janet and Max moved to New York City. She found work at an advertising agency and rented a big apartment in Greenwich Village, and he worked as a messenger and lived in a fifth-floor walk-up on the Upper West Side. "We'd go out, and I'd always have to pay for him," she says. Max finally got a job at an agency doing theater advertising, which brought with it invitations to theater openings. When he moved into Janet's neighborhood, the two began living a more Will-and-Grace-like existence. "We had a lot of fun. We went to movies and went shopping and did everything that they do," Janet remembers.

Max, though, was tired of living a double life, and announced he was moving to Los Angeles. In L.A., away from his "girlfriend," he could come into his own. And the next time Janet visited him in Los Angeles, he announced to her that he was gay. "It was huge," she recalls. "Traumatic and dramatic and sad, but also a relief." But relief soon turned to anger, as she began to resent the years she spent feeling unattractive and pining for Max while he was figuring out that he liked men. And just as depicted later in **WILL & GRACE** episode "Lows in the Mid 80s," they didn't speak for more than a year.

David, who had attended Wesleyan University, remained in touch with both Janet and their mutual friend Max, and it was he who made them ultimately realize that although they may not have been a couple, they had been the best of friends. "He really pulled us together," Janet says. "There was a caucus and a treaty and a meeting, and it was all very dramatic at the time. And then we were in each other's lives again, maybe with a little more caution initially, but then right back." The real-life Will and Grace couldn't stay mad at each other for very long.

Max had his chance to be resentful, too. In the mid-1990s, Janet met her "Leo" in David Bromberg, whom she describes as "this smart, funny, sexy, quirky Jewish writer guy." When the two married in 2000, Max helped hold the chuppah for the bride and groom. "It wasn't planned, but the way we were facing, it just happened that the pole that Max was holding was right behind David, so I was looking at them both when I was saying my vows. It was so funny. I remember Max just giving me a look like, '**Can you fucking believe this?**' and I was like, '**I know!**'"

The Start of Something Big

When Max and David look back, they credit Janet Eisenberg with being the catalyst for their collaboration. In the fall of 1988, Max, at age twenty-three, began the process of coming out to the people close to him. After he told former girlfriend Janet that he was gay, the two didn't speak for over a year.

"She was the most important thing in my life, and she totally stopped talking to me," Max remembers. "Here this great friend in my life was gone, and David was still very close with her. So the only way I could hear about her was through David. It created a real connection between Dave and me." During that year, 1989 to 1990, Max and David made their first attempt to write together.

A failed attempt, as it turned out. They toiled as assistants by day—David for director Sydney Pollack, Max for **CANDID CAMERA**'s Allen Funt—and during off-hours couldn't quite click. "Dave said to me that he didn't think our sensibilities lent themselves to one another," Max remembers. Fortunately, Max refused to throw in the towel even after David took off for a solo career in New York City. At Max's insistence, David agreed to a one-month trial period in the Big Apple; if they successfully pounded out a few scripts, they'd go back to L.A. together and give it another shot.

The determined duo met every morning and wrote two "spec" scripts, sample episodes of **MURPHY BROWN** and a brand-new show called **SEINFELD**. When their month was up, they returned to Los Angeles and, like something out of Hollywood legend, landed their first writing job the day they arrived. That **DENNIS MILLER SHOW** gig led to another job, on the 1992 sitcom **HEARTS AFIRE**, created and produced by Linda Bloodworth and Harry Thomason. The show lasted until 1995, though Max and David did not.

"It was a very odd job," Max explains, "because Linda writes everything, and we were really just window dressing." After thirteen episodes, the producers decided it was curtains for Max and David. After a brief stint in New York writing for ESPN's **ESPY AWARDS**—which Max remembers as "a comedy in itself" as he struggled to hide the fact that he, like his future creation Will Truman, knows nothing about sports—the team moved on.

While working on the Shelley Long sitcom **GOOD ADVICE** in 1993, Max and David unknowingly met some future members of the **WILL & GRACE** team. Their bosses on the short-lived show were executive producers Michael Patrick King (who would later work on the first season of **WILL & GRACE** and go on to write and executive produce **SEX AND THE CITY**); and Tom Palmer (whose wife, Katie, would become a **WILL & GRACE** writer).

Prior to getting fired by Michael Patrick King, Max and David learned a lesson about themselves. "It's funny," Max notes, "because I'm the louder one, and David's more soft-spoken and more of a gentleman. But it turns out he's unable to be in a writing room unless he's running it. He cannot speak unless he's the king." And so, Max and David decided to create their own show. "And that's when our career really went into the toilet," says Max.

"I actually still have a Grey Poupon jar on my desk at home," Max says. "We used to fill it with quarters, and there would always be enough money in there to get us a head of lettuce, rice, ranch dressing, and refried beans and tortillas. All of our money had run out, and we had no job prospects. But we would still get together every day like we had a little career."

Two breaks helped Max and David fill the mustard jar. First, Max's college friend, comic Anthony Clark, suggested that they write a series for him. Then they met agent Scott Schwartz, whom David calls "the knight in shining armor in our story."

Scott signed Max and David as clients, and soon got them jobs on both HBO's long-running comedy series **DREAM ON** (where they met future **WILL & GRACE** writers Rob Lotterstein and Ellen Idelson and casting director Tracy Lilienfield) and NBC's 1995 Thursday sitcom, **THE SINGLE GUY**. "We finally felt like maybe we belong," David remembers. And then something incredible happened for the two still-unproven writers: Scott Schwartz sold the Anthony Clark series. On March 21, 1996, Kohan and Mutchnick's first original series, **BOSTON COMMON**, premiered on NBC.

They'll Always Have Boston

At twenty-eight and thirty respectively, Max and David were among the youngest writers ever to create and run their own network sitcom. "I remember getting the list of things we had to do," remembers Max, "and I didn't even know what some of the things were." For crew, they often turned to friends, hiring, for example, Max's college acquaintance Lori Eskowitz-Carter—who now works on **WILL & GRACE**—to put together the show's wardrobe. It was also during the **BOSTON COMMON** days that they hired some future core members of the **WILL & GRACE** team, such as producers Tim Kaiser and Steve Sandoval.

BOSTON COMMON lasted only a season and a half, but in that short time, Max and David gained that all-important experience of running a prime-time sitcom, and jumped to the next level in the eyes of the industry, breaking into the elite group of writers with an "overall development deal" to create their own shows.

The Birth of Will & Grace

"We went into development at NBC," David Kohan remembers, "which basically means you waltz into the office at the crack of eleven-thirty, talk about what you did the night before, then it's time for deciding what to get for lunch, then it's time for ordering lunch, then it's time for picking up lunch, then it's time for eating lunch, then it's time for a nap. Then it's late already, and time to go home."

Despite that busy schedule, Max and David found time to brainstorm their idea for a replacement for **MAD ABOUT YOU**. In discussing the dos and don'ts of romantic comedy, David says he remembered Sydney Pollack's words: "'The love story is over once the boy and girl kiss. The love story is really about the obstacles toward consummating love.' So Max and I talked about coming up with a romantic comedy with an insurmountable obstacle. And for that third couple 'Will' and 'Grace,' we found it right away."

After Warren Littlefield's pronouncement to focus on the gay-straight neighbor couple, David talked his partner into getting personal. At first, Max was reluctant to depict his private relationship with Janet on-screen, partly because doing so would make him a poster boy. "I wasn't as loud and proud at that point in my life," he explains, "and I didn't want to be associated with the whole gay culture." But David encouraged him to be bold. "David was much more comfortable with it," Max says. "And one of the reasons I'm so comfortable and at ease in my sexuality and where I am in my life is because of David Kohan. Every gay man needs a straight man in his life to remind him what he can do." So the duo turned their idea into a first draft—and then immediately realized something was wrong.

"We found that Will had a bitchy tone because we were trying to cram every kind of gay man into one person," Max explains. "He was everything—campy, serious, flamboyant, and conservative," David adds. "We realized we had to break up this two-headed character. So Jack was born of Will's rib."

As they sculpted Will and Grace's world, its creators continued to pull in details from their own lives. "From our friends' little catchphrases to my relationship with Janet at the center of the show, we truly relied on our life experience," Max says. Finally, they handed their creation in to NBC.

Where There's a Will, There's a Way

Hollywood is a small town, and for a while, Max and David's much-discussed new script had a lot of "heat" on it, but before long, the heat started to cool. "The network seemed to be very pleased," Max remembers, noting that one executive in particular, David Nevins, became **WILL & GRACE**'s earliest champion. "But then its profile seemed to be dropping. I think they were scared of it."

Luckily, during an L.A. visit, Bob Wright, the chairman of NBC's parent company, General Electric, asked David Nevins for his three favorite scripts, and **WILL & GRACE** was one of them. Won over, Bob Wright insisted that Max and David's pilot take the next step.

NBC executive Don Ohlmeyer offered the duo a "cast-contingent deal"—meaning that the show would go on only if the creators could cast the two lead roles to the network's satisfaction. The network gave Max and David $25,000, promising, as David remembers, "If you find a Will, then maybe we'll take this a step further." And so, the race to find the actor to play network television's first gay leading man was on.

The Reading of the Will

"**WILL & GRACE** was a hot script around town, and actors wanted to read for it because the characters were so well-drawn," remembers casting director Tracy Lilienfield. She already had a Will in mind. "I knew I wanted Eric McCormack to come in," she recalls. "He is everything I saw in Will—elegant and smart, plus he's brilliantly talented, funny, and handsome." Happily, after Eric's first audition, Max and David agreed.

With everyone convinced they had found their Will, Tracy offered a "test option"—a standard industry contract in which in exchange for getting to audition for the network bigwigs, an actor guarantees a seven-year commitment. But, unwilling to sign away such a huge chunk of his life, Eric said no.

"I understood that Eric was probably also concerned about what right did he have to play a gay character, and would he be stereotyped that way forever, but still, I was pissed," David remembers.

"When I heard Eric was passing, I called his manager and begged and pleaded," recalls Tracy. But eventually, with their "cast-contingency" looming, the **WILL & GRACE** team was forced to move on. All told, the producers considered over 200 leading men, including Will's future friend Rob, Tom Gallop. "There were some we thought we could live with," Tracy says, "but the network said no."

Time was running out. "I had to keep Max and David from saying, 'It has to be Eric McCormack,' because as clearly as we could understand it, it was not going to be Eric McCormack," Tracy says. "We had tried to move on, but were stuck. And just then, I got a call from Eric's manager saying that he might be interested again, and we quickly zoomed him right back into the part."

Eric left his audition for the NBC honchos convinced that it had gone badly. "I went home that night and told my wife that it wasn't going to happen—and then I got the call from Max and David saying, 'How would you like to be our Will?'"

"When we got Eric on board," Max says, "I remember Don Ohlmeyer telling me that he reminded him of my boyfriend, Paul. And I thought that was a good sign." Max was especially impressed with Eric's portrayal of a gay man. "He did it in a way that no one had ever played it before—with a certain level of integrity, and with nothing stereotypical about it, yet it was evident that this was a gay man. It just speaks to his pitch-perfect acting."

Enter the 800-pound Gorilla

Once Eric was in place, Ohlmeyer, still unsure about **WILL & GRACE**, sought the advice of the preeminent sitcom guru, James "Jimmy" Burrows. The son of **GUYS AND DOLLS** playwright and director Abe, Jimmy had amassed the industry's most impressive sitcom resume, from working on **THE MARY TYLER MOORE SHOW** to directing **TAXI** and **CHEERS**. Having directed the nascent moments of **FRIENDS** and **FRASIER** among many others, Jimmy had long been known as the go-to guy for pilots with promise. Now he was about to pass judgment on **WILL & GRACE**.

Max and David braced for the worst. "I felt that it was something that only the two of us could write," says Max. "We didn't want someone else coming in and fucking it up." And so, in a car en route to a meeting with Burrows at a Beverly Hills café, the two writers girded themselves to refuse the guru's help.

"We agreed we were going to be tough with this guy," David remembers. "We were going to say, 'We know you're the great Jimmy Burrows, and thanks, but no thanks.' So we sat down with Jimmy, and there he was, reading through the last two pages. He looked up and said, 'Yeah, I like this script. I think I want to do it.' And Max and I quickly said, 'Okay!'"

"And then the great thing about the story," Max adds, "is that Jimmy then got up and left us with the check."

"It was all about it being a really good pilot script," Jimmy explains. "It's a story with heart. Even though you know they can't, you want Will and Grace to get together."

"The thing about me," Burrows adds, "is that I'm an 800-pound gorilla. I will die protecting writers, and I'm willing to go to the network and tell them to take their hands off." Now, with the 800-pound gorilla by their side, Max and David began the search for Will's three friends.

Jimmy Burrows plants one on Matt Damon (inset) and on set.

Elusive Grace

With a "cast-contingency" still looming for Grace, the producers cast a wide net for their leading lady. Thirty-eight actresses auditioned for Max and David in L.A.—including Leigh-Allyn Baker and Megan Mullally—and another thirty-six in New York; 105 more read just for Tracy or her New York associates. No one seemed right.

The team brought several actresses to NBC for approval, but the network turned them all down. However, NBC did let Tracy know that there was one actress they were interested in, even though she was still committed to an ABC series, **PREY**. But when rumors flew that **PREY** was about to meet its maker, Tracy arranged a meeting with Debra Messing.

The very choosy Max and David immediately loved Debra, but the actress was both loyal to **PREY**, which she hoped would survive, and tired from that show's exhausting schedule. To convince her to audition for the role of Grace, the show's creators resorted to a creative tactic: they showed up at her house with a bottle of vodka, and talked all night.

The vodka did its job. "And this led to what is now the legendary audition for Grace Adler," Max says. The first-choice candidate for Grace was scheduled to meet Tracy and the producers at Burrows' expansive Bel Air abode to read opposite Eric McCormack. The problem: There were three different first-choice candidates. And each didn't know that any others existed. "We promised three women that they could get a shot at reading with Eric alone," Max says. "Well, we did do that. Except we did it three times, back to back."

Candidate number one was Nicollette Sheridan. "She was very sweet, and almost too sexy," Eric says. Candidate number two, a Texan from a hair-care commercial, felt wrong, too: "I didn't feel I could spend seven to nine years of my life with her." And then came Debra. "We had immediate chemistry," Eric remembers. "She was also the first of all the actresses I read with who laughed in the scene as Grace. And it made me think, 'Oh right, they're friends. Grace finds Will funny.' Nobody else had done that before. They were so busy playing the sardonic comedy of it, they forgot to have a good time."

For Max and David, seeing Debra in action was a particular relief. They had courted her sight unseen; now they knew she was actually right for the part. "Everybody in the room flipped out," Max remembers, "because it was clear—there they were." The arrangements were made, the papers were signed, and Max and David got the word. "I got the call that Debra had said yes," Max says, "and I remember thinking, 'Oh my God, this is going to work.'"

Just Sean Hayes

Tracy knew that she had a Jack in her back pocket. She had met with Sean Hayes a few times and found him "adorable," but "a tough cast." When she read the **WILL& GRACE** script, she knew she finally had the right fit. "I knew 100 percent that Sean was Jack," she says. Unfortunately, thanks to a network executive's miscommunication, Sean was 100 percent sure he was...Will Truman. It took all of Tracy's persuasive powers to convince him that he was meant to be Jack. After his audition, Max and David—who had seen several other actors, including Alexis Arquette—were convinced, too.

"We had people coming in here who were so way out campy," says David. But Sean brought to the potentially bawdy role a special dignity...and more. "He is in his way a total naïf," David says. "I think that sweetness he has is what's appealing about him." Tracy also notes that Sean's immense likability allayed some of their fears about how America would take to such a flamboyant gay character. "Sean just lights up a room in a way that it was obvious Jack needed to."

The producers so enjoyed Sean's audition that they asked for an encore. "I'm sure that he knew he had just blown us away," Max remembers, "because as he was leaving the room, he turned around and said, '**Stop looking at my ass, Mutchnick!**' and then closed the door. That was a pretty nervy thing for an actor to say." Of course, it was an actor who knew he had just won the role of a lifetime.

Capturing Karen

As they proceeded, the **WILL & GRACE** team realized that they had inadvertently saved their hardest-to-cast role for last. When it came to finding Karen Walker, Tracy had no idea where to start.

The script called for a "stereotypical socialite," Tracy says. And so, they auditioned the obvious: "lots of tall, thin, blond, elegant, WASPy, New York types." In casting, Max, David, and Tracy usually try not to envision a particular physical type, preferring to be "turned on by an actor's voice," as Tracy describes it. But no voices were turning them on. And then they realized: it must be the writing. "It was the least well-conceived role," Tracy admits, "and that started to be clear to us when we couldn't find the right person."

With the role reconceived, Tracy thought of Megan Mullally, whom she had known from her **DREAM ON** days. Megan came in, and Max and David liked her for the part. The only person unconvinced was Megan. Says Tracy, "Megan is pretty well known for being picky." Tracy knew that Megan's true passion lay in theater, "where she was happy to work in hole-in-the-wall theaters that nobody went to." But despite her doubts about Megan's enthusiasm, Tracy called her back in to read for Jimmy Burrows.

Whenever Tracy asked Jimmy Burrows whom he wanted if he couldn't have Megan Mullally, Jimmy always answered, "Megan Mullally." To him, there was no other choice. Still, Megan resisted. So Tracy raised the stakes, setting up a test-option deal for Megan…and no one else. "I almost never have only one person to test," Tracy explains. "The network frowns on it because if they don't like the person, then you're left with nothing." Nevertheless, Megan refused to commit.

The day of the test arrived, with no one sure that the reluctant Megan would even show up. When, after a coaxing phone call from Tracy, she did, she impressed everyone so much that they promised her the role before she even got back in her car. "I walked out of the room right afterward and called her," Tracy says. "I asked, 'Did I ruin your life?' And Megan answered, 'I hope not.'"

"I don't think for a while Megan was ready to believe that she was a character actress instead of a leading lady," Max says. "But the best move she's ever made in her life was accepting this part. It's that rare, rare case where those two things collide: the perfect part with the perfect actor. Thank God we got her to come in and read." Because now, finally, **WILL & GRACE** had all four of its stars.

And Now Just a Few Minor Adjustments…

During the week before the pilot filming in March of 1998, **WILL & GRACE** continually evolved. Max and David found themselves having problems with the scene in which Grace, having left her fiancé, comes to Will's office in her wedding dress. Grace couldn't find the right words to say…and neither could the writers. So they asked Eric and Debra to do an improvisational exercise during which they said what they thought their characters felt. "I realized that night that we were in for a real treat," Max says. "We were with actors on a sitcom who could inform us as to what was the best way to write this scene. You never really get that opportunity."

The actors, too, spent the week fine-tuning their performances. Sean Hayes remembers suggesting a gasp after Will accuses Jack of being just like his mother. "Max sarcastically said, 'Yeah, something nice and small like that.'" But Sean did it anyway, and it got a laugh. "Then, through the rest of the week, I made it bigger and bigger, because that's where I saw the laughs coming from," he remembers. "So that's how I think the character became so over the top. And after all, as someone once said, nobody ever paid to see somebody 'under the top.'"

"It was a home run," Jimmy Burrows recalls of the test showw. "They screamed when Jack came in, they *oohed* when Grace told Will to go to hell. They loved and were invested in the story. You don't have to be smart to know that it was lightning in a bottle."

As is his custom, Jimmy videotaped the test show that night, creating a "lost," alternate pilot, never to be aired. In that pilot were several other characters—including a series regular (Will's straight law partner, Andy Felner, played by Cress Williams)—who, after that fateful night, were never to be seen again. After seeing the strength of their foursome in action, the producers knew that Andy and company were unnecessary.

Lights, Cameras, and Fabulous Action

As their big night arrived, Max and David resolved to apply the hard lessons learned from **BOSTON COMMON**. For example, they agreed to reach out more to others. "We don't need to feel like we're the only people participating in the process," Max says. "We're not. And the show is as fantastic as it is because of everybody who is involved in it."

What happened after the show set the tone for Max and David's future relationship with the network. "The pilot had gone really well, and some network people started to make things up and find things that weren't broken," Max remembers. That's when the 800-pound gorilla stepped in. "[Jimmy] said, 'We're done. You don't get to talk to these guys anymore.' Jimmy's role as our protector started that night, and there was never an issue again with the network from that moment on."

After the shoot, the **WILL & GRACE** crew and NBC execs partied. Even though the pilot's fate was still uncertain, Tracy Lilienfield remembers the evening's celebratory tone. "All week long, people had kept saying to each other, 'Is this show as good as I think it is?' Now, Warren Littlefield came very close to telling us that the show would be on the air."

Eric McCormack also recalls the network president's enthusiasm. The year before, Eric had been cut from a lead role on the network's **THE JENNY McCARTHY SHOW** before its first episode aired. "Then, after we shot the **WILL & GRACE** pilot," he says, "Warren came up to me on the stage, beaming with pride, and said, 'Now aren't you glad I fired you?'"

The Road to the Peacock

Word quickly spread that **WILL & GRACE** was a hot new fall prospect. Max says that he knew it was a good sign when a "fifteenth generation" videotape of the show circulated its way back to his own office. "Anybody who read the pilot knew that it was going to go," remembers series executive producer Tim Kaiser. "One look at these characters and you could see in them the potential to grow." And the show had that certain something that might have scared off rather than attracted a network in earlier days: "It was very timely for the network to have 'a gay show,'" Tim says.

Although the Gay and Lesbian Alliance Against Defamation (GLAAD) boosted the show's status with its blessing, NBC underplayed the gay angle. During a May showcase for advertisers in Radio City Music Hall, the network's **WILL & GRACE** presentation conveniently forgot to include that one little fact. "Will and Grace," the voice-over said, "not a couple. A couple of friends."

Other than at a critics' convention held the July before the show aired, Max points out, no one had taken issue with the show before, and no one has since. "That really spoke to the fact that we weren't trailblazing, but just riding the wave," he notes. "From the start, **WILL & GRACE** had all the same advertisers as every other show on NBC. The network had no issue with the show, and neither did Madison Avenue."

It was with this faith in the network's support for the show that Max was able to answer the most difficult of the critics' questions that day in July: How real, and how honest, would the depictions of Will and Jack be? "I said as a gay man, if I'm comfortable with it, that's all that matters," Max says. "And that was the philosophy that we owned from that point on. We had a confidence about what we were writing because it was our truth. And because it was truth, we ended up writing something that people really liked."

SEASON

ONE

AT FIRST, THE NEWEST DEBUT INTO NBC'S FALL '98 MONDAY NIGHT COMEDY LINEUP SEEMED TO BE JUST ANOTHER SHOW ABOUT ATTRACTIVE YOUNG URBAN SINGLES, PERFECTLY SLOTTED AT 9:30 TO FOLLOW *CAROLINE IN THE CITY* (ALSO PRODUCED BY JIMMY BURROWS'S COMPANY, THREE SISTERS).

"I had told the network," Jimmy remembers, "please do not put us on Thursday. Put us somewhere where the ratings number we need to get is a shoe size rather than an IQ." The strategy worked; Will & Grace's share began to climb. NBC executives quickly moved the potential hit to its troubled Tuesday lineup, following Just Shoot Me *at 9:30. The show continued to pick up ratings, and in April 1999, got its first shot at the sitcom Holy Grail: a few temporary tryouts in the flagship Thursday lineup.*

Wooing America

While the network worked to pick up viewers, the show concentrated more specifically on picking up fans, by being careful not to alienate first-time visitors to Will and Grace's gay Manhattan world. "It was our goal to lead America to believe that Will would recant this 'terrible disease' of being gay and marry Grace," Jimmy explains. "There was a kiss in the pilot and a parallel kiss in the last episode of the season, and that was deliberate. In television, it takes a long time for the word to get out, for people to tell other people, 'You should watch this show.' And a lot of people wouldn't watch **WILL & GRACE** because it has gay characters. But if we could get them involved in the humanity of these people, they would see how funny it was. And it worked."

While series creators Max Mutchnick and David Kohan agree that they were particularly careful in the show's early days in handling sensitive issues, they were not trying to suggest a consummate-able romantic relationship between their leading man and lady. "The kisses were kind of a tease, but we didn't want to be dishonest," David admits. "We did recognize that Will and Grace getting together might be a rooting interest for the audience, but we never wanted to give the impression that this is something that could or would happen."

"We were taking baby steps," Max says. "This was a sensitive area in the wake of Ellen, and we wanted the audience to fall in love with the characters, so we didn't want to do anything too aggressive or offensive. We used the same compass that helped me navigate my way through my own coming out to my family: I always made sure my family wasn't uncomfortable, and we thought of the American public in the same way."

Where am I? What am I doing?

As Max explains, the story lines for early episodes were drawn solely from the writers' own experiences. "That was the way that we knew what we were writing. We were always up against the problem that Will's sexuality itself was considered provocative, and we never wanted to be in the position of teaching anybody about anything. We knew we'd get to stay on the air a lot longer by just being funny and telling stories that were personal and therefore fresh and original."

David remembers that it was hard to find the right balance for the show—particularly in its first six episodes, which had to be completely rewritten when director Burrows didn't think their plots were clear enough. "We didn't necessarily know what we had," David says. "The pilot had a real premise to it, but now what? Initially the show was conceived as a romantic comedy with an insurmountable obstacle for the lovers, but how do you show that exactly? We had built differences into their characters—neat versus messy, WASPy versus Jewish—but what are the issues that are going to create conflict, and was there enough stuff there to create whole stories?"

"It's been said that in the first season of a show, your job is to write the pilot twenty-four times," Max explains, "and that's what we did. We found the 'money scene,' and so we knew every week that Will and Grace would have a fight at the act break, and make up at the end."

"We were also learning a voice," he explains. "You discover things along the way, like the funny way Megan says, 'Where am I? What am I doing? What's going on?' When we hit on a rhythm or pattern or sound that worked for these four characters, we went back to it over and over again."

"It's not like we said to ourselves in the beginning that Karen and Jack are going to branch off and become a burlesque, fun-house mirror of Will and Grace," David adds. "But when they met for the first time in the second episode, we realized the natural chemistry they have and the comic potential of their scenes together. From that moment on, we knew that another couple had been born."

When Max Mutchnick needs a logo for one of his new sitcoms, he knows he can keep it all in the family. His brother Josh, a graphic designer, has created that all-important first impression—the logo—for all of Kohan and Mutchnick's series, from **BOSTON COMMON** to **GOOD MORNING, MIAMI.**

The opening credits for **WILL & GRACE** were designed by Bonnie Siegler and Emily Oberman of the New York design firm Number Seventeen. They animated Josh's logo, overlapping Will and Grace's names to represent how intertwined the main characters' lives are.

At the start of Season Four, when the producers wanted to add images from the show they went back to Number Seventeen, and these are the opening credits viewers still see today.

(101) THE PILOT

Written By:
DAVID KOHAN & MAX MUTCHNICK

> **WILL:**
> *"Wow, let's have a look at that ring. Oh, it's beautiful. When is the stone being put in?"*

[Wh]en Grace accepts an unexpected marriage proposal from her [best] friend, Danny, Will risks their friendship by telling her she's [ma]king a mistake. Grace tells Will off and goes ahead with her [plan]s, but later ditches Danny at the altar. Although at first Grace [accu]ses Will of wanting her to be lonely just like he is, she later [apo]logizes and takes comfort in his promise that she'll someday [find] her perfect match.

RECURRING CHARACTERS *(first appearance of)*
Tom Gallop *as* Rob
Leigh-Allyn Baker *as* Ellen
Ellen Idelson *as* Will's Secretary, Ellen *(voice-over)*
Gary Grubbs *as* Harlin Polk
Todd Eckert *as* Jurgen Franzblau

> **WILL:**
> *[...] ck, blind and [dea]f people know [that] you're gay. [Dea]d people know [that] you're gay."*

[SE]AN HAYES: During the shooting of the pilot, I didn't tell anybody, but [I wa]s really flu-y and achy because I was so tripped out that I was on a TV [sho]w. It was nerves beyond the universe.

[The]re was a big, long break in the filming, and Jimmy Burrows said, "Sean, [plea]se sing a song or something." Back then, I was like, "WOOHOO! I'll [do a]nything!" I had a friend who was visiting from Chicago and she plays [guit]ar, and so she played and I sang this song we had written about some [old s]hows we remembered....

[Her]e's [some of] the song:

> *Kimberly held up a store, and Arnold didn't grow no more,*
> *and it takes diff'rent strokes to move the world.*

> *The black boys didn't give a damn and that's when they added Sam*
> *and it takes diff'rent strokes to move the world.*

[ERI]C McCORMACK: There was a moment when we had just finished [shoo]ting the pilot, where the audience was letting out, and Debra and I were [sittin]g on Will's couch looking at each other. I said, "Are you thinking what [I'm t]hinking?" and she said, "Yeah—we're going to be doing this for a very [long] time."

[FYI]: Will's off-screen secretary, Ellen, is played by series writer [Elle]n Idelson, for whom Ellen of Rob and Ellen is also named.

---

(102) A NEW LEASE ON LIFE

Written By:
DAVID KOHAN & MAX MUTCHNICK

Will convinces Grace to find an apartment of her own. When she falls for one in far-off Brooklyn, however, Will changes his tune and asks her to move in with him. This has the happy side effect of displacing Will's current roommate, Jack, and his pet parrot, Guapo. Jack meets Karen, and the two hit it off famously.

RECURRING CHARACTERS
Gary Grubbs *as* Harlin Polk
Ellen Idelson *as* Will's Secretary, Ellen *(voice-over)*

SEAN HAYES: I remember Megan and I both just laughed uproariously when we were told that we were going to bump bellies. I think the idea came about because one of Max Mutchnick's friends always did that.

ERIC McCORMACK: One of the great moments for me was after we shot this first regular episode, we were taking our bows and the assistant director walked over and handed us tomorrow's script. It was a great feeling to realize that the job isn't over, and there's always going to be another one to do. And not just a feeling that, great, I can pay my bills, but that this character is going to live and evolve.

> **GRACE:**
> *"What just happened? We were having fun, playing Regis, and suddenly, I'm supposed to grow up, get my own place, and pay bills? I hate you."*

MEGAN MULLALLY: Sean and I had really hit it off right away. By the time we got to the first episode, we were really primed for our first scene together. Karen is the woman Jack has always wanted to be, and from their first scene together, they have quite a mutual infatuation—they're almost like boyfriend and girlfriend in a weird way. I instinctively wanted to play up how this gay guy and straight woman are totally flirting. I had an idea, and told Jimmy I wanted to get up on the chair and stick my ass in his face as I got something out of my purse. I was thinking, "What's the furthest you would ever go when you meet someone and flirt with them?"—and that's pretty far. I just had the instinct that if Karen was going to flirt, she'd go all the way.

> **WILL:**
> *"Oh, you are so Markie Post in every single Lifetime movie."*

FYI: When Will turns on the TV, Conan O'Brien's guests include twelve-year-old pin bowler Jhoni Marchinko, named for the series' writer and eventual executive producer.

(103) HEAD CASE

Written By:
DAVID KOHAN & MAX MUTCHNICK

Grace wants a bigger bathroom, so she suggests tearing down the wall between hers and Will's; the redesigned bathroom will be large, but it will have to be shared. The new roommates have to confront their bad habits so that their relationship will not go the way of so many past failures. Until they finally smooth things over, Will and Grace take out their aggravation on Karen and Jack.

RECURRING CHARACTER
Gary Grubbs *as* Harlin Polk

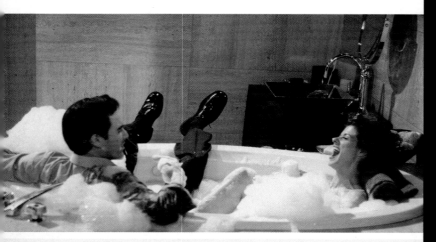

DAVID KOHAN: Jimmy Burrows was very strict about our stories in the beginning. He had come from a certain way of telling stories, and even though this one seemed straightforward to Max and me, Jimmy couldn't wrap his head around it. In these beginning episodes, we were still learning how to work together, and we ended up with a lot more give and take as time went on.

FYI: Jack's line to Will's unseen secretary, Ellen ("You're my new best friend—call me every five minutes") was also used in another *Will & Grace* episode ("Lows in the Mid 80s," again by Jack) and was also uttered by Anthony Clark's character Boyd in Kohan and Mutchnick's previous series, *Boston Common*. It's a personal favorite catchphrase for David Kohan.

> **KAREN:**
> *"Are you insane? You can't share a bathroom with the person you're living with. Honey, do you know where Stan's bathroom is? God, I don't even know where Stan's bathroom is."*

(104) WHERE THERE'S A WILL, THERE'S NO WAY

Written By: JHONI MARCHINKO

Grace blames Will for her lack of interest in dating, figuring tha since she's having so much fun with Will, there's no need for fun with anybody else. Having declared a moratorium on fun with V Grace goes out on a date and realizes that Will isn't the source o her problem. Will, of course, makes her earn her way back into his good graces. Meanwhile, Jack, who has never paid income taxes in his life, learns what a true friend Will is when the I.R.S comes calling.

GUEST STAR
Julian McMahon *(FX's Nip/Tuck) as* Man in Elevator

RECURRING CHARACTERS
Steve Paymer *as* Steve *(first appearance)*
Todd Eckert *as* Jurgen Franzblau

> **WILL:**
> *"Do you have ANY idea how the government works?*
> **JACK:**
> *"No, but I get a littl funny in the tumm around the Washing Monument."*

SEAN HAYES: The first time that sticks out in my head that I improvised anything physical with my character was when I was in Will's office in this episode, and the line is "I'm bored—can we talk about something else?" a did a headstand on a chair. And that came out of, "Well, if I'm bored, I sho probably be doing something. So I'm going to do calisthenics."

> **GRACE:**
> *"1099—Bo Derek, Barbara Feldon."*
> **JACK:**
> *"See? Why can't the government do that?"*

DAVID KOHAN: Both in the pilot and in this episode, we had the same character playing poker with Will and Jack. He's never even mentioned by name, so we figured, why not give him an idiotic name? So we chose "Jur Franzblau." The actor, Todd Eckert, was a cousin of our secretary.

FYI: This episode marks the first time we see Will kiss any man he gives Jack a peck on the cheek when he tells him he'll pay Ja $2,000 tax bill.

105 WILL ON ICE
Written By:
MICHAEL PATRICK KING

106 WILLIAM, TELL
Written By:
WILLIAM LUCAS WALKER

l's birthday wish is for a quiet dinner with his two best friends, when Grace and Jack discover that they both like figure ting, Will's birthday celebration turns into a surprise trip to ampions on Ice" at Madison Square Garden. Feeling excluded his own birthday, Will storms out. Grace later tells Will that he o longer a little boy who has to put the needs of others before own; he is a grown man and a friend who is entitled to speak for himself.

GUEST STAR
Rudy Galindo *as* Himself

)NI MARCHINKO: Karen was much different in the pilot, and I remem- the moment when she started to develop her persona. It was in this ;ode, when Karen says, "Honey, what's this?" as she critiques Grace's t while dialing to get a reservation at Balthazar. And then we kind of went, , that's who she is!" She's going to have an amazing power over this nan, she's a fashion guru, a fabulous New York society woman, a drunk, all that. She really wasn't any of those things in the pilot.

1: Rudy Galindo was the first star to make a cameo appearance himself on the show.

WILL:
"I just found a gray chest hair. So depressing. I went to bed young, and I woke up Ari Onassis."

KAREN:
"The nastiness comes so easily to your people."

Grace and Jack swap "Will secrets" after Grace hires Jack to fill in for the vacationing Karen. Grace learns that Will once slept with "a client," and becomes convinced that Will is keeping a deep dark secret. Her suspicions deepen when Will slips away for a discreet meeting with "a client"—who turns out to be Karen. When Grace confronts them, she learns that Karen is secretly considering divorcing her husband. Grace tells Will that it changed her whole life when he told her he was gay, and ever since, she has felt that any secret he keeps from her must be just as life-changing.

DAVID KOHAN: One of the things about Will and Grace is that they have inappropriate boundaries. Each tells the other everything, and if one doesn't, it means something. The thing that we wanted to do initially in this episode was to have Grace worry about something more specific from the start— namely, that Will might be hiding that he was HIV positive. Since the last time Will kept something from her it ended up being a big deal—his coming out—we thought her mind would logically take her somewhere like that now. We shied away from it because we didn't want to make the episode too heavy. The basic comic conceit of the episode is that it's a parallel to a couple where one suspects the other is having an affair, the joke being that here, it wouldn't matter since they're not a romantic couple.

FYI: This episode starts to relay some of Will and Grace's backstory by revealing how Will came out to her: in college, over Christmas break. The show's writers were inspired by this reference when they later showed this moment in the third-season episode "Lows in the Mid 80s"—but in that episode, Will comes out to Grace at Thanksgiving, not Christmas.

107 BOO! HUMBUG!

Written By:
JON KINNALLY & TRACY POUST

On Halloween, Jack and Karen, dressed as Body and Soul (Karen's a sexy catwoman; Jack's *Starsky & Hutch*'s David Soul), can't convince Will and Grace to abandon their low-key, grown-up evening on the sofa for a trip to the Greenwich Village parade. No sooner have Jack and Karen departed than Harlin drops off his two kids for Will and Grace to baby-sit. All goes well downtown, where Karen is the apple of every drag queen's eye and Jack's Hutch finds himself a Starsky. Unexpectedly, all goes well uptown, too, as Will and Grace reconnect with the spirit of Halloween fun while trick-or-treating with Harlin's kids.

RECURRING CHARACTERS
Gary Grubbs *as* Harlin Polk
Steve Paymer *as* Steve

> **WILL:**
> *"And remember, wear reflective tape, get lots of candy, and don't put anything in your mouth that isn't wrapped."*

DAVID KOHAN: We came up with this concept because in the first season, we looked for comedy by casting Will and Grace in roles that would be new to them—often lovers, but here, as parents. We also loved the idea that a West Texas oil man like Harlin—he could even be George Bush's friend—has no qualms about leaving his kids on Halloween night with Will, his gay lawyer. At the time, in 1998, we felt like we were making a small statement.

FYI: At the Halloween parade, the drag queens reveal to Jack and Karen the secret for finding your drag name—the name of your first pet, and the first street you lived on. Karen's is Shu-Shu Fontana, and Jack's was Glen 125th.

108 THE TRUTH ABOUT WILL AND DOGS

Written By: **DAVID KOHAN & MAX MUTCHNICK**

> **WILL:**
> *"Is that him?"*
> **GRACE:**
> *"No, it's veteran character actor Charles Durning."*

Will doesn't want a puppy, but when Grace brings one home despite his objections, he's soon as smitten as she with the new arrival. Taking care of the puppy forces big changes in their live When Jack and Karen puppy-sit to allow Will and Grace a night to themselves, Will discovers that he is too worried about the puppy to enjoy a movie. Grace tells him that he is putting all of his love into the puppy when he really should start dating again Will agrees, and they both conclude that they aren't ready for th responsibilities of puppy ownership. Luckily, Jack has fallen for the adorable pooch, and happily gives him a home.

RECURRING CHARACTERS
Tom Gallop *as* Rob
Leigh-Allyn Baker *as* Ellen
Gary Grubbs *as* Harlin Polk
Klaus Von Puppy *(first appearance)*

LEIGH-ALLYN BAKER: On the day that this episode filmed, my shower door broke and severed two of the tendons in my foot. I knew if I went to t hospital, I wouldn't be able to shoot the show. I had a friend drive me to th show with my foot literally taped together. I told them that I wouldn't be ab to walk out of the scene, and everybody was really nice about it—they just ended the scene with me standing up with my weight on one leg, looking like I'm ready to go.

> **KAREN:**
> *"It was either this or my neighborhood watch meeting. And if I have to hear Marlo Thomas one more time: "Phil recycles this. Phil recycles that…"*

FYI: The guy who sits next to Will at the movies says, "Hey, we m at Jon Kinnally's party," referring to one of the series' writers.

109 GRACE REPLACED

Written By:
KATIE PALMER

...ace has become very busy at work and has no time to hang out ...th Will. So when Will hits it off with new neighbor Val and starts ...ng all the things with her that he used to do with Grace, jeal-...sy rears its red head. When Grace learns that Val is nursing Will ...ough an illness, it's time for a prime-time network catfight, the ...peal of which is sadly lost on Will. After the hair-yanking and ...thes-tearing subsides, Grace finally realizes that Will doesn't ...nk anyone could ever replace her, and that it's good for him to ...ve a new friend. Meanwhile, when Jack is sentenced to commu-...y service for slapping a meter maid, he doesn't know which is ...rse: picking up trash, or the uniform he has to wear in which ...do it.

KAREN:
"Gosh, I don't think I've ever been stressed out. I mean, why would I be? I got practically no responsibilities, my job's a breeze, and I got a killer rack!"

RECURRING CHARACTERS
Tom Gallop *as* Rob
Leigh-Allyn Baker *as* Ellen
Molly Shannon *as* Val Bassett *(first appearance)*

WILL:
"Ahh, yes. The homosexual is he leading exponent of the underpant hybrid."

...VID KOHAN: The story of Will befriending someone who makes Grace ...lous would, you would think, lend itself to casting someone just like Grace, ...maybe even a better version. But we thought, what happens instead if the ...oman is just someone who happens to be there in the building, and is nuts? ...at way, we can play the jealousy stuff, but after that's done, we have the ...medy from Val being crazy. We always loved Molly Shannon—we would ...me back in to work after seeing her on *SNL* and recount how funny she ...s. We wanted to use her because she's so talented and funny, often while ...ting crazy.

 ## 110 SECRETS AND LAYS

Written By:
DAVA SAVEL

The gang drags Will to Karen's cabin in Vermont to take his mind off of what would have been his upcoming anniversary with Michael. Once there, Grace struggles to keep a rekindled high school romance out of Will's sight so that he won't feel even more alone. Jack tries to distract Will by taking him to the only gay bar in the woods, but Will returns early and catches Grace in the cabin with her lumberjack. But Grace's fears prove unwarranted; although he doesn't know when he'll be ready to move on, Will doesn't feel bad that Grace is ready now.

KAREN:
"Honey, Campbell brought the wood in. Looks like he'll be leaving with it too."

GUEST STAR
David Sutcliffe *(I'm with Her)* as Campbell

GLENDA ROVELLO: I based my idea of what Karen's cabin would look like on photos of some of the cabins of the super-wealthy, like Spielberg or Costner, that I've seen in magazines such as *Architectural Digest* or *Elle Décor*. They're always so amazing, done on a grand scale, non-urban yet finely appointed and genteel at the same time. They all use the same kind of modern, rustic language to create these perfect pleasure palaces.

FYI: *Happy Days* dad Tom Bosley filmed an appearance as an older gay man whom Will and Jack meet in the Vermont gay bar, but the scene was later cut.

Written By: DAVID KOHAN & MAX MUTCHNICK

When Harlin hires Grace to decorate his new apartment, she goes overboard with her theme of "Cowboy Chic." Although Will has promised to butt out, he assumes that Harlin hates Grace's work and inadvertently talks Harlin into firing her. As Jack, with Karen's help, makes his singing debut at open mic night at The Duplex nightclub, Grace learns that Will was responsible for getting her fired and forces him to sign a contract that he will from now on mind his own business.

HARLIN:
"Oh, darlin', whatever I don't get, I just figure is gay."

RECURRING CHARACTER
Gary Grubbs *as* Harlin Polk

MAX MUTCHNICK: A character like Harlin was a very useful tool for us in the beginning. We were being very deliberate in showing that a grown-up who is a Fortune 500 businessman and who is from the South is comfortable with his lawyer Will's sexual identity. It may be different to him, but it's not necessarily anathema. Now that we've had more time to establish these characters and people have grown comfortable with them in their living rooms, I don't think we need a character for that function anymore.

DAVID KOHAN: One of the things Max does for people he likes who work with him is to get involved in their lives. One time, Max recommended a decorator he liked to my then wife and me. She came in to redo our bathroom, and when the costs ran up and we had a problem, Max felt responsible. We decided to put that into a story: what happens when you're trying to do two friends a favor, but then you're responsible on both ends? This was a good story, especially for a controlling person like Will, who would not be able to do what you need him to do—butt out and let you work it out for yourself.

JACK:
"Hey, hey! It's not the 'Will and Grace' show! It's called 'Just Jack!'"

FYI: Does the red sweater Karen is wearing at the office look familiar? It's the same sweater we saw her pull out of a shopping bag to show to the cash-strapped Grace a few episodes earlier, in "A New Lease on Life." Says Lori Eskowitz-Carter: "I do often shop in advance, so if there is an episode where a character goes shopping, the props department would come to me and say that they need stuff for her to pull out of a bag."

Written By:
DAVA SAVEL

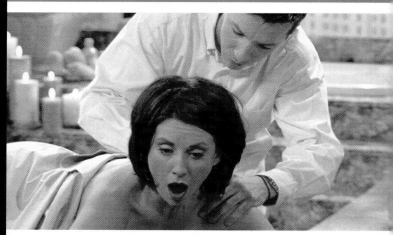

Grace has a chance to buy her office space and asks Will for legal help. When the landlord tricks her into agreeing to a high price, Will plays rough by threatening to tell other tenants how the landlord took advantage of a weak and naïve victim like Grace. The landlord backs down, but Grace feels awful. She pretends to be a helpless emotional wreck who no longer wants the deal at all, and ends up negotiating an even better deal for herself. Will learns that when it comes to business, Grace can take care of herself. Meanwhile, Jack delights Karen by using her for massage therapy practice.

JACK:
"I've finally found my life's calling, and it involves these two hands."

WILL:
"Ah, so you'r going to be self-employed

DAVID KOHAN: This is basically a story about respect: Will doesn't respe Grace's abilities, and we had to find some way that Grace could have a victory at the end. Her ability to manipulate the men by crying may have not been the best choice because it relied on the stereotypical "girl thing," and even at the time, we were apprehensive about that moment, but the audien really responded to it. They didn't see it coming.

FYI: When Will and Grace compare how hard it is to be in busine for a gay guy versus a girl. Will says, "Don't make me get my frie Jhoni over here—because we both know the only card that trump the gay card and the girl card is the gay girl card." This is anothe reference to Jhoni Marchinko, one of the show's writers.

annual design contest is imminent, and Grace is blocked. Will prises her by hiring a maid, April, to unclutter Grace's environnt and hopefully unclutter her mind. It works a little too well: ace soon comes to believe that she can't create without April rby, and even Karen starts to resent Grace's reliance on April. anwhile, Jack poses as a lawyer in Will's office to impress a guy wants to date and Will begrudgingly poses as Jack's assistant.

After Jack's effeminate behavior at the gym embarrasses Will in front of a client, Jack overhears Will referring to him as a "fag." Upset, Jack acts stereotypically straight around Will until Will realizes that his discomfort with Jack's openly gay behavior may really be due to his own fear of coming out completely. Meanwhile, Grace suggests to Karen that she talk to a girlfriend about her marital problems with Stan. Karen decides to talk to Grace, and the two enjoy a drunken evening of shared confidences. The next day, Karen regrets their night out together.

KAREN:
"You're giving the maid a key? You're going to be buying your jewelry back from hobos."

GUEST STAR
Wendie Jo Sperber (*Bosom Buddies*) as April

VID KOHAN: Max and I had seen Cyndi Lauper on *Mad About You,* and ught she was great. We went to her apartment in New York and asked to be on the show. We wrote the character of April, a more blue-collar d from Queens, with her specific voice in mind. But when Cyndi got to the le read in L.A., she was disappointed in the character—she had a vision ind that was more of a "surf punk." Our visions were too different, and it n't work out.

AM BARR: This is the episode I'm least proud of. In the end, it just ned out to be an uninvolving story, that Grace had this psychotic design se around her and that there was so much at stake for her pulling off esign competition.

LINDA RITZ: When the first draft of this episode was written, the ers didn't know what kind of design Grace was going to put together for showcase. I found an image of a very Zen room, and suggested it to m, and they loved the irony that Grace was near hysterical from trying ut together a room that's all about meditation. Very rarely do the writers e any specifics for sets or props into the show, because it's much more of haracter-driven show. Usually, if they comment on something on the set, appens because it's something I provided that they then decide to e jokes on.

WILL:
"Now listen, Swishburger, this is not like your old gym. Look around. Nary a nipple ring in sight. No men in Flashdance collars. And behold… women!"

a Favorite Episode of…

MAX MUTCHNICK: To this day, I think this is one of the best episodes we've ever done, and Michael Patrick King was a big force behind it. Some of the harshest criticism we used to get about *Will & Grace* came not from straight America, but from inside the gay community. The word "fag" is the "nigger" of the gay community, and this story used the word so effectively to show the internal oppression within the community and also Will's self-hatred and shame. This was also the only episode where sponsors ever backed out of the show, and because of the controversy, it aired only once in the show's prime-time run.

KAREN:
"You know what those rocks need? A little scotch."

JACK:
"I haven't worked out in two days. I'm fat. Je suis fatty gay."

SEAN HAYES: There's a majority of America that still doesn't even know any gay people or care to—or they don't think they do—and so this episode was educating them without them knowing it. That's why I liked the episode—and why NBC was very afraid of it.

115 THE BIG VENT

Story By:
JON KINNALLY & TRACY POUST

Teleplay By: **JHONI MARCHINKO**

A new heating vent in the floor gives Will and Grace a direct channel to the soap opera—like lives of their downstairs neighbors. Completely engrossed in the infidelities below, they forget all about Jack's request to read the play he has written as part of a class he is taking at The Learning Annex. Realizing that his friends have let him down, Jack rewrites his play and, with Karen's help, hires two actors to dramatize Will's and Grace's failures as friends.

JACK:
"I guess maintaining the thirteen shades of red in your hair keeps you so busy, you don't have time for recreational reading."

116 BIG BROTHER IS COMING
PART 1

Written By: **DAVID KOHAN & MAX MUTCHNICK**

Will is the most surprised person at Jack's surprise party when h estranged older brother, Sam, shows up at Grace's invitation. Th brothers' first steps toward mending fences are complicated whe Grace and Sam share a secret kiss. Jack has to deal with both th revelation that he is 30 and not 29, as he had previously miscalculated, and the disdain of haughty boutique salesmen. The latte problem is taken care of with the help of Karen and her respect-inducing credit card.

GUEST STAR
John Slattery *as* Sam Truman

WILL:
"Ma'am, the Schmenkman 5 is so good, you get juice out Hume Crony

DAVID KOHAN: I was talking in the writers' room about the beginning of my relationship with my now ex-wife, and someone asked me, if somebody close to me had warned me before we got married that they foresaw problems, would I have responded to that? I said no way, because I was in love and that's all there was to it. The only possible result would have been that I would have become resentful of the person who said something to me. So we decided on that being the backstory between Will and his brother, and then we were able to bring Grace in both to resolve their differences and to further inflame them when she starts to fall for Sam, the straight version of the guy she really loves. The episode highlighted the differences between how each of them deals with problems. One of the reasons Will loves Grace so much is because, unlike his, her emotions are out in the open. I love that moment where Grace takes charge to reconcile them, then rolls her eyes and says, "Goyim!"

FYI: This episode marks the first time we see Will's bedroom.

GRACE:
"Sam, come on. It took you 5 years to get here, and you're only 15 feet apart. That's like 3 feet a year. Merchant-Ivory films move faster than that."

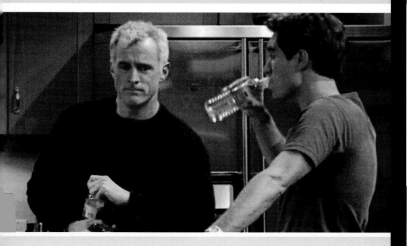

rmented by guilt over sneaking around with Sam, Grace confides
Karen, who is unsurprised that Grace would fall for the straight
rsion of Will. Of course, Karen can't keep the secret for long, and
ills it to Jack while trying to cure his depression about turning
. She also hires him as her personal assistant. When Will learns
e truth about Grace and Sam, he becomes wildly possessive and
enates Grace by speaking about her as if she were his property.
ck helps Will accept whatever Grace and Sam want, but Grace
cides not to pursue the relationship.

GUEST STAR
John Slattery *as* Sam Truman

> **KAREN:**
> *"How can I
> put this delicately?
> I think you went
> with Sam because he's
> the Will that'll touch
> your boobies."*

---

118 THE UNSINKABLE MOMMY ADLER
Written By: ALEX HERSCHLAG

Grace is afraid of what her visiting mother, the overly theatrical
Bobbi, will have to say about her living with a gay man. When
Bobbi, who unexpectedly applauds their relationship, suggests
that they marry despite their differences, Will laughs it off and
says that even if he were straight he wouldn't marry Grace. At
lunch, Grace has just finished criticizing her mother's star attitude
and her need to be the center of attention when Will arrives and
explains that he wouldn't marry Grace because of her need to be
the center of attention. Grace sees that she and her mother are
more alike than she had realized. Meanwhile, Jack helps Karen
deal with the possibility that she might be pregnant.

RECURRING CHARACTER
Debbie Reynolds *as* Grace's Mother, Bobbi Adler *(first appearance)*

FYI: The *Star Wars* joke is a reference to Debbie Reynolds's real-life
daughter, Carrie Fisher, who played Princess Leia.

JHONI MARCHINKO: I suggested Debbie Reynolds to play Grace's
mother. First of all, my parents love her, and I thought she would bring in a
whole new generation to watch the show. And we imagined that Grace would
have a really narcissistic mother, and I knew from *Postcards from the Edge*
that obviously Debbie could play that. She's ended up being so great that we
always try to use her at least once or twice a year.

> **BOBBI:**
> *"Let's go
> shopping. We'll
> spend your dowry.
> Might as well
> put it to
> some use."*

FYI: When Bobbi Adler's stole gets stuck in the door during
her final exit, it's a joke that wasn't planned. Look closely at Eric
McCormack's and Debra Messing's faces when this happens—
that's real laughter.

119 ALLEY CATS

Written By:
JHONI MARCHINKO & ALEX HERSCHLAG

Grace hates to lose. So much so, in fact, that her competitiveness is driving away friends Rob and Ellen, who can no longer enjoy even a simple game of Charades with her and Will. At Will's request, Grace tones it down, but as Rob and Ellen pull ahead of them in a bowling match, it becomes clear that Will is every bit as competitive as Grace. The two decide henceforth to be a single-minded, unbeatable (and probably intolerable) team. Meanwhile, after learning CPR from Jack, Karen saves a man's life when he collapses in Grace's office.

GUEST STAR
Lucky Vanous *(yes, the Diet Coke guy)* as EMS Worker

RECURRING CHARACTERS
Ellen Idelson *as* Will's Secretary, Ellen *(voice-over)*
Tom Gallop *as* Rob
Leigh-Allyn Baker *as* Ellen

a Favorite Episode of…

LEIGH-ALLYN BAKER: This is my favorite episode to date, and it wasn't originally even about Rob and Ellen. I think it was about a gay couple Will and Grace played games with and were overly competitive with, and we had only a few lines in one scene. But after the table read, they decided to rewrite the story to be about us. It was exciting because the whole episode was so last-minute. Everybody was a nervous wreck, but I was so excited because I actually had something here to sink my teeth into.

KAREN:
"Honey, silk collar, blue collar. They don't even mix in the washing machine."

GRACE:
"Once you let Jeannie out of the bottle, there's no way she's going back to that circle couch."

120 YOURS, MINE OR OURS

Written By:
ELLEN IDELSON & ROB LOTTERSTEIN

There's a new cute guy in the building, and both Will and Grace think they've got the inside track to his heart. Determined to figure out which of them is right, they enlist Jack and his usually infallible "gaydar" to figure out the guy's sexual preference. All they succeed in doing is acting so nutty that they drive him away completely. Meanwhile, Karen enlists Grace's help in figuring out the right way to get rid of an incompetent employee.

GUEST STAR
David Newsom *as* Peter

RECURRING CHARACTER
Earl Schuman *as* Karen's Limousine Driver *(first appearance)*

KAREN:
"As Gandhi once said, 'You're only as strong as your weakest servant.' I think he said that. Or maybe it was, 'Wow, this sand is hot!'"

SEAN HAYES: Jack claims to know whether Peter is gay or straight, but I myself have never thought about it. I guess I'd have to say that he's probab[ly] gay, since Jack thinks everybody is gay. After all, as Jack always says, "Ther[e] are no straight men, only men who have been without Jack."

a Favorite Episode of…

MAX MUTCHNICK: I consider this episode one of my favorites, and the irony is that it's the one thing I had told every writer who had been previous[ly] interviewed by us for the show that we would never do—the episode where Will and Grace both try to date the same guy. I don't believe in bisexuality, and I didn't want to pursue that story line, which seemed too obvious and clichéd, anyway. But then one of the brilliant writers in the room presented the idea, including that last beat, where Jack knows whether the guy is gay or straight. We would very often build episodes around a wonderful momen[t] and if we came across a moment as interesting as that, it was worth puttin[g] aside our initial reservations to write to that end.

...hen Grace falters at an interview with famous publicist ...than Barry, Karen saves the day by proving herself Nathan's ...me-dropping match. After an inspection of Grace's own ...artment, Nathan is about to turn her down when he meets ...ll and is smitten. Nathan offers Grace a deal: the job in ...change for a date with Will. Will reluctantly goes along for ...ace's sake, but after a horrible first date, neither Grace's pleas ...r Jack and Karen's demonstration of the art of kissing ...meone you don't find attractive can keep Will on board. Grace ...gathering her things from Nathan's in anticipation of getting ...ed when Will, true friend that he is, arrives for another date. ...rtunately, Nathan decides that Will's faked clinginess is a ...rn-off, so the relationship ends but Grace's job continues.

Will is upset over Grace's dinner plans with former fiancé Danny, but promises to do his best to butt out. Karen meets him at the office and they arrange to rescue maid Rosario from deportation by marrying her to Jack. In the morning, when Will runs into an undressed Danny, he realizes that Grace and Danny shared more than just dinner. During Jack and Rosario's wedding ceremony, Grace tests Will's feelings by pretending to have fallen back in love with Danny even though she actually dumped him. Will's anger leads them both to question whether they're too passionately involved in each other's lives. Realizing that neither of them has moved on, they decide not to continue living together.

GUEST STAR
Franklin Cover *(The Jeffersons)* as Minister

RECURRING CHARACTERS
Ellen Idelson *as* Will's Secretary, Ellen *(voice over)*
Shelley Morrison *as* Rosario *(first appearance)*
Tom Verica *(American Dreams)* as Grace's
ex-fiancé Danny *(first appearance)*

GUEST STAR
Miguel Ferrer *(Crossing Jordan)* as Nathan Barry

...ONI MARCHINKO: The idea for this episode came from the fact that ...x had once gone on a date with a similarly well-known and powerful guy. ...didn't hold the cards over a friend, like Nathan Barry did for Grace. Max's ...erience was just a tiny germ, and we built a story from that.

a Favorite Episode of...

SHELLEY MORRISON: This was the first episode I did, and it's still my favorite. I loved the story line of the marriage. In rehearsal, I had asked Sean while we were standing in front of the minister to play with my makeup, and he said sure. Then, when he touched my face when we did the take, I smacked him. By the look on his face, you can see that he didn't expect it. From then on, we have always thrown things at each other that we wouldn't have done in rehearsal.

JACK:
"Poor, poor ...alous you, stuck ...side the nunnery ...e all the other girls ...a around in their ...niniskirts and ...take the Pill."

WILL:
"I'm standing here making out with a girl. That's the international symbol for not moving on."

...I: When Karen and Nathan talk about their friends in common, ...a power circle where everyone is just by first name, Karen men-...ns "Eve and Dennis"—named for first-season writers Eve Ahlert ...egan Mullally's real-life best friend) and Dennis Drake.

JEFF GREENSTEIN: We always have had so many mythical characters on this show, because Stan was invisible and Rosario was invisible—Karen's entire world was invisible. We do have to populate the world these people live in, so that led to us meeting Rosario. Meeting Rosario was a big, big thing for us when it happened. And Shelley is amazing. She brings a deadpan quality to her character, where all she has to do is walk into a room and say one word and she's funny. And I cannot think of one other character ever who can be funnier with sunglasses on than with them off.

...: Nathan is upset that designer Antonia Hutt is traveling in ...rrakech and is unavailable to work on his project. Antonia Hutt, ...eal-life designer, is the partner of series executive producer, ...ni Marchinko.

WILL & GRACE &

JACK & KAREN

WILL & ERIC

Acting for Two

Calgary native Eric McCormack didn't know he was carrying on a family tradition when he entered Toronto's Banff School of Fine Arts at Ryerson University. Then one day he found a 1952 scrapbook detailing his father's days at the same school. "He had graduated as an actor from the television and film program and he had never told me," Eric told **INSIDE THE ACTOR'S STUDIO** in 2003. "I confronted him with it, and he said, 'Well, no big deal, I wasn't as serious as you were.' We got up from lunch and said good-bye, and in the middle of the mall in downtown Toronto he turned around and he was crying. He hugged me and he said, 'I'm very proud of you.' And he walked off and we've never discussed it since. But I sort of feel since that day that I'm acting for two."

Sorry About That, Chief

The acting bug bit Eric early. "There was some point between third and sixth grade where **GET SMART** went from being my favorite show to being something where I realized, 'Oh, this is a living. People make a living at doing this.'" Although Eric would go on to perform half of Shakespeare's canon on stages throughout Canada, something always led him back to sitcom. Ultimately, the Bard couldn't hold a candle to Don Adams.

Cops and Outlaws

As Eric transitioned into television in the early 90s, he appeared in a number of American shows shooting in Toronto and Vancouver, such as **TOP COPS**, **THE HAT SQUAD** and **COBRA**. "I can't say anything that I did in that period wasn't pretty much awful," he admits. After piling up a number of forgettable credits, Eric won the part of Confederate bad boy Colonel Clay Mosby in **LONESOME DOVE: THE OUTLAW YEARS**.

"That was just great," Eric remembers. "I had a beard and long hair, and it was a whole other me." **LONESOME** assistant director Janet Holden must have a thing for the bad boys…she married Eric on a boat in Vancouver's English Bay in 1997.

Ross... but No Cigar

LONESOME DOVE was unexpectedly cancelled after its second season, so the renegade who had it made shaved his beard and plunged into a comedy...of errors. For three years, Eric appeared in sitcom pilots that never went to series, and was fired from the cast of the only one that did: 1997's **JENNY**. But his most heartbreaking near miss came in 1994, when he and David Schwimmer were the two finalists for the part of Ross Geller on **FRIENDS**.

Following guest spots on **ALLY MCBEAL** and **VERONICA'S CLOSET**, and a recurring role as Jenna Elfman's boyfriend on the short-lived 1996 ABC series **TOWNIES**, Eric was called in to read for **WILL & GRACE** by casting director Tracy Lilienfield. His big break had finally come...and he almost blew it.

Summoning the Will to Be Will

"The moment I first read the **WILL & GRACE** pilot script, I knew that it was great, that it would last a long time, and I really knew that it was going to be mine," remembers Eric. "And it scared the hell out of me when I realized this would be my epitaph. If I did this show, my life would be measured in 'Before Will' and 'After Will.' Will would be my Sam Malone."

Will Truman had set off a soul search in Eric McCormack. "Everything just sort of hit me at once," he confesses. "Fear of success and fear of being pigeonholed and fear of growing up. Worrying about playing gay was the least of it." In fact, Eric suspected that playing television's first high-profile gay leading man might be an advantage, a way to stand out and win recognition...maybe even win an Emmy. But with great visibility would come great responsibility—becoming a spokesman for the gay community—and Eric wasn't sure he wanted it.

So he walked away. Fortunately, as Eric points out, in every romantic comedy the breakup is merely a prelude to the inevitable happy ending. "I had to go away from this part, to set it free, and if we both loved each other it would come back," he says. "I woke up one morning and said to my wife, 'I've made a horrible mistake, haven't I,' and she said 'yeah, I think so.'"

The part was still available. And now, so was he. Eric came back to **WILL & GRACE** like a man who'd turned a corner, committed to meeting his destiny without hesitation or apology, and was determined to embrace the privilege and responsibility of playing a gay leading man on network television, come what may. "When I woke up that morning," he says, "I knew that I had been avoiding the future. It was my future, and it was mine to ruin or to make happen."

Will and Eric, a Perfect Match

All Eric knew about Will Truman was that he came from an intact Connecticut WASP family and that he had brothers; anything else would have to wait for future scripts. But Eric didn't sweat the details. He felt at home in Will's skin right from day one. This comfort came as a welcome relief for an actor who'd grown accustomed to auditioning for roles as standard-issue sitcom slobs. "I didn't know how to play those guys," explains Eric. "I'll die, and you will never have heard me in eighty years say the word 'dude.'" In Will Truman, the real Eric could finally shine through.

"Until I got this part, I was never fully comfortable playing a leading man," Eric admits. Leading men tended to be narrowly defined characters who risked turning off audiences with behavior that was not stereotypically macho. Eric, a straight man who describes himself as "culturally gay," had usually felt it necessary to hide characteristics such

as his lack of athleticism, and his love of show tunes. Colonel Clay Mosby, for instance, was probably unfamiliar with the Rodgers & Hammerstein oeuvre. But finally, Eric could unleash the queer side of the straight guy: "I feel free as Will to be funny the way Eric normally is, to burst into song if I want, and to find parts of myself for Will that I couldn't always tap into."

Changing His Will

Will Truman may have liberated Eric, but it's also true that Eric wound up liberating Will.

"In the first season," remembers Eric, "I had so many people come up to me and point out the irony that the gay guy on the show is really the straight man." Eric took offense at the time—after all, he did get his share of jokes—but a look back at Season One finds Will very often the setup man for other characters' punch lines. Eric thinks it took a while to find Will's quirks…and for the powers-that-be to feel confident enough to unleash them. "There was a certain reticence to play Will as too gay," he asserts, "from Max Mutchnick, from Jimmy Burrows, and from the network. So Will ended up being a little neutered and a little straighter."

But as Eric relaxed into the role, the role relaxed right along with him. Many of the fun traits that now seem quintessentially Will are actually Eric's own, written into the character by his keenly observant colleagues. And during the rare rehearsal weeks when Will still feels too straight, Eric's always ready to share his diagnosis and suggest a cure. "The day before we shoot," he says, "I'll go to the writers and say I need more jokes, maybe two more punch lines."

Will's Sex Life…or Lack Thereof

Will's a great looking guy with a good job, a fantastic apartment, immaculate taste, and a recipe for olive tapenade that's been known to bring grown men to their knees. So why can't he get a date?

When the series began, Will had just left a seven-year love relationship, so for a while it made sense that he needed time to heal. "It was nice to show that he really was heartbroken and picky, but that only buys you so much time," Eric remembers. That's when Will started to date, though many fans didn't realize it. "I used to say to the writers that in every episode if I can just say 'Ugh, I had coffee with this guy today, what an idiot' it's enough to remind us that he's out there trying," says Eric. But six years later why isn't this hottie the most sought-after thing on the Upper West Side besides H&H bagels?

Eric can think of two reasons. First, Will carries a heavy burden…the heavy burden he used to carry around his waist. "I love that fat-boy past that they gave me," he says. "So they tend to write Will as a nervous date. I think it explains why it doesn't work out all the time, or ever."

Second, even if a date goes well, viewers are unlikely to see it. "It drives me crazy that Karen can make out with people for a minute and a half, and Leo and Grace can make out," says Eric, "but if I actually had a kiss with somebody, it would have to be negotiated with the network." With some fans clamoring for on-screen love connections, and others adamant in their opposition, it's no wonder Will doesn't get much action. Who could take the pressure?

Though it frustrates him, Eric sees a silver lining in Will's lack of love interest. A new relationship would take Will away from his friends. "I'd miss being able to play with Debra, Sean and Megan," Eric says. "I never wanted a boyfriend to take that away." He thinks he's found the perfect solution: "If we just get Will a boyfriend who is not famous, then we don't have to use him all the time." Or, if a prime-time lip-lock is in the stars, Eric wouldn't mind a big star that burns out fast: "I said to the producers, 'Look, let's get this over with. Let me have a good two-episode arc with someone really hot and famous, and let's make out.'"

"Who's next week?"

One of the perks of being on **WILL & GRACE** is that those hot and famous stars keep dropping by. Gene Wilder, Sydney Pollack, and John Cleese particularly thrilled Eric with their special appearances. "It's amazing when we have these people on this show," he says. "Gene Wilder came on and said he had wanted to do the show because he thinks it's wonderful, and I thought, 'That's amazing—*you* watched *me* on TV!'"

Eric freely admits to being spoiled by success. In the early days, he couldn't believe his good fortune when Sydney Pollack did a guest shot—**"TOOTSIE** is a huge film for me!" he gushes—but these days the show is an embarrassment of riches. "We were having people like John Cleese, Minnie Driver, and Geena Davis all in one show," says Eric, "and by then we were blasé, thinking, 'who's next week?'"

"Will & Grace" —Reality TV?

One thing that Eric will never grow blasé about is **WILL & GRACE**'s unique blend of fantasy and reality. Sometimes the writing is so true to life, such as when Will and Grace finish each other's sentences, that the acting feels effortless, and unrehearsed scenes come out perfectly the first time through. Other times, someone—usually Karen—comes out with a comment that positions her squarely in a fantasy world. Eric credits "the genius of these writers and the genius of Burrows" for keeping all the elements in balance. He shares the fans' enthusiasm for Will's unlikely world, where moments of raw emotional honesty live across the hall from interludes of exhilarating silliness.

Extracurricular Activity

Eric has never entirely vanished into the **WILL & GRACE** universe. Even while participating in the casting sessions to help find his costars, he often spent nights shooting his scenes in the 1998 movie **FREE ENTERPRISE**. He has since appeared in the film **HOLY MAN** in 1998, as Mel Ferrer in the TV movie **THE AUDREY HEPBURN STORY** in 2000, and in several independent films. During his summer 2001 hiatus from the show, Eric made his Broadway debut as Harold Hill in the acclaimed Susan Stroman-directed production of **THE MUSIC MAN**, for which he temporarily relocated to Manhattan's Upper West Side, home of Will Truman.

In his spare time, Eric has also started to explore directing as a possible future career. During his summer 2004 break, he directed and starred in a movie he also wrote, **WHAT YOU WISH FOR**, for the Disney studio. "People have asked if I am ever going to direct this show," he says. "And I say I hope not, because none of us would ever want Jimmy Burrows to leave, not even for one episode. There's an amazing continuity here with him at the helm, and with the fact that the writing staff has mostly remained the same. It is out of that continuity and that comfort, at least for me, that great things come."

Among those great things have been Eric's three Emmy nominations for his portrayal of Will Truman, and in 2001 he won the award for Outstanding Lead Actor in a Comedy Series. In 2003, he received the Vanguard Award from GLAAD, the gay advocacy group that recognizes positive portrayals of gay characters in the media.

But Eric's greatest prize is his son, Finnigan Holden McCormack, born on July 1, 2002, in Los Angeles.

"WHEN I'M IN WILL'S KITCHEN, I FEEL LIKE I'M AT HOME COOKING."

GRACE & DEBRA

Stacey & Grace

Debra Messing's dreams came true the day she won the title role in her high school's production of **ANNIE**. She'd been smitten by the adorable moppet—and a life on the stage—at the age of seven during a family visit to their native New York City from their new home in rural East Greenwich, R.I. "I could not believe there were people live, in front of me, dancing and singing with that kind of joy and energy," she recalls. "I felt it go through my body, and I wanted to leap up on stage and join them." For years she'd contented herself with dance classes, performing arts summer camp, and playacting with her brother in the backyard. Now at last the girl who'd been singing show tunes from the age of three was where she belonged: center stage. There was just one small—make that tall—problem: "I was very tall from a young age," Debra remembers. "Here was this 5'6" orphan and the 5'8" Daddy Warbucks. It didn't quite work, but I loved every second of it."

A good student and "good girl with a capital G," Debra felt like an outsider in high school, at home only on the stage. "That was the only place I felt it was safe and comfortable and freeing and dangerous all at once," she says.

After graduating summa cum laude from Brandeis University as a theater major, Debra joined the ranks of New York's struggling stage actors. While understudying Mary-Louise Parker and Polly Draper on Broadway at night, she began auditioning for TV work during the day, and landed her first role as a midwife on **ANOTHER WORLD**. Then, when Debra "clicked" with **NYPD BLUE** producers during their visit to film New York exteriors, she landed a guest-starring role that soon grew into a recurring character. As her career gathered steam, Debra won roles in her first Off-Broadway play, Paul Rudnick's **THE NAKED TRUTH**, and her first film, the 1995 Keanu Reeves vehicle, **A WALK IN THE CLOUDS**.

Earlier, Debra had been turned down for a new Fox sitcom called **NED & STACEY**. Now, as the film made her a hot property, network executives once again wooed Debra, who nailed the job at her second audition. The show's creator, Michael Weithorn, explained why he'd passed on her the first time around: he thought she was a nice Midwestern girl,

and Stacey needed to be a neurotic Jew from New York. "I said, 'Midwest? I've never even been to the Midwest,'" Debra remembers. "'I'm a neurotic Jew from New York!'"

Playing Stacey—a character similar to Grace Adler "but with a harder edge and more anger," Debra says—gave her the experience and the confidence that would serve her well later on. "I had never been on a sitcom stage before," she explains, "and I felt like I was being thrown into the ocean and had to learn how to swim. During the first six months, the producers would come up to me and say, 'Debra, you're screaming,' because I thought I had to project loud enough for the person in the back row."

After **NED & STACEY**, Debra made two appearances in the **SEINFELD** canon as Jerry's ideal yet elusive girlfriend Beth Lookner, then landed a lead role in the 1997 sci-fi series **PREY**. Luckily, **PREY** was short-lived, leaving Debra available to step into Grace Adler's oversized shoes.

Imperfect Grace

Debra had one major concern: Grace seemed a little too perfect. Like Eric McCormack, Debra fretted that her character might end up being a "straight man." Debra knew she wouldn't be satisfied in a part that required her only to be charming and pretty while she set up the other characters' jokes. She wanted Grace to be like the television characters she grew up enjoying—those who reflected real life, and all the imperfections that come with it.

But there aren't a lot of straight men on **WILL & GRACE**, and Debra quickly realized she had nothing to worry about. "Max and Dave said from the very beginning that they didn't want her just to be arm candy. They said she's going to have her own business. She's going to have funny love triangles and we're going to meet her family. That was all really important to me, and it gave me complete faith in them." Reassured that she and the show's creators shared the same vision, Debra made the multiyear commitment to the role that would change her life.

Right away Max and David made good on their promise. "I was happiest when Grace started to show moments where she was a little too hotheaded or passionate," recalls Debra. "There is often an ugly side to perfectly decent, funny, lovely people, where this little devil comes out."

Picking Grace's Battles

It's a good thing Grace has flaws— what else would she and Karen have to talk about? Believe it or not, Debra enjoys the put-downs. "It's throwing dog poo on the pretty girl," she says. "I like it even more now because Grace has more confidence in her ability to give zingers back."

These days Grace can give as good as she gets—to a point. "I like her fighting back, but I don't like it when she crosses the line," she says. "Out of the mouth of a heterosexual woman, some of these insults can have more of a bite to them than if they were out of the mouth of, say, Jack. In a couple of episodes there were originally some barbs coming out of Grace's mouth that I didn't feel were Grace-like at all."

"I have lived with this character for six years now and I can feel when some jokes cross the line," Debra says. When a line dissatisfies her, the writers often have alternatives standing by. Sometimes they try it more than one way and let the audience decide. "It's very interesting, on show night, to see what happens," Debra says. "We do get groans if Grace is too mean. Karen can say anything to Grace, but if Grace fights back, it has to be done in a way that still has a little touch of loser to it."

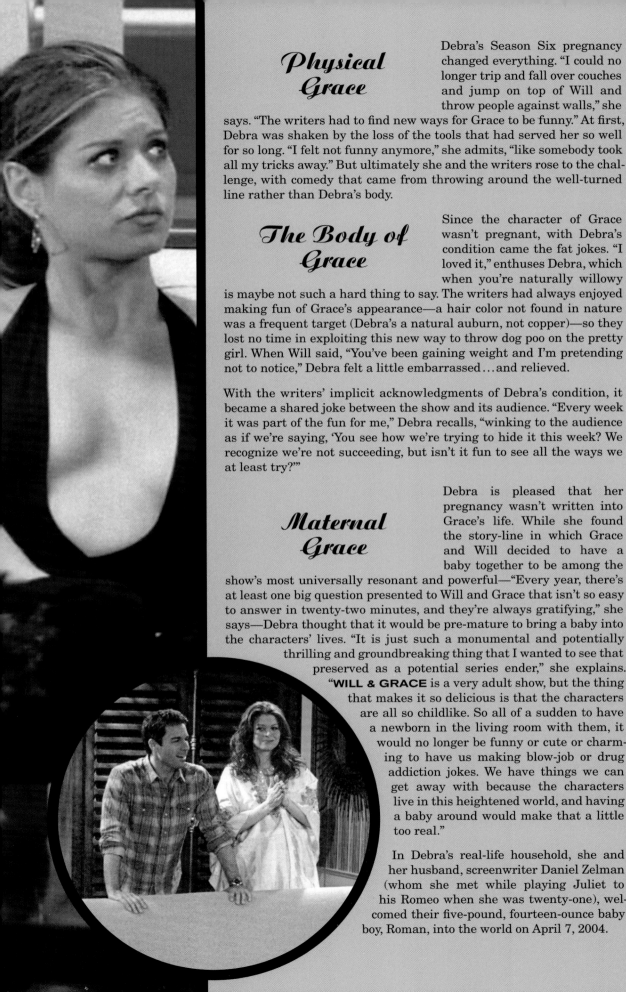

Physical Grace

Debra's Season Six pregnancy changed everything. "I could no longer trip and fall over couches and jump on top of Will and throw people against walls," she says. "The writers had to find new ways for Grace to be funny." At first, Debra was shaken by the loss of the tools that had served her so well for so long. "I felt not funny anymore," she admits, "like somebody took all my tricks away." But ultimately she and the writers rose to the challenge, with comedy that came from throwing around the well-turned line rather than Debra's body.

The Body of Grace

Since the character of Grace wasn't pregnant, with Debra's condition came the fat jokes. "I loved it," enthuses Debra, which when you're naturally willowy is maybe not such a hard thing to say. The writers had always enjoyed making fun of Grace's appearance—a hair color not found in nature was a frequent target (Debra's a natural auburn, not copper)—so they lost no time in exploiting this new way to throw dog poo on the pretty girl. When Will said, "You've been gaining weight and I'm pretending not to notice," Debra felt a little embarrassed...and relieved.

With the writers' implicit acknowledgments of Debra's condition, it became a shared joke between the show and its audience. "Every week it was part of the fun for me," Debra recalls, "winking to the audience as if we're saying, 'You see how we're trying to hide it this week? We recognize we're not succeeding, but isn't it fun to see all the ways we at least try?'"

Maternal Grace

Debra is pleased that her pregnancy wasn't written into Grace's life. While she found the story-line in which Grace and Will decided to have a baby together to be among the show's most universally resonant and powerful—"Every year, there's at least one big question presented to Will and Grace that isn't so easy to answer in twenty-two minutes, and they're always gratifying," she says—Debra thought that it would be pre-mature to bring a baby into the characters' lives. "It is just such a monumental and potentially thrilling and groundbreaking thing that I wanted to see that preserved as a potential series ender," she explains. "**WILL & GRACE** is a very adult show, but the thing that makes it so delicious is that the characters are all so childlike. So all of a sudden to have a newborn in the living room with them, it would no longer be funny or cute or charming to have us making blow-job or drug addiction jokes. We have things we can get away with because the characters live in this heightened world, and having a baby around would make that a little too real."

In Debra's real-life household, she and her husband, screenwriter Daniel Zelman (whom she met while playing Juliet to his Romeo when she was twenty-one), welcomed their five-pound, fourteen-ounce baby boy, Roman, into the world on April 7, 2004.

Grace in Love

Whereas Debra found her life partner early, Grace has only recently matured enough to really fall in love. Although Debra welcomed Leo's entrance into Grace's life as much-needed evidence that she had grown into someone capable of maintaining a real adult relationship after four years of failures, the change was at first frightening.

"I was fearful that the marriage might hinder the comedic prospects for Grace," Debra admits. "But these writers are just really smart and talented and they can mine anything. The marriage made Grace feel more grounded and a little sexier."

As Debra points out, Leo or no Leo, **WILL & GRACE** has always been a romantic comedy. Max and David's original idea—to follow Sydney Pollack's advice and craft a love story about a couple separated by an insurmountable obstacle—has been perfectly realized. "It was great to explore Grace's relationship with Leo, but whenever people at the show were interviewed, they always seemed to say something like, 'Well of course this can't last.' I think that was about reassuring the audience that it's okay to root for Will and Grace and to love them so much that you want them to be together, even though you know that it can't happen."

Her Inner Grace

Like the character she portrays, Debra has fallen hard for New York City. She loves the freedom of being able to walk the streets in anonymity. "There's something very safe about no one knowing you or caring about you or even looking twice at you," she says. Only a real New Yorker could turn her fellow citizens' complete disregard for her welfare into something to brag about.

Debra thinks she and Grace share many values in their personal lives, too: "Like Grace, I'm really a homebody. I love coming home, snuggling down with my husband—or Will, in her case—and watching movies, or cooking, or just spending quiet time together. Grace is a romantic, and I am, too. We both want to be married for the rest of our lives."

In fact, Debra could be describing herself when she says: "The thing I love most about Grace is that she is completely committed to whatever is in front of her. Whether that means she's a really passionate designer, and she's really competent and talented and disciplined, or she's going to be the best poker player, and she's going to win that thing at all costs. She always wants to be the best."

And Debra has joined the ranks of those recognized as the best. After three previous nominations, she won the Emmy for Outstanding Actress in a Comedy Series in 2003.

During breaks from the show, she co-stars with A-list actors in films like **ALONG CAME POLLY** with Ben Stiller and **THE MOTHMAN PROPHECIES** with Richard Gere. But most exciting for a Jewish girl from New York was the opportunity to work with one legendary director in particular, who handpicked her for his films **CELEBRITY** and **HOLLYWOOD ENDING**. As Debra told the *Jewish Journal of Greater Los Angeles* in 2002, "To star in a Woody Allen movie—as his girlfriend no less—has been a real-life Hollywood Ending for me."

Finally, the accolades that thrill Debra most are those that come from the fans. "Since this show began, so many people on the street have come up to me and said, 'I'm Grace and this is my Will and we've been living together for ten years,' It's something I think is very special and very real."

AMAZING GRACE

Before Grace, there hadn't been a Jewish leading lady who could be considered a role model—unless you wanted your kids to whine like **THE NANNY**—since Valerie Harper's groundbreaking **RHODA** went off the air in 1978.

WILL & GRACE creators Max Mutchnick and David Kohan, both Jewish themselves, have consistently aimed to confront any issues of faith head-on, rather than avoid them. "I always found it really annoying on **MAD ABOUT YOU** that you had 'Paul Buchman,' who was obviously Jewish, but it was never once mentioned," David explains. "It never made sense to me. It just goes to show how people in decision-making positions don't really know anything. Why, other than your own anxiety or discomfort or self-loathing, would you assume that people will have a problem with a Jewish character?"

Luckily, David and Max agree, their choices of religious denominations for their four characters never were an issue with the network; instead, they explain, they were free to leave these four questions to be answered by the gods of casting. "Debra is a proud Jewish American and we just incorporated it," Max explains.

Debra Messing, whose great-great-grandfather on her father's side was a cantor in Russia, remembers her excitement when Grace's ethnic identity first started to surface. The show's writers, many of them also Jewish, share her excitement. "I remember in the first season, when Will and his brother were mad at each other, Grace just said, '**Goyim!**'" says executive producer Alex Herschlag, "And that opened the floodgates."

In the Season Four episode "Bed, Bath & Beyond," Grace chants her famous prayer of loneliness. "That's one of my favorite episodes," Debra says. "The script called for a picture of Grace at her bat mitzvah, and I had a picture of myself at the *bimah,* in front of the torah with my grandfather, who is no longer with us. It was fun to be able to bring that in and laugh at myself in this dorky picture, and to contribute to that crossover of real and fictional. And the *'Baruch atoh'* line was one of the funniest they've ever written. I just knew at the moment I did it that I was making every single one of my relatives fall off the couch."

"It's one of the things I think is so subversive about the show, how Jew-y Grace is," series executive producer Jeff Greenstein explains. "Grace ended up having the only Jewish wedding I have ever heard of in the history of American TV, where she married a Jew in a Jewish ceremony. Show me any other show where the girl marries a guy who is wearing a yarmulke."

JACK & SEAN

Everybody Has a Sob Story

Shortly after Sean Hayes' first audition—at age five, for a United Airlines commercial—his father abandoned the family, leaving his mother to raise the kids on her own. "Everybody has a sob story, and that's mine," Sean explains. Although he continued an on-and-off flirtation with the theater world at his suburban Chicago high school, Sean's main focus was training to be a concert pianist. "I think I stayed with piano partly out of guilt over how much time and my mom's money I had already spent," he explains.

His dedication paid off in the form of a music scholarship to Illinois State University. "Coincidentally, they also have one of the greatest theater departments in the country," Sean explains. "So I studied music, but always ended up stopping by to see those funny theater people while I was walking to class. I was a groupie because I was afraid to cross over and admit to myself that I enjoyed acting."

Sean supported himself in college as a classical pianist, and performed in a pop band that was looking for that classical edge. When he finally did start auditioning for acting roles, he found a safe cover in being able to pose as a musician who was merely curious about acting. After college, Sean began working in the Chicago theater community, serving for a few years as the music director at the Pheasant Run dinner theater in St. Charles, Illinois, and appearing in several of their productions. "But it wasn't a cheesy place," Sean insists. "They actually put on really well-respected shows, which was kind of unbelievable."

A Commercial Success

Sean began going out for commercial auditions in Chicago and, as he recalls, "just got lucky and started booking commercial after commercial." After finding success in advertising and guest appearances on television shows, including **SILK STALKINGS** and **TOUGH TARGET**, Sean branched out into non-alliterative titles during the spring pilot season auditions.

Although he still hadn't had any formal acting training, encouraged by his success in Chicago, Sean moved to Los Angeles in 1995 with three theater friends—his Will, Grace and Karen—Mickey, Suzanne, and Ashley. "The thing I had going for me is that I had become a big fish in a small pond in Chicago by the time I moved," Sean says. "You can't get TV or film work there, but at least from the commercials, they had 'tape' on me," meaning that he had built a videotape resume to send to casting directors.

After a decidedly unglamorous start in L.A. ("the four of us lived in this run-down, literally rat-infested house, where the rent was $150 per person," he remembers), Sean again quickly found success by appearing in commercials—thirty-five of them, to be exact. During one Super Bowl, Sean turned up in two different high-profile ads.

In between jobs, Sean tried stand-up comedy, as a way, he explains, to "exercise any kind of craft that I could." Having cut his comedic eyeteeth with Chicago's legendary Second City improv comedy troupe, he did stand-up at The Comedy Club in Los Angeles, and helped form a sketch comedy group with Jeff Mayse and actor friend John Quaintance, who now writes for Kohan and Mutchnick's second NBC sitcom, **GOOD MORNING MIAMI.**

If paying his dues in stand-up and commercials wasn't motivation enough to find larger roles, the gig as an elf with the tour of the **KENNY ROGERS CHRISTMAS SHOW** might have been. "I spent my days writing letters to producers, and following up on leads from *Backstage West,*" Sean remembers, "I lived with blinders on." Thank goodness Sean didn't know when to fold 'em; he eventually landed an agent as well as parts in several independent films.

Sean's Hollywood Screen Kiss

Sean got his big break as the title character in the 1998 Film **BILLY'S HOLLYWOOD SCREEN KISS**, about a gay photographer pining for a man (played by Brad Rowe) who may or may not be gay. It was this film that then brought Sean to the attention of **WILL & GRACE** casting director Tracy Lilienfield, who recruited him to read for the career-making part of Jack McFarland in January 1998.

Playing It Gay

But those Pheasant Run dinner theater people can be choosy. Sean had his concerns, "specifically about going from a gay role, in **BILLY'S HOLLYWOOD SCREEN KISS**, to an even gayer role." The decision to become Jack boiled down to a question of business more than heart. **WILL & GRACE** was an NBC Studios show for NBC, it had legendary director Jimmy Burrows at the helm, and its creators already had a show on the air. Besides, he says, "I wasn't working, so it would have been stupid for me to turn the part of Jack down."

Tapping His Inner Jack

The kid who'd once hid his theatrical leanings had leaped into one of the most overtly theatrical roles in television history. Sean credits live audiences for helping him find new depths of energy and outrageousness. "On tape night, it's like a rock concert," he says. "It's fun to just let loose and let the energy take you, and not care where. You feel this electricity and can be uninhibited, not caring what other people are going to think, and not being afraid to fail."

Flamboyance Is in the Eye of the Beholder

Part of Sean's fearlessness involves making choices that he knows will be seen as flamboyantly gay, and when he's shrugging or batting his eyes or pursing his lips he never worries about stereotypes, only about getting laughs. He wonders, though, why so much physical comedy gets labeled "gay." "A lot of the physicality to me isn't any different from Robin Williams or Martin Short or Jim Carrey or Steve Martin," he says. "Any kind of physicality of movement from a man can be construed as gay. It fascinates me."

Funnily enough, Sean very often isn't thinking about playing Jack gay, he's thinking about playing him like a teenage girl. "He's everything a teenage girl is," Sean explains. "Teenage girls are so giddy and laugh at anything and are so dramatic about everything, and I think that is hilarious." Sean's director thinks Jack is simply a facet of the man who plays him: "Jimmy Burrows says that Jack was always within me, but that he's just unleashed me."

Bonding Through Chemistry

Some things can't be faked, and the perfect chemistry with his cast mates (what Sean calls "just like lightning in a bottle") is as authentic as it appears. "It's truly amazing that we all ended up together," he says, "because we all have the same sense of humor. What are the odds of that?"

Jack's relationship with Karen, in particular, reflects a strong real-world connection. It definitely wasn't love at first sight…in fact, at their first table-read together, Sean had Megan all wrong. "My initial impression was that she was kind of distant," he remembers. "For some reason, that always happens with people who turn out to be the closest in my life—I never have great first impressions of them, and then they turn out to be my best friends." Sean thinks it was inevitable that he and Megan, "two people who are both so open with themselves, and share the same sense of humor on such a deep level," would eventually click. "We just get it," he says, "We even finish each other's sentences. The relationship that Will and Grace have on-screen, we have in real life."

Part of that connection is a shared approach to their profession. "Megan and I both work on instinct," reports Sean, "whereas Eric and Debra are more analytical." Are Sean and Megan ever intimidated by their colleagues' formidable acting educations? Well, no. "Between you and me, there's not too much to know," he says, attributing the magic between himself and Megan as much to instinct as to preparation. "The two of us do a lot of coordinated movements on the show, like when Jack and Karen make a simultaneous exit or jump up and down, excited. A lot of that is thought out and choreographed, but a lot of it comes from our just being simpatico."

Whatever his method, Sean's unique brand of inspired madness has won recognition and reward. In the series' first six seasons, he was honored with two Screen Actors Guild Awards, a TV Guide Award, an American Comedy Award, and five Golden Globe nominations for his portrayal of Jack. And in 2000, Sean won an Emmy for Outstanding Supporting Actor in a Comedy Series.

Sean's television accomplishments have led to a burgeoning film career as well. Most recently seen in **WIN A DATE WITH TAD HAMILTON**, in 2003 he appeared in the independent feature **PIECES OF APRIL**, and also voiced The Fish in **CATS AND DOGS** and appeared in person as Mr. Humberfloob in

THE CAT IN THE HAT. In 2002, he received critical praise for his portrayal of Jerry Lewis in a high-profile CBS television movie **MARTIN & LEWIS**—something the **WILL & GRACE** writers won't let him forget, as they constantly throw Jerry Lewis references and impressions into the script for Jack as an in-joke. It was a hyperactive part Sean seemed born to play; like Jerry Lewis, he exhibits excesses of antic energy on the set, both in character and out. Between scenes on show nights, the show DJ often plays *The Flight of the Bumblebee,* and Sean races around the set as if being chased by bees.

And then there was the incident in 1998 just before the show's premiere, when cast and crew sat through a required seminar on sexual harassment. At its conclusion, Sean thanked the instructor, professed his newfound sensitivity—and then walked out of the room with his pants around his ankles. It was right in character.

"**Sean is joie de vivre personified,**" Eric McCormack told *People* magazine in 1999. "**If a week goes by without him dropping his pants, he's in a bad mood.**"

JUST JACK

The fall of 1998 saw the debut not only of the oft-quoted sitcom **WILL & GRACE**, but also of the even more oft-quoted fictional cabaret act, *Just Jack*. From its first appearance in the fourth episode in Season One, "Between a Rock and Harlin's Place," the name of Jack's one-man-show-within-a-show—and its accompanying signature gesture, of two open hands framing the face—became a fan favorite faster than you can say… **"Just Jack."**

The (mostly imaginary) accolades Jack Mc Farland received for *Just Jack* led to sequels and further finger movements, such as *Jack 2000* (two raised fingers on one hand, fingers curled into a zero with the other, with the eyes in between) and *Jack 2001* (you get the picture.) In the third-season episode "Last of the Really Odd Lovers," Jack announced he was even planning an upcoming *Jack 2002*—just as Sean Hayes himself was tiring of the whole bit.

Series co-executive producer Jon Kinnally recalls riding on an up escalator with Sean, "and everyone passing us going down started doing the *Just Jack* hands. "It's my **'Dyn-o-mite,'** or my **'whatchu talkin' 'bout, Willis,'**" Sean laments. Those shows, however, rode their phrases until they dropped, whereas the **WILL & GRACE** writers had the sense to stop—or did they? "Well, I requested that they stop," Sean admits.

While Sean is flattered to have had such an impact on fans, he fears that a hand gesture, improvised one day at rehearsal, could become too big a part of his legacy. "It's bittersweet. Thank God it's there, and yet I want it to go away," he says.

KAREN & MEGAN

Dying on Stage

Megan Mullally spent the first six years of her life in Los Angeles—and the next 20 or so working her way back. After her father, Paramount contract player Carter Mullally, Jr., grew frustrated with acting, he brought his wife, Martha, and their daughter back to his hometown of Oklahoma City. There was no performing arts program at her private Episcopalian Cassidy School—"They hadn't been invented yet in Oklahoma City," she laments—so Megan studied ballet for five hours each night after school. One day she made an important discovery about herself: "I realized that my favorite ballet roles were the ones where I was required to act," she says. "Having a mad scene and then dying onstage was the best part."

Acting Came Later

It's hard to believe now, but Megan was shy. It wasn't until her under graduate years at Northwestern University that she summoned the nerve to really try acting. "It freaked me out, because I didn't know I was so inhibited," she remembers. "Nobody in Oklahoma City had been rolling around on the ground pretending to be a peanut, because everybody was in their madras shorts and Izod shirts, and that just wasn't done."

Turned off by the experience, Megan transferred out of the school's renowned theater department—and has to this day not taken any acting classes—but she did continue to perform in college shows. After building up her confidence, she dropped out of Northwestern to pursue her career full-time. "My parents were very supportive," Megan says, even her actor father, who had once warned her not to follow in his footsteps. "When I was little and I had told him I might want to be an actress, he said, 'Don't do that—it's too hard a life.'"

A Long String of Short Series

After a six years in Chicago theater, Megan moved to Los Angeles, and won her first regular television role on the short-lived 1986 sitcom **THE ELLEN BURSTYN SHOW**. She felt a little over her head. "It was great getting to work with Ellen Burstyn and Elaine Stritch," she reports, "but I was twenty-seven, and very green. I had a lot of natural ability, but I didn't have the experience to back it up."

During the next twelve years, she was cast in many more series—all of which quickly fizzled: **MY LIFE AND TIMES**; **RACHEL GUNN, R.N.**; **FISH POLICE**. Bit parts in the films **RISKY BUSINESS**, **ONCE BITTEN**, **QUEENS LOGIC** and **ABOUT LAST NIGHT** kept her afloat in the 80s, along with guest shots on the television dramas **CHINA BEACH** and **MURDER, SHE WROTE**.

By the 90s, she was guest starring on almost every TV comedy you can think of: **NED & STACEY** (where she first met that series' star, Debra Messing), **ALMOST GROWN**, **HERMAN'S HEAD**, **DEAR JOHN**, **THE NAKED TRUTH**, **SEINFELD**, **FRASIER**, **MAD ABOUT YOU**, **WINGS**, **CAROLINE IN THE CITY** and **JUST SHOOT ME**.

Turning Karen Down

Small wonder, then, that Megan was burned out on sitcoms by the time Karen Walker came along.

"I'd done a million pilots, and eight trillion guest spots," says Megan. "I had gotten to the point where I vowed I wasn't going to audition for any sitcoms. Then I had no money, and beggars can't be choosers, so when they sent me the **WILL & GRACE** script, I read it."

The only trouble was, her audition was for the role of Grace, and Megan wasn't quite right. When her agent asked her to come in a second time and try out for Karen, she read the script...and said no.

"In that original script, the role of Karen was totally different from what it is now," Megan recalls. "This was a small part that seemed to be too reminiscent of Christine Baranski on **CYBILL**." But at her agent's urging, Megan took another look...and had a brainstorm. "I had an idea of a little twist I could put on the part to make her a little more interesting, by playing against the rich, sarcastic thing and instead playing her a little more...*weird*."

By the time Megan read for Max and David, they'd forgotten her audition for Grace. When she was finished, they'd forgotten everyone else's audition for Karen. Megan nailed the part in funky vintage clothes that Karen wouldn't be caught dead in. Max and David begged her to wear something "a little more Madison Avenue" to her network test, the final approval required to get the job. "I said, 'Are you kidding me?'" she remembers. "Listen, if you want to come over and go through my closet, we can go to a rock club, but we're not going to any Madison Avenue." Frankly, she didn't think there'd be a network test.

"My first choice that year was to play Carrie on **KING OF QUEENS**, which ended up going to Leah Remini," Megan says. **WILL & GRACE** still wanted her, but the feeling wasn't yet mutual. "This sounds so crazy in retrospect," she admits. "Two hours before the test, at two p.m., Tracy Lilienfield called me because she knew I was thinking of not showing up. And I was home in my pajamas, eating scrambled eggs—no makeup or hairdo or anything."

With the minutes ticking by, Megan made up her mind to go for it. She dressed quickly and hurried to the test. "When I walked in the door, they all cheered and clapped," she remembers. "And that was where my doubts suddenly ended."

Finding Karen's Voice

"I had had the instinct to do Karen's voice at the audition, but I was sure that they would think it was too weird," says Megan. She held back at rehearsals, too, fearful that she'd get herself fired, especially over an instinct that she couldn't explain. But she remained certain she was right, and as she worked the voice in slowly over **WILL & GRACE**'s first few episodes, she realized why. "My regular speaking voice is very laconic, and this is farce," she explains. "Her chirpy voice just seemed right for the pace and energy of the show—plus I think it's funny that somebody who is that critical of others would have such a bad flaw that doesn't seem to bother her in the slightest."

That Funny Feeling

Unlikely as it sounds, it wasn't until Season Three that Megan felt comfortable with comedy. Despite her resume, she'd always thought of herself as a good actress who could communicate a writer's comedy, but not her own. But in the right role, surrounded by supportive and courageous cast mates, Megan finally owned her greatness. "Being on this show has taught me about taking chances and trusting that what I instinctively feel like doing will be funny," she says.

That Killer Rack

Speaking of taking chances, offering your décolletage to prime-time audiences probably qualifies. "I don't think I had ever shown cleavage more than five times before playing Karen," Megan confides. She's still hasn't grown accustomed to letting it all hang out. "Even just recently I said to Sean, 'Is there not enough fabric in the world? Do they not have skeins of fabric large enough to cover my chest?' Each time "the kids" make an appearance, their legend grows. "My breasts have become mythologized," sighs Megan. "People think I have this huge Pamela Anderson chest. But I'm like a 36B—**that's not big.**"

Living the High Life

Another area where fantasy doesn't resemble reality is in Karen's excesses. "When Max told me that Karen was always drunk, I was panicked," she admits. "I thought, 'Oh my God, she's drunk? Do I have to act drunk?' And he said, 'No. With Karen, you would never be able to tell.'" So Megan inhabits a character who is perpetually under the influence, but who never shows it. Not very realistic, but a congruent part of that strangely innocent, consequence-free fantasy world into which **WILL & GRACE**'s characters—particularly Karen and Jack—often slip. Anyone inclined to take Karen's exploits literally should consider her rap sheet, as described by Megan: "Not only does she drink, but she does practically every drug there is. She carries a gun, she has committed murders, she's part of a gang, she's friends with both Ol' Dirty Bastard and Candice Bergen. She has mob ties, she used to be a stripper, she did a porn video... You can't take her background all that seriously."

Karen's Omnisexuality

Everyone knows Karen is a wild woman. But there's one department where she's shown plenty of restraint: despite a past that includes a three-way marriage with Connie Chung and Maury Povich, she managed for the most part not to cheat on Stan. Megan says the writers wanted Karen to defy expectation when it came to her marriage: "They wanted people to believe that as fat and hairy and obnoxious and gassy as Stan was, Karen really loved him."

Of course, there was that one moment of weakness…but how can a gal be expected to resist Rip Torn? "Karen likes the silver foxes," says Megan. She herself enjoys being mismatched with older romantic interests. And—who knows?—they may not be mismatches after all. "You're not supposed to know how old Karen is, because she's supposedly had like 735 face-lifts," Megan muses. "So Karen could be seventy and look the same age as these guys. Meanwhile, I've never done anything with plastic surgery. I don't even have pierced ears."

And, as viewers well know, Karen's got a taste for the vixens as well as the foxes. The references to Sapphic satisfactions started with Grace: "There was something early on where Grace has me bend over and I say something like 'Honey I tried this once in college'—but soon we saw Karen turn down Martina Navratilova's proposal; and because she doesn't understand what breast-feeding is, she came on to a woman nursing her baby in a bar. Megan suggests we not scrutinize Karen's sexuality any more closely than her personality's other pleasure-seeking parts. "You can't analyze it, really," she says. "There are just certain things that turn her on and you never know what they're going to be. But when she's turned on, she's all the way."

Life imitated art when Megan created a media stir in 1999 by telling gay magazine The Advocate that she considers most people —including herself—to be bisexual. Not long after, she grew close to Nick Offerman, an actor eleven years her junior, and the two married in a small ceremony in September 2003 at the home they share with their champagne poodle, Willa.

Her professional achievements have been similarly rich. Megan won the 2000 Emmy for Outstanding Actress in a Comedy Series, the 2001 American Comedy Award for Funniest Female Performer in a Television Series, and in 2004 became the first performer to win three consecutive Screen Actors Guild awards. Apart from the trophies, Megan has also won roles in the theatrical films **MONKEYBONE**, **STEALING HARVARD** and Disney's **TEACHER'S PET**.

Somehow, Megan finds time for her love of music and theater. In 2002, she released a musical CD, **BIG AS A BERRY**, with her L.A. band Supreme Music Program. In the spring of 2003, she and Nick appeared together in Kelly Stuart's play **MAYHEM**, and later that year she performed in a sold-out, four-week run of her self-conceived, one-woman musical, **SWEETHEART**. An apt title for a gifted actor with prime-time America wrapped around her finger.

SEASON

TWO

"We moved Grace out because I'm a big believer in evolution in a comedy series," Jimmy Burrows explains. "I learned that on Cheers. At the end of our first year we got Sam and Diane together, and everybody said it was the worst possible choice. But our defense was that if Sam Malone can't get a girl in bed after a year, then he's not a cocksmith. Characters have to move and change. Grace has to say, 'I think it's a little pathetic I'm living with a gay man.'"

Award Winning Season

The new living arrangements could also drive a new season's worth of plots. David Kohan explains, "Our stories could then come from them questioning what it would be to get them to the point of thinking that life is better together than apart." Moving Grace across the hall was the perfect "compromise effort," satisfying the characters' drive to find romantic relationships, and the audience's desire for Will and Grace to stay together.

Now that NBC had picked up the show for a second season, the writers were free to make long-ranging plans for their characters' futures (as opposed to thinking in thirteen-week blocks of time). Several strategies were put in place to broaden the scope of the show beyond Will and Grace's own relationship (and living room) as well.

First, they gave Will a new job in a corporate firm, where he would have to answer to a difficult boss. "Nobody sparks particularly to law stories, but everyone understands that there's a certain drudgery to working in a corporate office under a boss," reasons David. And if that boss could be a love interest for Grace, all the better. "We realized that getting Grace involved with his boss is a good way to integrate the Will-and-Grace story with stories about Will's career," says David.

"By then, someone had to have a boyfriend," Max adds, "and we thought we would start with Grace, because that would be a safer bet. But I also remember that we were no longer afraid of the fact that Will was gay. I remember saying, 'It's time to give this gay man a real voice.'"

So Will began to get some—mostly implied—action in Season Two, if not true love. And thus began an unofficial **WILL & GRACE** tradition:

at the start of each of the next few seasons, the producers would be asked, *Is this the year Will finds a boyfriend?*

"This was about the time," Max remembers, "that it was dawning on us that we had four of the best actors ever to step onto a sitcom stage… it was always a problem to find people who could stand up to them. We found ourselves firing one actor after another who came on the show, and we never found boyfriends who could hold up to Will or Grace, just in terms of talent."

Jack, in the meantime, had met his match. "Marrying Jack off to Rosario just before the start of the second season was the most subversive homosexual move that we could have made," Max says. "We were able to explore so much more about Jack's homosexuality through his heterosexual marriage. And that was an arc that Sean played particularly well, because he had something to play all year."

After the second season drew to a close, the show received the ultimate validation in the land of television: **WILL & GRACE** won the 2000 Emmy for "Outstanding Comedy Series." Sean Hayes and Megan Mullally also won "Outstanding Supporting Actor" and "Actress" awards, and Eric McCormack and Debra Messing had been nominated for their leading roles.

"This award really indicates a whole new meaning to the phrase 'acceptance speech,'" Max said, clutching his new Emmy at that night's ceremony. Then, looking at the trophy, he added, **"I finally met a girl I want to sleep with."**

201 GUESS WHO'S NOT COMING TO DINNER

Written By: DAVID KOHAN & MAX MUTCHNICK

...at's the point of Grace moving across the hall if she spends as ...ch time at Will's as when she lived there? When Grace bursts in ... Will while he's lounging nude on the sofa, the two quarrel. Each ...clares his/her independence, and to prove it, Will asks out a guy ... met at a bookstore, while Grace throws a disastrous dinner party ...thout Will's help. Meanwhile, to avert I.N.S. suspicion, Karen ...akes Jack move into Rosario's quarters in her manse in the sky.

> **KAREN:**
> *"They're like Siamese twins who are joined at their boring personalities."*

RECURRING CHARACTERS
Shelley Morrison *as* Rosario
Tom Gallop *as* Rob
Leigh-Allyn Baker *as* Ellen

...HELLEY MORRISON: When I came to the table read for the first show ...the second season, I noticed a gift sitting on the table, which turned out ...be for me. It was from the four actors, but Eric had picked it out. The card ...d, "To the fifth Beatle." And inside was an original *Flying Nun* lunch pail ...h my picture on it.

...IC McCORMACK: One of my favorite scenes we ever did was where I'm ... the phone with a guy from Borders Books. It was the first time in the show ...ere I felt completely confident in the part. I'd cut my hair and I felt like the ...d for the first time. The first season will always be really charming, but for ... the second season was when this show became really funny and where I ...n felt like I became funny.

> **WILL:**
> *"I got a call from my friend at the I.N.S. yesterday, and apparently the marriage between a 30-year-old gay man and a post-menopausal Salvadoran maid flagged something in their computer."*

...I: When a preview copy of this episode was released, Karen's ...e—"Hey, you're on the clock, tamale. Get to work."—sparked ...troversy and protest from Latin groups. NBC initially apolo-...ed, and redubbed "tamale" with the word "honey" for the show's ...st airing. But when the show aired in syndication, the change ...s undone, with the network taking the position that they had ...erreacted earlier.

202 ELECTION

Written By:
ADAM BARR

> **JACK:**
> *"A little tip. When you shadow, a good rule of thumb is less is more. Okay?"*

Grace challenges Will for the presidency of the Tenants' Association after she learns that the office has its perks, such as determining who gets to have a working fireplace in his or her apartment. It's a low-down, dirty campaign, with Grace baking goodies and Will handing out flashlights to bribe the electorate. After the vote deadlocks, Will and Grace race to St. Luke's Hospital, where Grace wins over the ailing Mr. Munitz and his tie-breaking vote. Over at Karen's, Jack is devastated when Guapo flies out a window that Karen left open. Jack lets Karen soothe her conscience by treating him to shopping sprees, but ultimately is tricked into admitting that Guapo long ago returned, safe and sound.

RECURRING CHARACTERS
Shelley Morrison *as* Rosario
Marshall Manesh *as* Mr. Zamir *(first appearance)*
Klaus Von Puppy
Guapo

> **ROSARIO:**
> *"When I prayed to the Madonna for a husband, maybe I should have been more specific."*

FYI: Alan March, who plays one of Will's neighbors at the Tenants' Association meeting, is the cousin of series executive producer Jhoni Marchinko.

FYI: There is an informal tradition among the *Will & Grace* writers that Adam Barr will write the opening episode of each season. "He's very fast, and writes terrific drafts," Jeff Greenstein explains.

ADAM BARR: *Election* is near and dear to my heart because it introduced the character of Mr. Zamir. I actually ran that casting session and picked him myself, from among three or four other Middle Eastern ethnic types. (He was far and above the winner.) I loved that he had an indistinct point of origin about him.

FYI: Will's neighbor Mrs. Pressman hints that her umbrella may have been stolen by Tim Kaiser in 12B. The potential thief is named for one of the show's executive producers.

203 I NEVER PROMISED YOU AN OLIVE GARDEN

Written By: JON KINNALLY & TRACY POUST

WILL:
"Yeah, it's family style! Later, the waiters come over and tell you what a disappointment you are to them."

At an uncomfortable dim sum dinner, Rob and Ellen start to miss their favorite restaurant, the Olive Garden, and decide to leave Will and Grace to eat with the "weirdos" at the group table. Becoming fast friends with the hip Manhattan couple, Naomi and Kai, Will and Grace invite them over for cocktails and an evening out on the town, without realizing they had made plans with Rob and Ellen for the same night. Meanwhile, Karen asks Jack to accompany her to her stepkids' elementary school for a discussion with the principal. There, he befriends a young boy who mirrors himself as a child, helping them both face their fears.

GUEST STARS
Tamlyn Tomita *(The Joy Luck Club)* as Naomi
Steve Valentine *(Crossing Jordan)* as Kai

RECURRING CHARACTERS
Tom Gallop *as* Rob
Leigh-Allyn Baker *as* Ellen

TOM GALLOP: As a thank-you for bringing us back again and again throughout the season, Leigh-Allyn and I got the producers a gift—a gift basket from the Olive Garden.

LEIGH-ALLYN BAKER: My dad always wants to go to the Olive Garden, and I'm always too embarrassed to go in now. Because as soon as we step inside, he'll say, "You know, my daughter did an Olive Garden episode."

FYI: Jack reveals that as a child he was teased and called "Jack McFairyland." The writers had been waiting to use this joke—it's the reason why they gave Jack the last name of McFarland in the first place.

KAREN:
"Honey, my time is precious. Call me when one of them gives birth at the prom."

FYI: The redheaded secretary who comes out of Principal Daley's office to retrieve Karen is Debra Messing's stand-in, Amy Crofoot. She also appears in the second season episode *Acting Out* as the NBC receptionist.

204 POLK DEFEATS TRUMAN

Written By:
JEFF GREENSTEIN

When Harlin announces that he is about to buy a cable company, Will dumps all his "little clients"—even Grace's Aunt Honey—in order to be able to concentrate on Harlin's business full-time. But when Harlin fires Will, leaving his practice in a shambles, it turns out that Grace's warnings against Will's arrogance were right. Meanwhile, Grace helps Karen when Stan puts her on a budget. Their ill-advised trip to a Paramus, New Jersey outlet mall—and Karen's budget crisis—ends when a frustrated Karen calls Stan and threatens to show up at the next society dinner in rhinestone jogging suit.

JACK:
"I think the first thing you're going to buy me is color contacts. I need new eyes for fall."

RECURRING CHARACTER
Gary Grubbs *as* Harlin Polk

JEFF GREENSTEIN: The reason why Grace has such a ferocious reactic to Will's treatment of his clients is because he is the ethical standard of the friendship. It's always hardest when your friends with the most integrity are the ones to disappoint you.

WILL:
"You know the old saying. 'Give Jack a fish, he eats for a day Teach Jack to fish, he brings home a fisherman.'"

...e to shadows and camera angles in a newspaper writeup ...Grace, her breasts look enormous. When an old boyfriend, who ...st happens to have seen the photo, calls Grace and invites ...r to a showing of his watercolors at a local gallery, Grace decides ...at she needs to have those big boobs when she meets him in ...rson. Karen introduces Grace to the miraculous "Liqui-Bra," and ...the gallery show, Grace's new fluid boobies do the job—until, ...ring a hug, Karen's brooch punctures the bra. When Grace finds ...t that her old flame was just interested in her for her boobs, she ...uirts her bra water all over his watercolors. Meanwhile, Jack is ...gered when he learns that Will had a fling with his old boyfriend, ...lter. But when Will arranges to have Walter show up at the ...llery to show Jack that he's sorry, it turns out that Walter wasn't ...actly the guy Jack was remembering.

GUEST STAR
...cott Patterson *(Gilmore Girls)* as Grace's ex-boyfriend Donald Dorio

a Favorite Episode of...

BRA MESSING: I've been made fun of my entire life for my small ...asts, so it was fantastic to play that out in a comedy in front of the entire ...ld. I felt like I was saying, "Small-breasted women, unite! We're going to ...ke it." I look at *Das Boob* as an ode to Lucy. And the very first scene of the ...sode, I think, is probably one of the best "A" scenes that has ever been ...ten. It ends up with Jack, Will, and Grace all feeling each other's breasts ...l comparing them. The timing of that was intricate. We spent about a half ...r on just the choreography of feeling each other's breasts, because you ...n't want it to be too sexual or too long. It was exciting because it was one ...he first times where we were pushing that boundary.

...: The Zelman Gallery, where the art opening is being held, ...named for Debra Messing's husband Daniel Zelman. The Zelman ...llery makes another appearance in Season Six in *"A Gay/ ...cember Romance."*

WILL:
"I haven't been with a woman in some time, but I'm pretty sure they're not supposed to do that."

KAREN:
"It's the oldest story in the world: Boy meets Girl, Boy wants Girl to do dominatrix film, Girl says 'Naked?' Boy says 'Yeah,' Girl says 'Forget it.' Boy says 'Okay, then just wear this rubber dress and beat the old guy with a scrub brush.' Girl says 'How hard?'"

GUEST STAR
Terry Kiser *(Weekend at Bernie's)* as Carl

After an unemployed Will tells Jack that a trained monkey could do Jack's job as a cater-waiter, Jack challenges him to replace a waiter who called in sick. But when Will arrives at the Waldorf-Astoria, he learns that he's going to be serving at a function for the American Bar Association. Unable to face his former colleagues as a waiter, Will pretends to be a guest. But when an old law school buddy insults Jack, Will comes to his defense. Meanwhile, Grace turns the tables on Karen when she discovers that, a few years back, Karen made a few "specialty" films for men who appreciate a clean diaper and a strict maid. After an unsuccessful attempt to retrieve the tapes from sleazy producer Carl, Karen returns to the office and quits. However, that day, without Karen's knowledge, Grace had scoured the seamy underside of Manhattan and bought up all of the remaining tapes.

MEGAN MULLALLY: This was the first time that anything that really out-there had been revealed about my character, and I loved it. I loved that she did fetish films. Whenever I'm at the desk in Grace's office, we try to think of different bits of business for me to do. When Grace first shocks Karen by playing the sound on the porn film, my first instinct was to fall out of the chair. But Jimmy Burrows came up with the bit that we ended up using. They rigged my compact with baby powder, and when I choked, I blew the powder everywhere.

JACK:
"Tonight, I'm supervising an event at the Waldorf-Astoria. I will have eight men under me. How great is that?"

WILL:
"Eight men? What did you do—write the gay Make-a-Wish foundation?"

Will decides to host Thanksgiving dinner at his apartment this year, and as a surprise to Jack, invites Jack's mother, Judith. During one of her patented "test-runs"—to see how long it will take her to get to Will's apartment holding a casserole dish—Judith shows that she obviously does not know that Jack is gay. With his friends' urging, Jack comes out to his mother during dinner, and finds out a secret of Judith's as well: Jack's father is not his biological father, and she doesn't know who is.

GUEST STAR
Veronica Cartwright *(L.A. Law)* as Jack's mother, Judith McFarland

SEAN HAYES: A lot of people do come up to me and say, "Thank you for that episode. It was easier—I popped that one in to show my parents after I came out."

KAREN:
"Honey, I think you're missing the silver lining here. When you're old and in diapers, a gay son will know how to keep you away from chiffon, and backlighting."

a Favorite Episode of...

MAX MUTCHNICK: I love this episode because of the gentleness we show between Will and Jack in the moment when Will tells him why it's important that he come out to his mother. I think it is such an effective, beautiful scene between two gay men.

JHONI MARCHINKO: I thought it was such a funny thing to do an episode where a character like Jack, who is so flamboyant and obviously gay, has a mother who doesn't know. I loved seeing Jack emotional, which was a new thing for the character. Sean struggled with it, though, because he's "the funny guy." He was nervous about just taking a breath and playing a real moment. Because it was so emotional, when Will and Jack were talking out on the balcony, it brought tears to my eyes. And we got letters from kids who said that they knew the episode was coming, so they watched it with their families and then came out. To hear that we changed someone's life and know that person has a relationship with his or her family—to me, that meant so much.

Grace braces herself for the worst when Bobbi, her meddlesome mother, announces that she's coming to visit, with an old summer camp friend of Grace's in tow. But Bobbi unexpectedly fixes Will up, instead of Grace, with the guy, and when the two hit it off, Grace is angry—until she realizes that she is actually reacting to the fear that her mother might have given up on her. Meanwhile, Jack and Rosario must convince a suspicious I.N.S. agent that they are really married. The newlyweds have their work cut out for them: the I.N.S. agent is an old lover of Jack's!

GUEST STAR
Peter Paige *(Queer As Folk)* as I.N.S. investigator

RECURRING CHARACTERS
Shelley Morrison *as* Rosario
Debbie Reynolds *as* Bobbi Adler

ROGER:
"Let's stop pretending. gotten farther your husba than you have."

PETER PAIGE: I was a total unknown, and I had been brought in to replace a guest star who had been fired. I was excited to be working with Jimmy Burrows, and on a new hit show. I got the okay after my first day that everyone was happy with my work. Then it was the night before tape night, and we were rehearsing the scene in my office, arguing about whether to keep Rorio in the country. We finished running through it, and Max said to the write "We really don't have the ending to the scene—we don't have a 'blow.'" And piped up and said, "Well, what if Karen just goes back to treating her like maid right away?" Max whipped around and looked at me with the deade eyes and said, "We never take suggestions from the floor." There was a lo pause while I was shrinking down to the size of nothing, and then he said, "But I gotta say, that's pretty good." To this day, when Max sees me, he say "You're the only guy I've ever taken a joke from off the floor."

FYI: When Will, Grace, Bobbi, and Andy Felner are at lunch, take a look over Grace's shoulder at the table behind them. The woman with the long brown hair later played a taxi driver in *A.I.: Artificial Insemination* and the cashier at the sub shop in *Fanilow*. (It's Karen's stand-in, Peggy Lane O'Rourke.) The man at Virgin Records who gives Jack a dirty look for his love of Cher is series writer Jon Kinnally.

(209) HE'S COME UNDONE

Written By:
ADAM BARR

...gued by sex dreams about Grace, Will brings her along to ...rapy. The session goes so well that soon Grace and the therapist ...secretly dating, although out of guilt, she will not sleep with ...1. Frustrated, the therapist begins exploiting Will's dreams in ...attempt to get Grace into bed. When Will discovers the affair, ...confronts Grace, using it as conclusive evidence that she needs ...lways be the center of attention. Meanwhile, Jack threatens ...ithhold his companionship unless Karen treats Rosario bet- ...But when Karen changes her ways, Rosario can't stand it and ...eatens to quit.

RECURRING CHARACTER
Shelley Morrison *as* Rosario

JACK:
"You're in love with me. You can't have me. You're fat. Ergo, Grace. It all lines up perfectly."

...AM BARR: In this episode, Jack says he, too, has dreams about women— ...ra, Bette, and Liza. In writing a show in which the central characters ...gay, we're always walking a careful line between current, hip references, ...:h can have a short shelf life, and older ones, which can be clichés. The ...sic gay references can be very funny, but we try hard not to overuse them.

(210) HEY LA, HEY LA, MY EX-BOYFRIEND'S BACK

Written By: JEFF GREENSTEIN

WILL:
"Nice job of protection, Grace. If you were a condom, I'd be pregnant now."

When Will's ex-boyfriend, Michael, asks Grace to design his apartment, Will tells her to go ahead and take the job. After all, he and Michael are over each other. Or are they? Will begins to suspect that Michael is using Grace to work his way back into Will's life, and realizes that he has his own unresolved feelings, too. Will confronts Michael, but ends up embarrassing himself in front of Michael's new boyfriend. At first, Will is angry at Grace for not warning him about Michael's relationship, but eventually realizes that it is truly time to move on. Responding to Karen's demands for more responsibility in the workplace, Grace lets her design one chair. But as Grace attempts to use a visualization technique to help Karen detail her design, Karen freaks out and abandons the project.

GUEST STAR
Chris Potter *(Queer As Folk) as* Will's ex-boyfriend Michael

KAREN:
"I've come to a decision. I'm going to decorate Michael's place. I mean, he's gay—how hard could it be? Chrome, black leather, a shower for six...done!"

DAVID KOHAN: We always knew we wanted to meet Michael at some point. We had put a lot of emphasis on this character, and he explained a lot about Will. It had even become a joke in the writers' room, as a rationale for anything about Will's behavior or dating life. We waited until the second season to do this episode, because at first we had tried not to hit the "I Miss Michael" thing too hard—we always thought it made Will too pathetic.

When big-shot attorney Ben Doucette backs out of a decorating deal that has already cost Grace time and money, she persuades Will to represent her in a suit for damages. Although intimidated, Will argues her case so well that Ben offers him a job. There's a problem, though: Will's first assignment is to get rid of Grace's lawsuit. Torn between conflicting obligations, Will ultimately chooses not to betray Grace. Ben is unexpectedly impressed by Will's moral fiber and, claiming it was all a test, lets him keep his job. Meanwhile, Karen and Jack act in a corporate video about sexual harassment, and Jack demonstrates his willingness to throw himself into a part.

Will's best friend from high school, Claire, asks him to donate sperm so that she can have a baby. When Will says yes, Grace is upset by the prospect of his fathering another woman's child. Karen concludes that Claire has stolen Grace's own backup plan, that Grace wanted Will to be hers alone should she ever need his sperm. Grace confronts Will at the sperm bank, accusing him of being too loose with sperm that by all rights belongs to her. Will is incensed by Grace's selfishness, but then realizes that if he someday does father a child, he would want it to be with her.

GUEST STAR
Megyn Price *(Grounded for Life)* as Will's high school best friend, C

RECURRING CHARACTER
Laura Kightlinger *(series writer)* as Nurse Shelia *(first appearance)*

RECURRING CHARACTERS
Gregory Hines *as* Ben Doucette *(first appearance)*
Jo Marie Payton *as* Mrs. Freeman *(first appearance)*

SEAN HAYES: It was really hard to get through rehearsing and filming the scenes of Jack and Karen making the sexual harassment video and sticking their tongues in each other's ears. We couldn't stop laughing, especially at rehearsal. It was that kind of laughing where you can't breathe and you're slapping the floor.

MAX MUTCHNICK: The term that Jack coins for a sperm donation, "macho gazpacho," was suggested by one of our cameramen, Glenn Shimada.

GRACE:
"I knew you when you were on the cus when you made me to Chippendale's ev Saturday night beca you said they made killer mai tai."

WILL:
"Of course. That ruthless bastard offered me a five-year contract, paid vacation, a huge signing bonus—all to make a dispute over slipcovers go away. How could I have been so blind?"

GRACE:
"Why do your people always go to sarcasm first?"

FYI: Will's line to Ben Doucette ("You mean I'm Willy Wonka and I just gave me the keys to the chocolate factory?") is a coincidental in-joke, since later, in "Boardroom and a Parked Place," Gene Wilder, the Willy Wonka of film, plays Doucette & Stein partner Mr. Stein.

FYI: Will and Claire recount how after the senior prom, they're driving to the beach when Claire made her move, leaning in clo and kissing Will—and Will crashed into a Dodge dart. This is a erence to the real-life story of Max Mutchnick and Janet Eisen "I ended up totaling Janet's father's car," Max says, "probably ju to distract her long enough so that we didn't have to have sex."

JACK:
"Of course you're freaked out. You can't just start sleeping with women. Who are you— Anne Heche?"

OH, DAD, POOR DAD, HE'S KEPT ME IN THE CLOSET AND I'M FEELING SO SAD

Written By: KATIE PALMER

l insists on being at an award dinner honoring his father,
orge, despite George's efforts to keep him away. At the banquet,
l discovers that George has never told his colleagues that Will is
, and that he's made everyone think Will and Grace are hus-
d and wife. Grace enjoys the charade, but Will is stung by his
er's lie. After Will confronts his father with his disappointment,
orge tries to make it up to his son with a well-intentioned but
pletely embarrassing speech about how proud he is of his gay
. Meanwhile, Karen helps Jack through his own daddy issues
arranging a meeting with the man whom she believes is Jack's
g-lost biological father. The plan goes awry, however, when Jack
l his possible father arrive before Karen does, and both assume
meeting is a blind date.

JACK:
*"I hit on
father—
I'm
oon-Yi!"*

GUEST STAR
Perry King (*Riptide*) as John Marshall,
the man Karen thinks is Jack's father

RECURRING CHARACTER
Sydney Pollack as Will's father, George Truman (*first appearance*)

X MUTCHNICK: Everyone fought David on this episode, and he was
vinced it was funny, so he made it happen. And to this day, it is one of
biggest laughs we've ever had in the house.

GRACE:
*"Well, my father's
never invited me any-
where, except that time
he had that lower
GI series. Don't think
Norman Rockwell's
gonna be painting
that one."*

: Among the people Will guesses will be at George's award
ner are "Buz and Rhea," named for David Kohan's parents.

ID KOHAN: People here were grossed out about the idea [of Jack
g on the guy who's supposed to be his father], and nervous that the
ence would be, too.

: Episode title is a reference to the 1959 Arthur L. Kopit play
subsequent 1967 film *Oh Dad, Poor Dad, Mamma's Hung You
he Closet and I'm Feelin' So Sad.*

ACTING OUT

Written By:
DAVID KOHAN & MAX MUTCHNICK

WILL:
*"One giant step
for man-on-
mankind."*

Jack is incensed when a kiss between two gay men scheduled to
air on network television doesn't happen. He vows to take his
complaint directly to the network, but finds little support from his
apathetic friend Will until Grace intervenes. Will and Jack storm
the NBC offices, but are taken even less seriously than the obviously deranged woman with them in the waiting room. Heading
home in defeat, they join a crowd around Al Roker during a live
broadcast of the *Today* show, where Will realizes that if they want
a kiss between gay men to air on network television, they might
as well take matters into their own hands. Unfortunately, Grace's
plan to let boyfriend Josh down easy by telling him she's in love
with Will falls apart when she and Josh then see Will and Jack
smooching on live TV.

GUEST STARS
Al Roker *as* Himself
Jeff Blumenkrantz *as* NBC executive Craig Vissay

RECURRING CHARACTERS
Gregory Hines *as* Ben Doucette
Jo Marie Payton *as* Mrs. Freeman
Ellen Idelson *as* Will's Secretary, Ellen (*voice-over*)
Corey Parker *as* Grace's boyfriend, Josh (*first appearance*)
Mary Pat Gleason *as* crazy homeless woman, Sally (*first appearance*)

JON KINNALLY: I liked *Acting Out,* because it was a very simple story,
plot-wise, and yet it was also subversive, in showing a gay kiss on TV in
the context in which it did. We had a lot of fun with it—and we got to go
to New York for free.

FYI: Jack finally explains his mystifying fat jokes about Will (who
is obviously svelte). When Grace defends Will, Jack tells her: "Hey,
hetero skinny is very different than homo skinny. You're not in the
club. You wouldn't understand."

JACK:
*"It's a gay
network, for
God's sake. The
symbol is a
peacock!"*

FYI: When Karen is in the bathtub, we see the feet of the
forever-mysterious Stan Walker—feet that in reality belong
to a production assistant.

215 TEA AND A TOTAL LACK OF SYMPATHY
Written By: JON KINNALLY & TRACY POUST

KAREN:
"On the piano, and put a little Michelle Pfeiffer into it!"

Ben Doucette gives Will an ultimatum: bring in a major new client by Friday, or be fired. With his deadline looming, Will makes a desperate bid to sweet-talk Karen into giving him the Walker, Inc. account. Drinks with Will go down smoothly until Karen realizes that Will has been playing her, and so she him through a series of retaliatory humiliations. Will finally has enough and storms away, only to learn the next day that Karen has brought the Walker, Inc. account to the firm and thereby saved his job after all. Meanwhile, Grace and Jack use an old teapot to try to get onto their favorite television program: *Antiques on the Road.* The discovery that the teapot is worth thousands sets off a fracas between the greedy friends wherein they accidentally cause damages of an equivalent amount and are forced to forfeit their treasure.

RECURRING CHARACTERS
Gregory Hines *as* Ben Doucette
Jo Marie Payton *as* Mrs. Freeman

JACK:
"Okay, now, do the face of someone who had something really valuable and ruined it with Lemon Pledge."

FYI: Four times during the run of the series, Karen has made small talk with a bartender she calls "Smitty." In this episode, "Smitty" is played by David St. James; in *A.I.: Artificial Insemination* and *Sex, Losers, and Videotape,* "Smitty" is played by Charles C. Stevenson, Jr.—although he seems to be working in a different bar each time; and in *Husbands and Trophy Wives,* a bartender who insists to Karen that his name is *not* Smitty is played by Richard Livingston.

216 THERE BUT FOR THE GRACE OF GRACE
Written by: MICHELLE SPITZ

Will and Grace visit a beloved old college professor who has recen retired, only to find him transformed into a bitter, resentful man with his own "Grace," a straight woman who's been a lifelong frier Observing the older duo's angry, dysfunctional relationship, Will a Grace get a glimpse of their own possible fate and vow never to le it happen to them. Meanwhile, Jack and Ben introduce Karen to t mysteries of the kitchen after Stan does the unthinkable: request home-cooked meal. Jack, desperate to outdo Ben at something, cha lenges him to a competitive tap dance. Not the brightest move wh your guest star is Gregory Hines.

GUEST STARS
Orson Bean *(Mary Hartman, Mary Hartman)* as Will and Grace's revered former professor Joseph Dudley
Piper Laurie *(Carrie)* as Professor Dudley's best friend and hag Sharon Timmers

RECURRING CHARACTER
Gregory Hines *as* Ben Doucette

MEGAN MULLALLY: Working with Gregory Hines, and being right there while he did his tap dance number in this episode, was really thrilling. It was fun flirting with him from behind the glass pane, which was Jimmy's idea—he said, "Honey, get behind the door!" Then we did that thing where I ran my finger down his face, which was my idea. It just happened in the moment.

BEN:
"Mrs. Walker, we've been through this befor Now, I am not a prowler am not a bartender. I am the black guy from Design Women. I am your lawy And maybe if you'd stop bobbing for olives for ha a minute, you might remember that."

FYI: Lost Scene: In this episode, Gary Beach, the flamboyant, cross-dressing theater director Roger DeBris from Broadway's The Producers, filmed an appearance as a future Jack-like best friend of Professor Dudley. But the scene was later scrapped. "The idea of that episode was great," David Kohan explains. "Wi and Grace were terrified of becoming these people, so it's funny that in walks this Jack-like character, too. But Gary Beach could not for the life of him remember two words." "To be fair," Max Mutchnick adds, "he had gotten cast that day, after both Joel Gr and Frank Gorshin had had the part and then quit. But it made for a really long night and ended up being the biggest meltdown we ever had on the show."

217 SWEET (AND SOUR) CHARITY

Written By: **GAIL LERNER**

...ace promises God that she'll do charitable works if she and Will ...[win] Joni Mitchell tickets on a radio call-in show. When they win ...tickets, Grace volunteers her time, and Will's, at a commu-...y center, where they are assigned to direct a children's theater ...[pro]duction of *Stone Soup.* But when the show time is moved back ...[and] is in conflict with the concert, Grace initially chooses Joni's ...w over the children's until guilt—not to mention Joni Mitchell's ...[sec]urity guards, who are not happy with Grace's singing along with ...concert—changes her mind. Karen, too, learns the meaning of ...[giv]ing until it hurts when Jack accidentally donates her favorite ...r of shoes to the community center's rummage sale, where the ... embark on a distasteful mission to get the shoes back.

GUEST STARS

Debra Mooney *(Everwood) as* Sister Roberta
Future Spy Kid Daryl Sabara *as* Broccoli Boy

RECURRING CHARACTERS

Shelley Morrison *as* Rosario
Mary Pat Gleason *as* crazy homeless woman, Sally

[SH]ELLEY MORRISON: When we were making this episode, Megan and I ...the scene in her walk-in closet, where she lifts me up and yells at me for ...[losi]ng her favorite shoes go missing. The writers rewrote that whole scene ...[t]ape night, and Megan and I had two minutes to learn two and a half new ...es, which had even more dialogue than usual because we were doing ...thing where we yell at each other at the same time. But, we were able ...o it.

[MA]X MUTCHNICK: This was the worst episode we ever did. There just ... no good way to talk about the "plight" of the rich white person who ...sn't do enough charity. We could never figure out a good angle to make it ... a believable problem, and because we couldn't find any emotional angle for the characters, we didn't write anything
that mattered. It sounded too ugly to hear Will and Grace
say outright that they don't do enough charity, so we
fudged our way through the episode, and it didn't work.

JACK:
h my God—
y closet were
this, I would
r have come
ut of it."

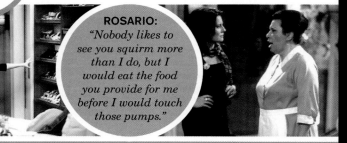

ROSARIO:
*"Nobody likes to
see you squirm more
than I do, but I
would eat the food
you provide for me
before I would touch
those pumps."*

---

218 ADVISE AND RESENT

Written By:
JON KINNALLY & TRACY POUST

Will overcomes his reluctance to let boss Ben fix him up on a blind date and meets a great guy. When the guy doesn't call, however, Will becomes convinced that he is a terrible blind date. Jack's advice on how to master the art of blind dating does little to ease Will's mind, but finally he learns that the whole thing was a misunderstanding: the other guy had been waiting for Will to make the first move. Meanwhile, Grace endures bad dating advice from Karen, who suggests that Grace withhold sex until her boyfriend Josh learns to be more assertive. Grace gives it a try and Josh breaks up with her. But when Josh realizes that Karen was behind Grace's scheme, he tells them both off and shows a tough side that finally turns Grace on.

JACK:
"I'm an expert. Will, I go on literally thousands of dates a year."

WILL:
"That doesn't make you an expert. That makes you an escort."

RECURRING CHARACTERS

Gregory Hines *as* Ben Doucette
Jo Marie Payton *as* Mrs. Freeman
Corey Parker *as* Grace's boyfriend, Josh
Kathleen Archer *as* lesbian delivery woman Molly *(first appearance)*

GRACE:
"He takes pictures of me sleeping. He thinks that's beautiful. To me, it's a little, 'The call is coming from inside the house.'"

TRACEY POUST: Kathleen Archer is a friend of our executive producer Jhoni Marchinko. She turned out to be so funny as the UPS woman that we brought her back a second time.

KAREN:
"Oh, hi, Pharmacist. No, honey, I don't need anything for the week-end. Unless the FDA has approved something new. Oh, terrif. Send me a bottle."

AN AFFAIR TO FORGET

Written By:
ALEX HERSCHLAG & LAURA KIGHTLINGER

When Rob and Ellen ask Will and Grace to be Best Man and Maid of Honor at their wedding, Grace confesses to Will that she and Rob once slept together. Will promises to keep the secret, but Ellen later overhears them talking outside the bridal shower Grace has thrown at her apartment, and angrily calls the wedding off. Will tries to be the voice of reason, but when Ellen throws him onto the bed, he realizes she wants more than advice: she wants Will to be her vehicle for getting even with Rob and Grace. Ellen's not the only one who's confused. At the bachelor party, Jack is appalled when the female stripper turns him on. Everything turns out for the best, as Rob and Ellen reunite and Jack learns the stripper isn't actually a woman.

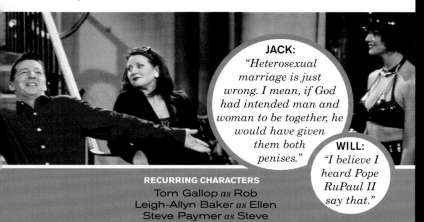

JACK:
"Heterosexual marriage is just wrong. I mean, if God had intended man and woman to be together, he would have given them both penises."

WILL:
"I believe I heard Pope RuPaul II say that."

RECURRING CHARACTERS
Tom Gallop *as* Rob
Leigh-Allyn Baker *as* Ellen
Steve Paymer *as* Steve

FYI: This episode marks the first and only time we see anyone use the door behind Will's kitchen to the building's large, immaculate service stairway.

LEIGH-ALLYN BAKER: The original script for the scene where Ellen tries to seduce Will called for me to be butt naked. Of course as the week goes on, it gets toned down. When it came time to do the scene in front of the audience, I didn't get nervous until I opened Will's nightstand drawer and realized I was holding a condom on national television. And then I had to have the sweater pop open. After the scene was over, I was really shaking, because it was a surreal moment where I had just taken my shirt off on TV.

FYI: Ellen's line—"Now I'm going to grind you like a fresh cup of coffee"—was suggested by actress Leigh-Allyn Baker.

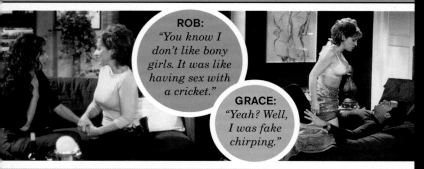

ROB:
"You know I don't like bony girls. It was like having sex with a cricket."

GRACE:
"Yeah? Well, I was fake chirping."

ALEX HERSCHLAG: This episode had a pretty dirty script, and my parents came to the filming. Afterwards, David Kohan went up to them and said, "That was a filthy show, wasn't it?" And my parents said, "We loved it."

MY BEST FRIEND'S TUSH

Written By: **ELLEN IDELSON & ROB LOTTERSTEIN**

JACK:
"Hey, mon frère, if your derriere cou use a little cush, n need to pout, the wo is out. It's Jack's Subway Tush!"

Grace despairs when she learns that she is in competition with famous interior decorator Helena Barnes for a lucrative job. It falls to Karen, who moves in the same circles as Helena, to build Grace's confidence by demonstrating to her that Helena is as human as the rest of us. Meanwhile, Jack persuades Will to help sell a new invention: the Subway Tush, a cushion that rescues backsides from hard subway seats. When investors prefer Jack's over-the-top style to Will's more professional approach, they mak Jack an offer: get rid of Will, and he's got himself a deal. Will is touched when Jack quits the project out of what seems to be loya but later learns that he quit because the investors found out he had stolen the idea for the Tush.

GUEST STAR
Joan Collins *as* haute designer Helena Barnes
Doug Ballard *(one of the history-making gay grooms on* Northern Exposure*) as* Robert Lilienfield

GRACE:
"I can't affo Louis Vuitt and her d poops in it

ADAM BARR: I remember one of this episode's writers, Ellen Idelson, coming in and doing the theme song for the Subway Tush in the writers' room, and we thought it was so funny, we made her do it four times. It was really catching—we found ourselves singing and humming it for months after.

FYI: Grace's client is named for the show's casting director, Tracy Lilienfield.

ROB LOTTERSTEIN: Having been a huge *Dynasty* fan, I was sooooo excited to meet Joan Collins and to get to talk to her. I finally did, at the tap when I was backstage at the Craft Services table. I turned around, and the she was. I mumbled, "Hi, it's so nice to meet you. I'm Rob, one of the write of the episode." She did smile politely, at least, considering I had a mouth full of ham.

(221) THE HOSPITAL SHOW

Written By:
ADAM BARR

WILL:
"If memory serves, he thinks he's God's gift to gay men. And if that's true, then God shops at the Newark Airport."

[Wil]l's miserable blind date is interrupted by the news that Karen's [hu]sband, Stan, has had a heart attack. Will rushes to the hospi-[tal], where he learns that Karen blames Grace for Stan's collapse [bec]ause she'd asked him to move furniture. Will, Jack, Grace, and [Ro]sario make bets on which one of them Karen will turn to during [her] impending emotional collapse. Stan's attack turns out to be [jus]t acute angina, but, tipped off about the bet, Karen takes her [rev]enge: she asks needle-phobic Grace to donate blood; Rosario, to [cle]an the hospital; Will, to work things out with his blind date; and [Jac]k, to cut up the credit cards she has given him. After confront-[ing] her friends about her disgust with their bet, Karen has a rare [mo]ment of vulnerability during which she shares with Grace her [fea]r of losing Stan. The moment quickly passes, however, as Karen [ma]kes Grace swear not to divulge their intimate moment to any-[on]e in the same breath as she resumes ridiculing Grace's clothing.

GUEST STARS
Dan Bucatinsky *(actor-writer from popular gay film* All Over the Guy*) as*
Will's annoying date Neil
Jennifer Elise Cox *(Jan from* The Brady Bunch *movies) as*
incompetent Nurse Trainee Pittman

RECURRING CHARACTER
Shelley Morrison *as* Rosario

a Favorite Episode of...

[AD]AM BARR: This episode—even more so in its original draft—is one of my [fav]orites because it's like one long sketch, with self-involved doctors, stupid [nur]ses, blood, needles...all that's missing is Harvey Korman and Ken Berry.

[DE]BRA MESSING: The only time, really, that I was ever out of control [lau]ghing during a scene in all of our years on the show was during this epi-[so]de. Jennifer Cox as the nurse taking Grace's blood had braces on, and a [lis]p, and take after take, when she would say, 'This is hard,' you would see my [fac]e start to crumble, and I couldn't get it under control. It ended up taking us [abo]ut an hour to finally get the scene.

[DA]N BUCATINSKY: I had auditioned to play a different role the prior [se]ason, and they had promised me a better one "down the line." I didn't think [it w]ould happen, but lo and behold I got the call to come in and play Neil. It [wa]s the week when Shelley Morrison officially became a series regular, so [eve]ryone was in a super-good mood, and she was over the moon.

---

(222) GIRLS, INTERRUPTED

Written By:
JHONI MARCHINKO & TRACY POUST & JON KINNALLY

After reconciling with crazy neighbor Val and spending a friendly evening, Grace notices that her music box is missing. Will immediately suspects Val, but Grace defends her and insists on breaking into her apartment to prove her innocence. After they discover the stolen music box and wrest it from the characteristically violent Val, Grace admits that her defense of Val was due to the delight of having a female friend. Elsewhere, Jack and Karen pose as a married couple to attend a meeting of Welcome Back Home, a group that converts homosexuals back to the straight and narrow. Jack's designs on group leader, Bill, bear fruit once it turns out everyone in the room secretly views the group as a gay pickup joint.

GRACE:
"Why is it always the hygienist? What is it? Is it the white uniforms, the latex, the gloves?"

VAL:
"I think it's because they're whores."

GUEST STARS
Neil Patrick Harris *(Doogie Howser, MD)* as "Welcome Home" leader Bill
Marianne Muellerleile *(Life With Bonnie)* as group member Jodie

RECURRING CHARACTER
Molly Shannon *as* Val

JON KINNALLY: The ex-gay story line was conceived after my roommate's boyfriend suddenly just dumped him, started going out with a woman, and eventually married her. I don't know if he went to an ex-gay ministry, but we used that in this story because "ex-gays" were in the news a lot.

KAREN:
"It looks like your new sweetie has turned his back on homosexuals—and not in the good way."

JIMMY BURROWS: We don't usually get political, we just make it funny. But I guess the show is political in the fact that, for example, I used to drive carpool on Thursdays with 13-year-olds and 14-year-olds, and when I would take them to school, they would all want to know what's going to be on *Will & Grace*. And it occurred to me—oh my God, these are teenagers and they're not homophobic all of a sudden.

MELINDA RITZ: All that the script for this episode specified is that Val is crazy and she has a collection of snow globes. In the course of shopping I got the big kitty, the blowup furniture, and the Keane paintings of girls with big eyes.

WILL:
"Okay, who are you? You're dating two guys, and they're seeing other people. This is not your life. You're not gay or French."

Will's effort to forge a more cordial relationship between Grace and Ben succeeds too well when the two start a steamy affair. But Will feels compelled to tell Grace when he sees Ben dancing with another woman on his conference table. And in an even more career-limiting move, Will also agrees to represent Jack in a suit against Karen; after Jack discovers Rosario is "cheating" on him, he wants a divorce but also wants to be kept in the lifestyle to which he has become accustomed. Under fire from Ben for both siding against wealthy client Karen and butting into his affair with Grace, Will quits. But no sooner has he done so than he learns that Grace knew about Ben's cheating all along, and is in fact cheating on Ben with Josh. What's more, Will's distraction has not only lost Jack's suit against Karen and stuck him with the now homeless Jack as a roommate, it has also cost him his relationship with possible boyfriend Alex, who has had enough of Will's excuses.

RECURRING CHARACTERS
Shelley Morrison *as* Rosario
Gregory Hines *as* Ben Doucette
Jo Marie Payton *as* Mrs. Freeman
Corey Parker *as* Grace's boyfriend, Josh
Marshall Manesh *as* Mr. Zamir
Guapo
Klaus Von Puppy

JACK:
"Rosario married me to get a green card. But as long as I'm married to her, I get a platinum card, a Barneys card, and a Hallmark card that says, 'Welcome to easy street!'"

FYI: Grace reads a wedding announcement for "Janet Eisenberg and David Bromberg." These are the names of Max Mutchnick's best friend from high school, the inspiration for the character of Grace, and her real-life husband, who were married the week the episode aired.

His life a mess, Will grabs a plane to the Caribbean, leaving Grace and Jack to realize that there's no substitute for their best friend. But Will proves too valuable to Doucette & Stein, so Ben follows him to a tropical island and agrees to make him a partner at the firm if he agrees to stay on the islands to set up Walker Inc.'s new offshore company.

GRACE:
"Obviously I didn't plan this thing with Ben. It just happened. It was just this wild chemical ripping of a pair of $50 panties kinda thing."

WILL:
"Thank you, Grace. That'll go next to the visual of my grandmother getting out of the tub."

FYI: Sean Hayes did not care for Jack's parrot, Guapo, since the temperamental parrot would peck while perched on his arm, requiring him to wear a pad underneath his shirt.

FYI: The hand reaching over to touch Karen's boob, supposedly belonging to Stan Walker, belongs to series executive producer Jeff Greenstein.

WHERE IT
THE

From left to right: Alex Herschlag, Jon Kinnally, Bill Wrubel, Jeff Greenstein, Tracy Poust,
Jhoni Marchinko, Gail Lerner, Adam Barr, Sally Bradford, Gary Janetti

ALL BEGINS: WRITERS

THE IDEAS

The show's four stars may seem effortlessly witty, but every joke, story line, and character begins its life as an itch in the fertile imagination of a **WILL & GRACE** writer. Each and every idea must then beat back formidable competition, proving itself over and over during a rigorous development process before it arrives in our living rooms.

It all begins in the hotbed of the writers' room. Here, wildly productive comedic minds pitch ideas at whiplash speed—a lucky few of which will be seized upon by the group, and embark upon the long journey to the screen. But just where does this stuff come from?

Believe it or not, even on **WILL & GRACE**, art imitates life. There's an old adage that says "write what you know," and the staff keeps a firm grasp on this dictum. They mine their own lives for inspiration, and cheerily admit to stealing from their friends' lives as well. Those who don't come up with a particular story chip in with contributions based on their own experiences. In the intensely collaborative writers' room, events from several contributors' lives may make it into a single episode—either as the main premise or as a subplot or a joke—and the person who writes it may not be the one on whose life it's based. A script has many parents.

Other times the comedy stork drops ideas right into the writers' laps. Take, for example, the episode "Acting Out," in which Will and Jack's live **TODAY** show smooch overcomes a network ban on gay kisses. That story came to life when Al Roker, responding to a gay marriage proposal during a live broadcast, reportedly said, "That's like something you'd see on **WILL & GRACE**." Says writer Alex Herschlag: "You can't have an idea more hand-delivered than that."

Keeping It Real

Writers take liberties with life. The real world may inspire story lines, but don't look for absolute realism on the screen. Authentic New Yorkers don't leave their doors unlocked so friends can burst in, and they don't pop back and forth between, say, a Soho office and an apartment on the Upper West Side. "You have to think of it in TV logic," says Gail Lerner. When life is crammed into a twenty-one-minute episode, there's no time to stop and smell the flowers…or buy a MetroCard or unlock a door. And so what if the writers play fast and loose with reality? "If it's funny," asserts Jon, "then it doesn't matter."

Not Even the Facts Are Straight

The same goes for continuity. Like most sitcoms, **WILL & GRACE** has a "show bible," a detailed record that helps the writers keep their facts straight from episode to episode. Unfortunately, admits Jeff, "none of us has ever read it." No surprise, then, that inconsistencies creep in. For example, in one episode Grace says that Will came out to her at Christmas; in another, that event takes place at Thanksgiving.

And good luck keeping track of Karen's husbands—when she married and how she ended the relationships. Says Jon Kinnally, "We do try to be consistent, but whatever makes for a good story will win out."

It's a Living

The original idea was to make Grace a designer so she could be out meeting interesting people for the writers to build stories around. It hasn't turned out that way. "The only reason Grace's job is interesting," says Jeff, "is because Karen lives there." Rich relationships between the primary characters make it easy to confine them to the usual locations. Great for the writers…and lousy for the characters' social lives. How can Will and Grace meet anybody when their creators never let them go anywhere?

Will's workplace is no better when it comes to stimulating the writers. "He's the worst kind of lawyer to write comedy for," says Jeff. "We don't even really know what Will does," adds Tracy Poust. Will may be well paid, but his bread and butter—drafting contracts and brokering deals—make even the most committed fan's eyelids droop. The writers' solution has been to make Will's office like junior high school…and Will the kid everybody hated.

Fresh Is Best

Many story lines on **WILL & GRACE** come from the writers' determination to keep things fresh. "We're pretty good about killing a story if we feel like we've already told something similar," says Adam Barr. New twists, like Karen's sudden Season Six computer competency, create joke opportunities. And when a theme, such as Will and Grace's friendship, feels played out, the show's structure itself is sure to change. Grace gets married, Stan passes away, and suddenly it's a whole new show. In Alex's words: "It opens up doors to emotional territory that we haven't explored before."

Similarly, when humor veins feel tapped out, the writers give them a rest. For example, it's the writers' decision—not newfound sensitivity—that's kept Jack from criticizing Will's weight in recent years. Likewise, when jokes about Grace and food began to sound too familiar, they went on the shelf…until Debra's pregnancy in Season Six, that is. When Debra gained weight, Grace's eating habits became fair game once more.

Fresh Meat

Fresh faces mean fresh ideas, so new characters continually join the **WILL & GRACE** world. Much is at stake when the show commits to a multi-episode character, so the writers spend a lot of time brainstorming the qualities that will bring out the best—and worst—in the series regulars.

Adam Barr, who created Rosario and Leo, is considered especially good at coming up with original characters. "We always joke, every time we need to create a new character, that there's another residual payment for Adam," says Tracy.

Casting can be another source of inspiration. "Once we know who the actor is, we have even more space to create jokes," says Alex. "Once Minnie Driver was cast as Lorraine, we were able to put in a lot of British jokes." The transatlantic taunts slowed only after the staff realized they'd used every single one they could think of.

Sometimes the casting gift keeps on giving. Lorraine, for example, was not intended to be a recurring character. But Minnie Driver's Lorraine, like Shelley Morrison's Rosario, excited everyone's imaginations. They had to have her back. As Jeff says: "Sometimes that combination of actor and character just turns out to be so fantastic that you use them again and again."

TO MAKE A LONG STORY SHORT-ISH

Grace Adler, originally from Schenectady, New York, was a freshman at Columbia University when she attended Nancy Jacobs's party on a starry rooftop across from Paradise Juice. Across the moonlit roof, she spotted a man whom she thought was the cutest she had ever seen, so she walked up and asked him for a drink. He held the funnel for her, and when Grace staggered back to Nancy's side, she famously predicted, *"That's the man I'm going to spend the rest of my life with."*

Will Truman, a typical college upperclassman in 1985, lived in a Columbia dorm with only the bare essentials—futon, stereo and cast-iron enamel fondue pot. One night he was stirring up a batch, and when the chocolate was coming to a gentle boil, a girl came to his door, sniffing. As he remembers it, he looked at Grace Adler, she looked at the chocolate, and the two have been together ever since.

In its first six seasons on the air, **WILL & GRACE** has pieced together an intricate backstory for each of its characters. Some life-changing moments occurred before the cameras, and some had occurred before the cameras even arrived into the lives of Will Truman, Grace Adler, Jack McFarland, and Karen Walker.

"To me, this is why you want to write television," executive producer Jeff Greenstein explains, "especially instead of writing movies. You get to write a big Russian novel over a period of years. In the second season, in "Seeds of Discontent," we planted the 'seed' where Jack mentions how often he has given sperm. We built upon that story idea and had a thirteen-year-old kid of Jack's show up the next season. Similarly, we planted in a mention in first-season episode "William, Tell" about the moment when Will told Grace he was gay, and began laying groundwork for the flashback story in "Lows in the Mid 80s," which we always knew we someday wanted to—and probably had to—tell."

MAX MUTCHNICK: I will never forget the moment, standing on the stage watching Eric and Debra do the scene where Will tells Grace that he's gay, and thinking that this is possibly the most exciting thing that will ever happen to me in my life. It was phenomenal actors speaking the words that have been written by an **A++ Writing Room**. I looked at the two of them and thought that they are as good as it gets. A minute prior, they were in the living room being funny with Debbie Reynolds, and then they walk into the kitchen and are instantly able to deliver the most poignant, life-changing scene.

FOR MORE ON THE BACKSTORY, SEE "LOWS IN THE MID 80S" (P. 87), AND "LAST EX TO BROOKLYN" (P. 165).

During that same fall of 1985, Jack McFarland was a high school junior who routinely hung out at college parties in order to meet guys who were less hung up about their homosexuality. At one such affair, given by never-again-heard-from friend Matt Stokes, Jack met Will. At the time, Will was overweight, and in deep denial about his own true sexual identity.

Will began dating Grace on that fondue-scented eve, and the two began frequenting Chippendale's every Saturday night, due to Will's purported fondness for their killer mai tais. Two months into the relationship, just prior to Thanksgiving, Will threw his own soiree in the dorm room he shared with his future accountant, Rob. At the party, Rob's future wife, Ellen, convinced her friend Grace that her romance with Will would become merely a friendship unless consummated immediately. Taking Ellen's advice, Grace began scheming to get Will into her childhood bed during their trip to her parents' Schenectady home for the holiday.

But at that same party, literally in the closet—for once—was Jack McFarland. Upon meeting Will for the second time, Jack said aloud the fact that dare not speak its name: Will Truman is gay. Angered at the suggestion, Will threw Jack out of his dorm room, but not before accepting Jack's card, which read, **Jack McFarland—Since 1969.**

When Will and Grace arrived at her parents' home, his relationship with Grace was quickly put to the test when she made a surprise appearance in his bed later that night. After some awkward attempts at kissing Grace, Will retreated to an Adler family bathroom and called Jack McFarland for help. But when Jack again suggested that Will just might be hiding from the truth, Will developed a new, albeit shaky, resolve to prove his heterosexuality in bed that night.

As Will and Grace resumed their fumbling attempts at fore-play, Grace—who had already done it three and one half times—came to the realization that Will was a virgin. Equally embarrassed by this new (true) label, Will confessed the "true" reason why he did not want to have sex with Grace: he loved her, and wanted to wait until they were married. Then, within seconds, they were engaged.

Before Will could even make it downstairs minutes later, the Adler household had already erupted into celebration. But the champagne did not get a chance to flow; while helping Grace retrieve it from the kitchen, Will admitted his homosexuality for the first time.

After blurting out the truth to her disappointed—but not surprised—family, Grace threw Will out of her family home that very night. Will made his way back to Manhattan from Schenectady, then went immediately to Jenny Von Sladecker's "Back from Mono" themed party. After loading up on vodka and Squirt, Will met Diane.

WILL:
"I think on some level I've always known. The guy toweling himself off in the Zest commercial always did a little too much for me."

GRACE:
"Oh great! The Zest guy knew before me!"

Attracted to Will because he was cleaner than everyone else at the party, Diane danced with him to Dead or Alive's "You Spin Me Round" before inviting him back to her place. They made love on Diane's futon that night. Diane didn't care that her hair was burning on her nearby hot plate, because, for the only time in her life, she had an orgasm.

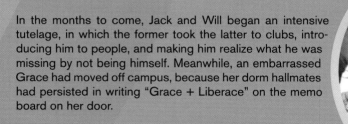

The next morning, Will was deeply ashamed, and he left, never to call her again. He then ran to the house that Jack shared with his single mother, Judith, and spent the day talking about Grace, crying so hard that he could barely iron his jeans.

In the months to come, Jack and Will began an intensive tutelage, in which the former took the latter to clubs, introducing him to people, and making him realize what he was missing by not being himself. Meanwhile, an embarrassed Grace had moved off campus, because her dorm hallmates had persisted in writing "Grace + Liberace" on the memo board on her door.

Exactly one year after their breakup, Will and Grace met once again at a D'Agostino's. They began a reconciliation; Jack admitted to loving Will, although he took it back when Will explained that he saw Jack more as a sister; and Will nearly missed being spotted by Diane at the freezer case.

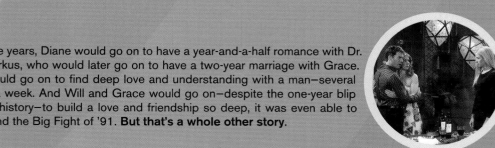

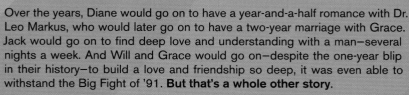

Over the years, Diane would go on to have a year-and-a-half romance with Dr. Leo Markus, who would later go on to have a two-year marriage with Grace. Jack would go on to find deep love and understanding with a man—several nights a week. And Will and Grace would go on—despite the one-year blip in their history—to build a love and friendship so deep, it was even able to withstand the Big Fight of '91. **But that's a whole other story.**

THE PROCESS

Once the initial ideas are in place, the writers hammer away at them to make sure they're sound. "A lot that comes out of the moment and has us giggling all the way home dies the next day," explains Adam. The primary question—is it funny?—isn't always easy to answer.

Ground Rules

"With each character, there are some lines you can't cross," says Tracy, "and we only find out what they are as we go." By consensus, a joke about Karen having once killed a man with a pair of scissors was changed to one about her having robbed a barbecue joint. "Armed robbery is okay," explains Jeff, "but she didn't kill anyone."

The rules are different for each character. Nobody would buy Will Truman as a barbecue bandit.

"In the beginning, I think the rules were most stringent for Will," says Jeff, "because everyone was concerned that he be respectable, dignified, and relatable and never be feminized or diminished."

Befriending Big Brother

Naturally, NBC has a lot to say about which jokes cross the line. But the writers think **WILL & GRACE** gets a lot of latitude because it's a nine o'clock marquee show that competes head to head with hip cable products like **SEX AND THE CITY**.

Gary thinks success has softened the censors: "There are still things we get away with that surprise me. Like at Stan's funeral, when Minnie Driver opened her legs and the silverware fell out? I never dreamed that that would make it in there."

"In the first season," says Tracy, "Max and David didn't want us to write any alcohol jokes for Karen. Now, that's practically all we do." "Blow" was a no-no early on; now drug references slip the censors' grip. But Max and David and the network step in when they feel the writers are overdoing it. "In 'Fanilow,' we couldn't have Karen going to Washington Heights to score coke," recalls Alex.

"The rules do change over the years," agrees Jon. "In the first season, Will calls Jack a fag in 'Will Works Out,' and sponsors got riled." Notes Alex: "Now we throw the word around as a joke."

The Method to the Madness

The **WILL & GRACE** staff writes by splitting into two groups and then presenting their work to each other by acting it out. If it sounds like fun, well, the writers feel the same way. They even credit themselves on extremely rare occasions with out-acting the cast: "My Karen is the best!" jokes Gary.

Actually, most of the writers have appeared on screen in bit roles, and have snuck their names into inside jokes. References to friends and family used to slip in, too, but at the legal department's insistence, those now rarely make it past a first draft. "Our best friend in the world may turn around and sue us because it's GE," says Alex. "Often at the last-minute before taping we'll get these memos that we have to change a name because they found someone with the same name in New York City."

BILL WRUBEL:
"When I got hired on the show, I feverishly tried to learn about the gay world. But when I got here I realized that the show is based on the emotional life that any person has, gay or straight."

When the **WILL & GRACE** writers get script feedback from NBC's Program Standards Department, they are often asked to change or omit specific jokes or references. In the case of Jack's line above, explaining how he won a gay spelling bee, both versions may seem equally naughty. Ken Samuel, the department's vice president who has overseen the show since its fourth season, admits that it's a fine line between which jokes hit the airwaves and which hit the cutting room floor.

"We try to put ourselves in the place of the average viewer of a particular show," Ken explains in determining what might be offensive. There are also different standards for different characters. Karen is quite clearly not a role model, so she can (and does) drink and take drugs with abandon in every episode. And shoot off her mouth quite a bit. "An equal-opportunity bigot," Karen is also given more leeway, when it comes to ethnic slurring, than Will and Grace, who may be used, along with Rosario, to put Karen back in her place.

Since so much of **WILL & GRACE**'s appeal is its edginess, Ken works closely with the writers to find creative solutions that don't compromise the show. "One of my favorite examples is the two Sandra Bernhard episodes," Ken notes. The network allowed Sandra to actually curse on set; then, rather than bleeping her expletives, the show used 'ambient sound'—a blender in one case, and an electric screwdriver in the other—to cover it up.

With **WILL & GRACE,** the network has also allowed the more frequent use of "queer," "fag" and "homo," even with their loaded histories. Ken notes that "Jeff Greenstein has explained it to me over the years as taking back the power of these words, but it's a difficult issue. We don't want to desensitize America to how hurtful those words have been. But by having Will and Jack use the words in each other's presence, hopefully the show is reframing their use.... Context is everything."

ACTION

There are no sure things in comedy. Magic in the writers' room sometimes fizzles outside of it. Jeff tells a story about a joke he loved: in a story line that was eventually cut, Karen asked Will what to serve a visiting Southeast Asian deposed dictator, and Will replied, "A man who murdered thousands in the killing fields…Orange Julius?" "I found it so funny, I had to leave the room," relates Jeff, "and of course the next day at the table read, an actual couple showed up in their Cambodian garb, and nothing was funny."

More often, though, actors add their own magic at table reads. Megan will find laughs in a line as simple as "What?" Sean's delivery of "It is an Eggo," will inspire a sequel: "It is Hot Pockets." And Debra's face after someone has insulted her is comedy treasure. Says Jeff: "You couldn't write anything funnier than that."

A writer enjoys a special feeling of accomplishment when an actor can't get through a line without laughing. On the flip side, when an actor can't get through a tasteless joke without gasping, there's nothing to do but pretend you're offended, too.

The Audience is Always Right

"We act like it just appeared on the page," says Gary. "It's times like that you realize, 'Okay, too far.'"

"By the time it gets to the night we film, it's hard to tell whether a joke is funny or not," admits Tracy, "so we let the audience decide." If a joke tanks, the writers immediately set to work on a replacement. "That's where this show is different from other shows," says Alex. "We huddle together between breaks in the filming and pitch new jokes."

After the long, difficult journey from conception through development to show night's blessed event, writing still sometimes boils down to what you can come up with on the spot.

JEFF GREENSTEIN:
"It was a scene between Will and Jack, and Jack said, 'We haven't danced to a show tune together since Reagan got shot,' and I thought 'Wow! I'm working on a different kind of show.' I knew I was part of something special."

WEDNESDAY
In just another way that sitcoms have their own reality, a **WILL & GRACE** week begins on Wednesday. Having received a delivered script at home on Tuesday night, the actors usually read through it at least once before they arrive on Wednesday morning, to get familiar with the jokes before they perform them out loud.

The eleven a.m. "table read" gathers the actors around a table, in front of the executive producers, writers, network executives, and crew to read the script aloud, in character. "I know not to worry if I'm not sure a joke works, or if I don't know as an actor how to find the humor in it. I know the writers will hear it and fix it," Eric McCormack explains.

Immediately after the table read, director James Burrows and the writers discuss the script. Around the table, they plan that afternoon's rewrites. The actors go home, and receive another script delivery that night.

THURSDAY
Thursday marks the first time an episode will be "on its feet," meaning with actors rehearsing on the actual sets. Starting at nine or ten a.m. and lasting until one or two in the afternoon, the actors again read and then "run through" the script as a group, along with any guest stars.

FRIDAY
After a Thursday-night rewrite by the writers, the cast and director will again gather onstage on Friday morning, and show the writers their progress. Then, it's time for another rewrite.

MONDAY
On Monday morning the cameras arrive onstage, and the director will "block" the show—determining the optimal camera locations and movements for capturing the action in each scene. On most sitcom sets, "blocking" involves putting masking tape "marks" on the floor to note the required positions for both actors and cameras at different points in the scene. But director Burrows prefers not to use marks, relying on his camera crews to be quick to anticipate the actors' movements.

TUESDAY
The big day usually begins at noon, with the actors again running through the show in front of the writers and producers. For easy scenes, they usually perform it just once; for more difficult scenes, twice. By two p.m., it's time for a break until six p.m., showtime.

The show is shot on film, in front of a live audience, with each scene shot at least twice. During breaks in between, writers often huddle together and continue to suggest changes to lines that solicited a disappointing audience reaction. In rare instances, where whole scenes don't get laughs, several writers will go off to write a new one, returning to give it to the actors to shoot at the end of that same night.

SEASON

THREE

In September of 2000, it was official: Will & Grace *had arrived. After a few substitute tryouts in its first season in NBC's landmark "Must-See TV" lineup, the show now was given a permanent home on Thursday night. And not just any home, but the 9 p.m. anchor time slot formerly held by* Cheers, Seinfeld, *and even the venerable hit,* Frasier, *which* Will & Grace *now displaced.*

Must See Will & Grace

Inside Bungalow 2 on the Studio City, California, lot where the show is filmed, the move injected a new confidence into the **WILL & GRACE** writers' room. "They tell you you're a hit once you make it to the third season," Max Mutchnick explains. "So we felt empowered, like we were on the way to something...that allowed us to open up, and to have the confidence to ask people like Cher to do the show. "

One of those bigger guest stars recruited was Woody Harrelson, playing Nathan, a neighbor and new love interest for Grace whose storyline would continue into the show's fourth season. "Because we could never realize a love story between Will and Grace, we were used to importing guest stars, but not someone as experienced as Woody," Max remembers. "That was our introduction to having two leading men onstage at the same time. It wasn't easy to write those episodes, with two such strong guys feuding over the attention of Grace and of Debra as an actress and of the audience. But I think that dynamic really served us well. "

In addition to deciding to end Grace's continued flings with Josh and Ben and to begin a new romance with Nathan, the writers also planned for Will to have his first long-term relationship in season three. But at first, they had trouble finding a suitable suitor.

"In the beginning, when I would be casting for the show, I would occasionally hear something from an agent where I could read between the lines that the actor didn't want to play a gay role," casting director Tracy Lilienfield remembers. "I would finally ask the agent, 'Should I ever call him again?' and sometimes they would say no. Now I haven't had that discussion in years. But I always deferred also to Max, the 'keeper of the flame.' He had a very good antenna about it. And together we always preferred to cast Will's partners or dates as not very stereotypically gay at all."

One of Max's first casting suggestions was Robert Downey, Jr., but the actor turned down the role. Luckily, the show did find that Mr. Right, and cast Patrick Dempsey as Will's new boyfriend, sportscaster Matt, to appear in three of the season's episodes.

With the start of the third season, the show continued to reach further into the lives of its four main characters, adding the actress playing Karen's maid Rosario, Shelley Morrison, as a regular cast member in the opening credits. But even as the show began to explore new territory, its writers also sought comfort in the familiar, and moved Grace back into Will's apartment. In addition to facilitating stories about Will and Grace's friendship, the move created a convenient place for Jack to park his khakis.

"There are a couple of things we wanted to do with Jack in season three," David Kohan explains. In addition to giving him his own apartment in which the writers could depict more of his life, "we wanted to expand on his search for his father. We thought that the idea of a character like Jack who is always so sure of himself, having an existential crisis would be really funny. "

The writers also decided to try expanding the bond between the two least-combined characters on the show, Will and Karen. "They were the two characters who were the furthest apart in terms of personality, and had the fewest reasons to interact," David notes. "But they always did so well in their scenes together. We loved the idea of Will working for Karen, and his resentment at having to listen to this woman he has no respect for. On the other hand, he's a good guy at heart, so he's the perfect one to step in to help her navigate her emotional life. Plus, the last episode of Season Two had been yet another example of us painting ourselves into a corner. We just wanted to get Will and Karen back from the Caribbean and back to New York, where they belong. "

301 NEW WILL CITY

Written By:
DAVID KOHAN & MAX MUTCHNICK

...up with Karen, Will returns from the Caribbean only to find ...Jack has replaced him in Grace's life. When Grace follows ...'s advice to date Ben, rather than Will's advice to date Josh, ...becomes very insecure. Grace finally assures him that he's ...placeable, and Jack explains the truth behind his conviction ...Ben's the man for Grace: Jack slept with Josh. At ...airport, Karen sticks Rosario with a bag of contraband that ...s her in jail. Karen then suffers physical guilt pangs at ...mention of Rosario's name until she finally frees her wrong-...accused maid.

RECURRING CHARACTERS
Shelley Morrison *as* Rosario
Corey Parker *as* Josh

...K MUTCHNICK: This is the second episode where we use the phrase ...layan whistle kids." My mother had married a man who had two children ...his first family, whom she would force my brother and me to talk to. ...d get on the phone with these kids, and we never understood a single ...they said, and we used to say it was because they spoke in hoots and ...s like they do across the Himalayan valleys. So we started calling them ...Himalayan Whistle Kids." It was a little bit of an exaggeration.

...N HAYES: For the Britney "Oops, I Did It Again" dance we had the ...eographers from the videos come in and teach us the moves. Thank God ...a is like me in that she likes to rehearse until it feels like second nature ...ur body, so you can concentrate on what you're saying rather than how ...e moving.

...I ESKOWITZ-CARTER: One of my favorite wardrobe pieces ...e show is the mustard-ruffled shirt that Debra Messing wears ...e show's opening credits for season three. I think it's ...chino. I thought it was so interesting and beautiful ...had a lot of texture and movement. With her hair ...ing in the wind and the ruffles, it really looked ...d on her.

JACK:
"Remember how I said there was something about Josh I couldn't put my finger on? Well... I put my finger on it."

...This was the highest rated episode in ...history of the series.

302 FEAR AND CLOTHING

Written By:
ADAM BARR

There are too many lunatics in the asylum after an attempted break-in at Grace's drives her into Will's apartment. Will leaves it to Grace and Jack to figure out who will stay and who will go, but when they decide that Jack will remain Will's roommate, Will takes charge and chooses Grace instead. Jack is hurt until they offer him a paid sublease on Grace's apartment. Jack and Karen finally patch things up (post-lawsuit) after Will reminds Karen that blaming Jack for taking advantage of her is like blaming a puppy for piddling on the carpet: you don't stop loving Jack for being Jack.

GUEST STAR
Derek Basco *as* Mipanko

RECURRING CHARACTERS
Shelley Morrison *as* Rosario
Klaus Von Puppy
Guapo

WILL:
"Did I just scream like a woman?"
GRACE:
"Don't flatter yourself. You scream like a girl."

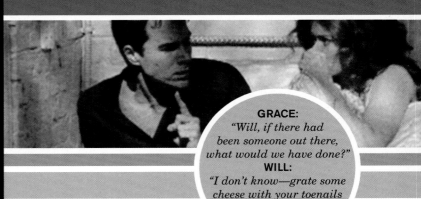

GRACE:
"Will, if there had been someone out there, what would we have done?"
WILL:
"I don't know—grate some cheese with your toenails and invite them in for quiche?"

(303) GIRL TROUBLE

Written By:
ALEX HERSCHLAG

Will's gay sensitivity seminar for the police department goes awry when Jack's anti-lesbian remarks chase away their lesbian costars and trigger an onstage brawl between the two of them. Will is mortified—until the cops thank him for the realistic illustration of the wounding power of words. At Grace Adler Designs, new intern Gillian emulates Grace until she decides that she would rather be like Karen. Grace is touched when she overhears Karen tell Gillian that Grace is the better role model.

GUEST STARS

Natasha Lyonne (*American Pie*) as Grace's intern Gilian
Megan Cavanagh (*A League of Their Own*) and Henriette Mantel
(Alice from the *Brady Bunch* movies) as lesbian couple Terry and Annie

RECURRING CHARACTERS

Louis Giovanetti *as* a Cop (*first appearance*)

> **KAREN:**
> *"I'm fabulous, okay. I'm an incredible dresser, I've got buckets of money, I'm a hoot and a half and I've got a killer rack."*

ALEX HERSCHLAG: This script changed a lot from my early conception of it. I originally wrote that, in the police sensitivity training class, although there was tension between the gay men and the lesbians, once one of the cops says something against them, they stick together. But the story just wasn't working, so it was changed. Then, in editing, some of the back-and-forth insults between Jack and the lesbians were removed, so that the episode ended up having Jack insulting the lesbians unprovoked. This was, at the time, the only episode NBC didn't repeat, and it was not one of my favorites.

> **TERRY:**
> *"I don't think that's funny."*
> **JACK:**
> *"Why, because Ellen DeGeneres didn't say it?"*

FYI: Grace mentions the "fabric board for the Flebotte House," which is named for TV writer Dave Flebotte, who worked with the writer of this episode, Alex Herschlag, on the sitcom *Ellen*.

(304) SWIMMING POOLS... MOVIE STARS

Written By: **KATIE PALMER**

While posing as millionaires shopping for high-end real estate, and Grace befriend Sandra Bernhard and inadvertently place a they can't afford on her apartment. After milking the friendship a while, they admit their deception to the angry star and learn they, too, have been tricked: Bernhard never liked them and was just trying to unload the apartment. Meanwhile, Jack takes time out of his online bidding war for Britney Spears's platform sneakers to advise Karen how to patch up her relationship with steps Mason. Karen attends Mason's swim meet and embraces him warmly, only to later realize she's hugging the wrong chubby kid.

GUEST STARS

Sandra Bernhard *as* Herself (*first appearance*)
Mitch Kaplan *as* her accompanist, Mitchie (*first appearance*)

RECURRING CHARACTER

Shelley Morrison *as* Rosario

> **WILL:**
> *"Look at this. Courtney Love probably peed in very toilet."*
> **GRACE:**
> *"Or at the very le around it. "*

JHONI MARCHINKO: Sandra Bernhard has been my best friend for alm fifteen years. I really wanted to have her on the show, and I wanted her to play herself, because I think that's when she's best. I also felt that it was that Will would be a fan of Sandra's, so we wanted to have him be one of ones to meet her. The story line came from real life, because Max and I we love to go out on weekends to open houses. Sometimes we'd have to co up with a story—especially in the first couple of seasons, when we were ir homes that we couldn't afford.

305 HUSBANDS AND TROPHY WIVES
Written By: KARI LIZER

[Wil]l and Jack are surprised to learn that hard-partying friends [Joe] and Larry have adopted a baby and are now happy home[bod]ies. When Will and Jack baby-sit so their friends can enjoy a [nigh]t out, Will's failure to get baby Hannah to sleep convinces [him] he'll never be a good dad. At first making Will's crisis worse, [Jac]k later reassures Will that he'll be a terrific parent; after all, [for] years he has been a good dad to Jack. A different crisis of [con]fidence is brewing at the yacht club, where Karen is about [to t]urn the same age as Stan's last wife when he [divo]rced her. Grace's attempts to boost Karen's [spi]rits fail dismally when Karen first thinks [Gra]ce is hitting on her, and then later uses [him] to make Stan jealous. When Stan then [has] Ben kicked out of the club, Karen feels [bett]er after all.

> **KAREN:**
> *"Well well well. Look what the cat cleaned up, showered, exfoliated, powdered, lipsticked, Gucci'd and dragged in."*

RECURRING CHARACTERS
Shelley Morrison *as* Rosario
Jerry Levine and Tim Bagley *as* the formerly swinging couple Joe and Larry *(first appearance)*
Gregory Hines *as* Ben Doucette

> **GRACE:**
> *"I wish I had a caddy. Someone to tell me about the hazards up ahead and carry my stuff."*
> **WILL:**
> *"I think I'm your caddy."*

[TIM] BAGLEY: When I first came to town, I worked as a page during one [of t]he last years of *Cheers.* I used to sit there and watch Jim Burrows direct. [He's] really great and I learned so much just by watching him…and now [her]e I was working with Jim Burrows.

306 GRACE 0, JACK 2000
Written By:
JON KINNALLY & TRACY POUST

Jack's new solo show, *Jack 2000,* is a dud until making fun of Will becomes part of the act. Hurt, Will stops sharing confidences and boycotts the shows until Karen tells him that *Jack 2000* will close without his help. Will offers to rescue the show, but Jack puts friendship first and looks for other audience members to abuse. Meanwhile, Grace's decision to break up with Ben fails to go as planned when Ben rejects the breakup. Grace reconsiders after Karen points out that with Ben she's happier than she's ever been. Grace's change of heart comes too late, though: Ben has decided to break up with her.

> **WILL:**
> *"What happened? Yesterday you were adding milk to your mochaccino to show me what pretty colors your kids would be."*

RECURRING CHARACTER
Gregory Hines *as* Ben Doucette

SEAN HAYES: Jeremy Forte, the actor playing Jack's heckler, had a delivery of the line "You STINK!" that still cracks me up when I think of it. So whenever we'd do another episode with Jack performing in that room, I'd ask Jimmy, "Can we get that guy back? The 'You STINK' guy?"

307 THREE'S A CROWD, SIX IS A FREAK SHOW

Written By: JHONI MARCHINKO

> **KAREN:**
> *"Hey, he's looking at baseball gloves. What do you know, Grace. You bagged a straight one!"*

Grace cancels a date with new beau Mark after a dermatology appointment leaves her with an angry sore on her lip. When Mark learns the reason for Grace's cancellation, he assures her he's not that shallow. Upon learning that Mark has six toes on one foot, however, Grace proves that she is precisely that shallow, breaking up with Mark but sparing his feelings by telling him it's because he's a Celtics fan. There's relationship turmoil on another front when Will and Jack learn they're both dating the same guy, Paul. Both vow to break up with him, but when Will violates their gentleman's agreement, Jack feels betrayed. Will drops Paul to spare Jack's feelings, but then, sure enough, finds him in Jack's apartment.

GUEST STAR

Ken Marino (from comedy troupe *The State*) as Mark

> **JACK:**
> *"You're Judas! This is exactly what he did!"*
> **WILL:**
> *"Hmmm…I don't know that the big problem there was a gay love triangle."*

JHONI MARCHINKO: The idea for this episode came out of my real life. Years ago, I was going out with this girl named Allison, and one of my best friends, Elaine, wanted to go out with her, too. When I said, "But I'm going out with her," she suggested, "What if we both did?" I thought it was weird, but I agreed. We said that the minute one of us liked her more than the other, the other one would back down. And then of course that's what happened—Elaine called me one day to say that she really liked Allison, so I broke up with her. It's funny because Elaine ended up being with Allison for two years, and out of that situation I met my current girlfriend, Antonia Hutt.

JEFF GREENSTEIN: Karen is incredibly sensual and has voracious appetites for everything, so I think she'll do it with anyone. Early on, Megan did an interview with *The Advocate* magazine where she talked about being bisexual, and as a writer you always try to incorporate things from the actors' lives, so we put in a few references. Here, we had Karen say she had once done something with a woman in order to borrow her Halston skirt.

308 LOVE PLUS ONE

Written By:
RICHARD ROSENSTOCK

Will and Karen laugh when Grace tells them she's been invited to join a couple in a mènage-à-trois. Since when would Grace, a.k.a. "Prudence McPrude," do anything so kinky? Grace decides to prove her friends wrong, and even patches up the kinky coup relationship when it unravels right before the big event. At the last moment, however, Grace finds she can't go through with it. Elsewhere, Jack takes a job at Banana Republic and falls for Ma a gorgeous customer who has the misfortune to be intelligent. Desperate, Jack and Will go "Cyrano de Bergerac," with Will feeding Jack lines through his headset to seduce the guy. It ends badly for Jack, who loses interest in the conversation he's channeling, but well for Will when the guy sees through the ruse and asks Will to give him a call.

> **WILL:**
> *"You're not around m You'd hit o Pope if he a better c"*

GUEST STARS

Jeremy Piven *(Ellen)* as Nicholas
Maria Pitillo *(Providence)* as Paula

RECURRING CHARACTER

Patrick Dempsey *as* Will's boyfriend Matt *(first appearance)*

> **JACK:**
> *"I'd say yes on the pants, yes on the sweater…and definitely yes on the other decision you're struggling with."*

FYI: The statue that Will tells Matt he was shamed into buying, Japanese Man with Fish, is actually a much-joked-about prop ne Will's TV nook, which was provided from the personal collection the show's set decorator, Melinda Ritz.

 309 / 310 — LOWS IN THE MID 80s PART 1 & 2
Written By: JEFF GREENSTEIN

...meeting with Pam, a heartbroken woman at a restaurant bar, ...ds Will and Grace to recount their romantic history. We flash ...ck to Will and Grace as college sweethearts, perfectly matched ...cept for Will's emerging awareness of his sexuality—an aware-...ss helped along by new friend and high-school student Jack, ...ose infallible "gaydar" has locked onto Will. When Will's despera-...n not to sleep with Grace leads him to propose marriage during ...Thanksgiving visit with her family, he realizes it's time to come ...an. Honesty has it price: Grace kicks Will out of her parents' ...use and doesn't speak to him again until a chance encounter ...he supermarket one year later. Will and Grace conclude their ...e despite Karen's interruptions with the story of how she chose ...n over a sultan, a jazz man, and Martina Navratilova, but Jack ...slip one final detail that Grace never knew: Will slept with a ...nan after their breakup. Grace is devastated until Will explains ...t he only did so in order to be certain of his sexual preference.

★ GUEST STARS
Martina Navratilova *as* Herself
Sara Rue (*Less Than Perfect*) *as* Grace's baby sister Joyce Adler
Ever Carradine (*Veronica's Closet*) *as* Pam,
who's dating an obviously gay guy

RECURRING CHARACTERS
Shelley Morrison *as* Rosario
Tom Gallop *as* Rob
Leigh-Allyn Baker *as* Ellen
Debbie Reynolds *as* Bobbi Adler
Neil Vipond *as* Bobbi's pianist, Julius (*first appearance*)

KAREN: "Oh cripes, honey. Let me give it to you in a nutshell. Your boyfriend's a big flaming feather-wearing, man-kissing, disco-dancing, Vermont-living, Christina Aguilera-loving, Mykonos-going… honey, take it home."

JACK: "Tom's queer, dear."

...FF GREENSTEIN: I remember when writing this episode how incredibly ...otional it made me. I just thought about the vulnerability of it from Will's ...int of view: you are carrying around the biggest secret you've ever had, and ...w not only do you have to say it out loud for the first time, but you need to ...y it to the person you adore.

...NET EISENBERG: I don't know if the thing about Will sleeping with ...woman afterward happened with Max in real life. In college in Boston, and ...en afterwards in L.A., there were a few women with whom Max was having ...se "faux-mances." In retrospect, he would say to me that he needed to get ...se to them and then come out to them so that he could practice.

311 — COFFEE AND COMMITMENT
Written By:
ADAM BARR

The fur flies when Will won't let Grace put her name on the gift he bought for the celebration of Joe and Larry's civil union. Will and Grace bicker like an old married couple all the way to Vermont and throughout the ceremony, until the words of love they read to the newlyweds remind them how much they love each other. At the ceremony, Karen's tough love helps Jack kick a coffee addiction, and he returns the favor by helping her survive the alcohol-free environment.

RECURRING CHARACTERS
Jerry Levine *as* Joe
Tim Bagley *as* Larry

KAREN: "Rule number one at a wedding. Find the sad sister, and you've found the booze."

TIM BAGLEY: I think that one reason the writers created Joe and Larry is so that they can write things that they might not want Will or Jack to do. They wouldn't want to write Will or Jack getting married—first of all, for plot reasons, but also because with the leads, it would be hard to focus on something like a gay wedding or adopting a child without getting preachy.

DEBRA MESSING: Sean can make me laugh doing any of his big physical stuff. One of my favorite things he's ever done was his bit in the beginning of this episode when he became addicted to caffeine. He walked in and did that huge monologue while drinking his coffee, and then turned right around and walked out. That was one of the most thrilling things I've witnessed in all of our years on the show. I couldn't stop laughing—luckily it didn't matter, because I was off-camera.

ADAM BARR: The reading at the end of Joe and Larry's ceremony that Will and Grace do, that sounds like vows, was something that I wrote and acted out in the writers' room with Kari Lizer's help. When my wife and I got married, we wrote our own vows, but ours had not been nearly as good as the reading was. In fact, after the episode aired, we got calls from people asking where it came from, and if they could have it for their own ceremony.

(312) GYPSIES, TRAMPS AND WEED

Written By: KATIE PALMER

"Psychic Sue" alarms Will with her prediction that he'll spend the rest of his life with a man named Jack. As Will and Jack negotiate the boundaries that might make their friendship last a lifetime, we realize that every condition has already been met, and that their life-long relationship would be merely as friends. Meanwhile, Grace is conscience-stricken after getting a waiter fired—so she hires him. Lenny's work is impressive—until Grace realizes that his new "clients" are there to buy drugs, not ottomans. At a restaurant, Jack's inflatable Cher doll attracts the attention of Cher herself. Jack dismisses her as a drag queen imitator, and Cher wins the ensuing Cher-off with a *Moonstruck*-inspired slap. ★

WILL:
"Sex is out of the question. I don't even like seeing your head poke through the hole in your sweater."

GUEST STARS
Cher *as* Herself
Camryn Manheim *(The Practice) as* Psychic Sue
Robert Romanus *(Fast Times at Ridgemont High) as* Lenny the waiter

SEAN HAYES: I have a friend who does all these impressions of all these famous people. The Cher impression always made me laugh because it was so bad and over-the-top and exaggerated and cartoony. I was just doing it at work one day in front of the writers, and then it just ended up in the show.

FYI: One of the two men at the table behind Jack, where Cher had been sitting, is the late makeup artist Kevyn Aucoin.

CAMRYN MANHEIM: I went to NYU a few years before Debra, and then taught her in a seminar where she was extraordinary. We became friends, and after she got *Will & Grace*, I told the producers I was a huge fan of the show and would love to be on it. Max and David made it happen. The first day I got there, I was reading my part and Jimmy Burrows said, "That's not funny—do something else." I thought to myself, "Good thing I have an Emmy or I'd be hurt by that." But he gets right to business because he works very quickly and lean, and has such an amazing eye for comedy.

FYI: Jack's Cher doll is actually a one-of-a-kind prototype for the doll, which was not due for release until the following May. Series cocreator Max Mutchnick kept the prototype, valued at $60,000.

JACK:
Um, I don't think I need a drag queen to define normal behavior, okay? But I will say this. The look? It's flawless."

FYI: Sean Hayes himself had helped to recruit Cher to do the show, having met her while presenting at an awards show.

(313) CRAZY IN LOVE

Written By:
JON KINNALLY & TRACY POUST

KAREN:
"My mother's crazy. That's why I had her committed. Well, she's not crazy so much as she just bugged me. She's a bitch."

Will takes batting lessons from Grace in order to impress his new sports-loving boyfriend, Matt. The plan comes to ruin when Matt switches their date from baseball to basketball, but it turns out that honesty appeals to Matt much more than an interest in spo[rts]. Across the hall, Grace's redecoration of Jack's apartment gets interesting when Jack and Karen find a forged note describing Gra[ce] as a dangerous psychotic. Grace plays "psycho" to the hilt, but la[ter] finds it hard to convince her friends that the note was faked.

RECURRING CHARACTERS
Patrick Dempsey *as* Matt
Marshall Manesh *as* Mr. Zamir

MATT:
"Don't tell me you're a Johnson fan."
WILL:
"Oh, I'm a big Johnson fan."

JON KINNALLY: Karen has said different things about her mother over th[e] years. She's in a home, she's dead—in one joke that got cut we even had had Karen pulling the plug on her mother's life support out with her foot. W[e] never worried about meeting her mother one day, because with Karen, it ju[st] doesn't matter. We never know if she's making it all up or filtering somethi[ng] through a drug-induced haze.

314 BROTHERS, A LOVE STORY
Written By: DAVID KOHAN & MAX MUTCHNICK

ll is appalled when Matt introduces him to his boss as "my
other," but so starved for affection is Will that he stands by his
n. Not until Matt blows a second chance to come clean does
ll realize that Grace is correct: he shouldn't stay in a relation-
ip that's based on a lie. Elsewhere, Karen's ire is aroused when
e discovers that Stan's will leaves huge sums to charity. Holding
ll responsible, she tracks him down to the secretly gay seafood
nt in Queens where he has just broken up with Matt and sub-
ts him to a tirade of double-entendres in front of Matt and his
mophobic boss.

RECURRING CHARACTER
Patrick Dempsey *as* Matt

KAREN:
*"Honey, why do I
need a will? I'm
gonna live forever.
That is the deal,
isn't it, Red?"*

GRACE:
*"If I knew why
straight guys did
anything, do you
think I'd be hanging
out with you
two homos?"*

JACK:
*"Tall, muscular
lovelies in nothing but
short-shorts and
matching tank tops?
Why would straight
guys watch this?"*

315 MY UNCLE THE CAR
Written By:
KARI LIZER

Grace has second thoughts after charging Will with selling her
late Uncle Jerry's lemon of a car. After a difficult negotiation to
buy back the vehicle from the cheesecake-baking nun who bought
it, Will agrees that in exchange for use of the car, he and Grace will
help her with deliveries. Another custody battle rages at Karen's,
where Karen and Beverly Leslie play pool for possession of Rosario.
Meanwhile, Jack's mother aids his search for his biological father
by informing him that he is "a black boy." Jack determines to honor
his African-American heritage, until his mother clarifies that he
is "a Black boy," son of one of the eleven brothers in the Irish-
Catholic Black family. ★

WILL:
*"Oh look,
it's
Notorious
F.A.G."*

GUEST STARS
★ Ellen DeGeneres *as* Sister Louise
Jimmy Burrows *as* Grace's Uncle Jerry *(voice-over)*

RECURRING CHARACTERS
Marshall Manesh *as* Mr. Zamir
Leslie Jordan *as* Beverley Leslie *(first appearance)*

TIM KAISER: In the scene where Karen and Beverley Leslie are fighting
at the pool table, we originally had had the idea to parody *The Matrix* using
special effects. We brought in guys who do a lot of the Jet Li and martial arts
scenes in town, and went through several days of demos on how to do the
scene. We even had a day of training for Megan. But then the writers got a
good look at the scene and realized that it looked like the show was jump-
ing the shark. It would have been fun to see Karen in black leather, raised up
seven feet in the air, but we realized it was a little too much.

KAREN:
*"Where have you
been?"*
ROSARIO:
*"Riding a llama in
Neverland. Where do
you think I was?
I was cleaning."*

FYI: This story was originally conceived for
the return of Joan Collins's character, Helena
Barnes, executive producer Jeff Greenstein
explains. "Oddly enough, when we replaced
her with Beverley Leslie, we didn't have to
change a single line." ★

LESLIE JORDAN: In that episode, when at the very end, Karen says to
Rosario, "Where the hell are my slippers?" Rosario was originally supposed
to say, "Follow your drunken footsteps backwards, and you'll find them." But
as it got late, somebody must have told Shelley to change it, because in one
take, she said instead, "Have you looked up your ass, you drunken fool?" It
gets bawdy around here…and sometimes that's the take that gets on the air.

(316) CHEATERS
Written By:
ALEX HERSCHLAG

Will doesn't want to hear it when Grace tells him she's discovered that his father, George, is having an affair. The Truman family's powers of denial are put to the test when Will and Grace share a meal with George and his new squeeze, Tina. At the end of the meal, George tells Will that he secretly wanted Will to confront him about the affair, and then thanks Will for telling him off. George's love life makes trouble for Karen, too, who enlists Jack to help her tail Stan with the limo when she mistakenly believes that he's the married man having the affair with Tina.

GRACE:
"I feel like a Jewish Jane Goodall, and you're 'Goyim in the Mist.'"

GUEST STAR
Dirk Shafer *(whose film* Man of the Year *depicted his being chosen as* Playgirl *magazine's first gay centerfold) as* auditioning actor Blaze

RECURRING CHARACTERS
Shelley Morrison *as* Rosario
Sydney Pollack *as* George Truman
Lesley Ann Warren *as* George's mistress Tina *(first appearance)*

ALEX HERSCHLAG: This was our first "supersized" episode, and when it was repeated they wanted to break it into two half-hours, so I had to add two extra scenes that had nothing to do with the story. They were the first scene in the coffee shop, where Will just mentions his dad is coming to town, and a scene where Karen and Jack hold auditions.
The idea for this story came from Max running into somebody who would laugh inappropriately, and I thought that was a good aspect for a character. It was written before the part was cast, so I think we lucked out to get Lesley Ann Warren, who did it so beautifully. One of the things I love on our gag reel is a moment from this episode, where Sydney Pollack's character gets nervous and tries to imitate Tina's laugh. He's such a dignified man that he couldn't do it without laughing himself.

MEGAN MULLALLY: I had the idea for the latest bit with Karen's pills in this episode. I just thought it would be funny that Karen would have an old-person pill keeper for her recreational drugs.

WILL:
"Gentiles' three gifts to the world: One, we make a great martini. Two, we keep retail stores alive. And three, we don't talk about things that we don't want to know about."

(317) POKER? I DON'T EVEN LIKE HER
Written By: MIMI FRIEDMAN & JEANNETTE COLLINS

Will's poker buddies want to ban Grace from their game and they delegate the job to Will. Will does his best, but relents when Grace spins a heart-wrenching tale about needing to win back h[er] grandmother's turquoise jewelry. When it turns out that Grace's competitiveness has turned her into a liar and a cheat—and tha[t] she bought the turquoise jewelry off a drag queen on the street—the men feign hostility toward one another and stage a fight tha[t] forces Grace to confess and quit the game. Deception's afoot at t[he] spa, too, where Jack poses as a masseur to trick Karen's friend Candy Pruitt into being a guinea pig for the surgical shoulder implants that Karen craves. The scheme works too well: Candy struts away with the last pair of implants and Karen's stuck wit[h] last year's model.

GUEST STAR
Christine Ebersole *as* Karen's nemesis, Candy Pruitt

RECURRING CHARACTERS
Tom Gallop *as* Rob
Jerry Levine *as* Joe
Tim Bagley *as* Larry

KAREN:
"She's gone to Mexico for face-lif[ts] so many times, I'll [bet] if you whacked he[r] head with a stick[,] prizes would fall out."

FYI: Christine Ebersole, who co-starred with Megan Mullally in the short-lived 1992 comedy series *Rachel Gunn, R. N.*, was cast when Candy Pruitt was created as replacement for Joan Collins's character, Helena Barnes ("My Best Friend's Tush," Season Two). Helena was originally going to reappear both here and in "My Uncle, the Car," where s[he] was replaced by Beverley Leslie. "Joan Collins didn't want to jok[e] about plastic surgery, she didn't play pool, and even though she [did] do the scene in 'My Best Friend's Tush' with the dog, she didn't like dogs," Tracey Poust explains. "Three problems for three different episodes."

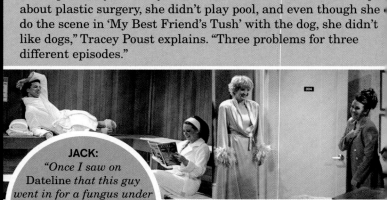

JACK:
"Once I saw on Dateline *that this guy went in for a fungus under his fingernail and he came back with no limbs. Luckily, he was ugly, so it wasn't that sad."*

318 ALICE DOESN'T LISP HERE ANYMORE

Written By: SALLY BRADFORD

JACK: "This is so tight. Now I know why Evita was such a bitch."

...ilty Grace drags Will to the funeral of Alice Robinson, a high ...nool classmate she used to ridicule. Intending to offer a post-...mous apology, Grace learns that it is in fact her former victim's ...andmother with the same name who has died, so she wants to ...ve, but Will insists that they stay, mostly so that he can hit on ...e bereaved grandson. Although the younger Alice initially rejects ...r apology, she eventually makes peace with Grace—until Grace ...rns her lip on hot coffee and begins to speak as if making fun of ...ice's speech impediment all over again. Karen helps Jack prepare ...videotaped acceptance speech after his solo show, *Jack 2001,* is ...minated for a MAC Award, the "most prestigious award in all ...lower Manhattan non-transgender Equity waiver gay cabaret," ...t then has to break the news to Jack when she finds out that the ...mination was in error.

GUEST STARS

Alice Kapp Horner (*Maggie Winters*) as Alice Robinson
Todd Stashwick as Gabe Robinson

ALICE: "For 20 years I have been afraid to talk because of my lisp. I've never even seen a single movie with Susan Sarandon or Sissy Spacek. But through it all, I knew that someday I'd be able to look you in the eye and say very clearly, 'You suck!'"

GRACE: "Well, on the bright side, she probably never had to see anything with Sylvester Stallone."

319 MAD DOGS AND AVERAGE MEN

Written By: ADAM BARR

Will can't bring himself to dump Paul because he loves Paul's dog, Pepper. When Jack loses Pepper at the park, a guilt-wracked Will agrees to go on a weekend trip with Paul. On the day of their departure, Will hears a "woof" in Paul's apartment and learns he's been scammed: Pepper is trained to run away and equipped with Doggie Lo-Jack. Meanwhile, Grace bristles at Karen's efforts to keep her away from Karen's attractive nephew, Sumner, until she learns that Karen thinks she deserves better.

GUEST STARS

Peter Jacobson (*A.U.S.A.*) as Will's dog-owning boyfriend Paul
Ellen Idelson (series writer) as the opera usher
Ellen Idelson's parents, Bill Idelson (*The Dick Van Dyke Show* writer) and
Seemah Wilder as the couple in the opera box

KAREN: "You know, I do have a family."

GRACE: "I know. I just always imagined they lived in pods somewhere in your boiler room...and they only came out at night to race from village to village stealing people's essences."

ADAM BARR: Every one of the writers has a pet of some sort, and we spend a lot of time talking about them—more than our personal lives. The idea of getting involved with someone because you really love their pet seemed natural to us.

320 OLD FASHIONED PIANO PARTY

Written By:
JHONI MARCHINKO & TRACY POUST & JON KINNALLY

Afraid that she and Will are drifting apart, Grace buys a piano so they can share their love of music. Will has had enough after two days, so Grace goes to desperate lengths to keep the piano fun coming. After her "old-fashioned piano party" bombs, Will and Grace cement their bond with a Captain and Tennille duet. Across the hall, Karen labors to keep Jack heartbroken after he begins to channel his misery into a steamy erotic novel.

GUEST STAR
Gigi Rice *(The John Larroquette Show)* as Grace's friend Heidi Doro

WILL:
"Have you been gargling with bong water?"

RECURRING CHARACTERS
Marshall Manesh *as* Mr. Zamir
Tim Bagley *as* Larry

TIM BAGLEY: I try not to break up on stage, but during the "Enough is Enough" number I did with Debra at he piano, I couldn't help myself. On every take, Megan would yell out "is ENOUGH!" and Debra and I would laugh, so we'd turn our heads away from the cameras. I remember feeling like I was so clever that I turned away so nobody could see—and then they ended u using a shot from behind us, so you can see me totally laughing in profile.

FYI: In one scene during this episode, Grace wears a black Ralph Lauren T-shirt with a large pink Polo pony. In a commercial break during the show, NBC ran a ten-second promo directing viewers to polo. com to buy a similar shirt, part of the proceeds from which were donated to the fight against breast cancer. By midday the next day, three thousand shirts had been ordered.

KAREN:
"But, honey, I've got to know what happens next. I'm addicted to these stories, which is odd, because I don't have an addictive personality."

FYI: One of the uncredited piano movers is set decorator Doug Devine.

---

321 THE YOUNG AND THE TACTLESS
Written By: JEFF GREENSTEIN

Grace is on the warpath after slovenly neighbor Nathan takes her wet clothes out of the basement washing machine. After scolding Nathan, Grace ends up coaching him on how to win back his girlfriend. Nathan's transformation of his apartment into a simulate Venice fails to impress his girlfriend, but does earn him a new one Grace. Elsewhere, Karen spoils Will and Jack's evening at a hot nightclub by saddling them with her ancient, supposedly impossible mother-in-law, Sylvia.

GUEST STAR
Ellen Albertini Dow (the rapping granny in *The Wedding Singer*) as Karen's mother-in-law, Sylvia Walker

RECURRING CHARACTERS
Marshall Manesh *as* Mr. Zamir
Branden Williams *as* Scott Sender, the young video clerk who Will dates briefly *(first appearance)*
Woody Harrelson *as* Grace's boyfriend Nathan *(first appearance)*

KAREN:
"Getting along with people, like Madison Avenue, is a two-way street."

WILL:
"Madison Avenue is a one-way street."

KAREN:
"Well, that explains why those two cops had Driver in a choke hold last night."

FYI: The show's producers at first envisioned Jack Black playing the difficult-to-cast part of Nathan, Grace's "inappropriate boyfriend." But when he was unavailable, director Burrows was able to call his old friend from his *Cheers* days, Woody Harrelson. The timing was so tight that Woody returned from France, filmed his first scenes in front of an audience on Monday night, and then filmed his second episode as Nathan the following night.

WILL:
"There's a roll of quarters in my top drawer right beside my eye cream and my pedicure kit. Wow, my dad would be so proud of me."

...ll is dating a much younger man, Grace is dating a guy she ...rself calls a pig and a child, and neither wants the other to ...ow. Once the truth comes out, they make a pact to simultane-...sly unload their embarrassing boyfriends. Will carries out his ...eakup, but Grace falls into bed with Nathan instead. Meanwhile, ...l turns into a stalker after she falls in love with Jack's solo ...ow. Jack chases her off, but when his show bombs without her, ... begs her to stalk him again.

RECURRING CHARACTERS
Woody Harrelson *as* Nathan
Molly Shannon *as* Val
Branden Williams *as* Scott Sender

...TER CHAKOS: Sometimes in editing, we can create a new joke. When ... guy at The Duplex asks Val to see her autographed breast again and ...ain (and that was one of our writers, Adam Barr, by the way), the scene ...ginally ended, and we cut away to something else. I thought it would be ...nny to do a quick cut back, after that next scene, to Adam asking Val yet ...ain, to create a joke suggesting that he had been asking her the whole ...e. That wasn't written or filmed that way. So I just took one of Adam's ...es from another take of the scene, and edited it into the show.

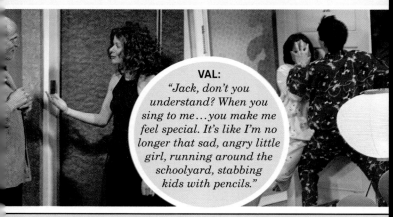

VAL:
"Jack, don't you understand? When you sing to me...you make me feel special. It's like I'm no longer that sad, angry little girl, running around the schoolyard, stabbing kids with pencils."

...I: Karen's description of Nathan as "the hottie who smells like ...e" is a reference to Woody Harrelson's pro-hemp political activism.

...I: Will gives his young date Scott a quick good night peck on the ...s—the first time we see Will kiss a man at all, and the network ...d producers opted not to promote it.

ELLIOT:
"I'm from Queens."
JACK:
"Yes you are, but we'll talk about that when you're older."

Will can't stand it when Grace invites Nathan to temporarily move into the apartment. He and Nathan are at each other's throats until a night of drinking steers them toward friendship. Grace, fearing that Nathan is about to tell her that he loves her, breaks up with him and arranges a trip with Will to Morocco. After learning the depths of Nathan's feelings, Will becomes convinced that Grace is making a mistake and intercepts her at the airport to challenge her to try to make it work. As Grace rejoins Nathan for an exchange of I-love-you's, Will runs into a cute guy he's admired for weeks and impulsively joins him on a bike trip to France. Jack rejoices when he believes he's located his biological father, Joe Black. When the man's widow arrives with the news that Jack's father died years ago, Jack is crushed. The unexpected arrival of a boy claiming to be Jack's son via a long-ago sperm donation sends Jack reeling, until he recalls the pain of not knowing his own father and chooses to be a part of the boy's life.

RECURRING CHARACTERS
Shelley Morrison *as* Rosario
Woody Harrelson *as* Nathan
Michael Angarano *as* Jack's son Elliot *(first appearance)*

NATHAN:
"Grace, if you're going to think I'm gay every time I pass out with men, you're in for a lifetime of heartache."

MAX MUTCHNICK: The idea behind introducing the character of Elliot was to be able to end the story of Jack searching for his father with a satisfying and emotional twist. When Jack finds out that his father is dead, he then realizes that he has a child. It was a way to express that the circle continues.

FAMILY & LOVERS &

FRIENDS, OTHERS

THE SIDEKICK

Shelley Morrison *as* Rosario

Since the day they met in 1985, Rosario has been Karen's maid, henchman—and, Karen will admit in times of weakness—friend. Not afraid to stand up to to the boss she has called "Count Drunkula," this tart-tongued "tamale" can dish out the salsa as well as she can make it.

Becoming a Fifth Banana

Long before she gave voice to Rosario, Shelley was best known as Sister Sixto in the 1967-70 Sally Field series **THE FLYING NUN**. In the late 90s, the burned-out native New Yorker and her husband, Walter Dominguez, loaded their dogs into a van and fell in with a band of Native Americans they met on the road. Fed up with the roles she was being offered—quick, name the older Latinas you've seen on screen lately!—Shelley told a tribal elder she was ready to call it quits. His response changed her life:

"He told me when I go to pray, I should be specific about what it is I would like to do. So I prayed that I could be in a good comedy, with good writing, that says something. Fifth banana, and if at all possible, shot in front of a live audience. This was on Sunday, and on Tuesday, my agent faxed me the first script with Rosario. Adam Barr wrote that episode, so thank you, Adam Barr! Blessings to you, your family and future generations!"

That Members Only Look

There's a lot of Shelley in Rosario's look. "I have macular degeneration," she admits. "I didn't tell them that, but Max went crazy for the sunglasses. I thought, 'Great—I'll be able to see what I'm doing!'" Shelley also wears her own lucky knee-high socks. Aside from the occasional nightgown or Members Only jacket, she wears the same thing in every episode, just like on **THE FLYING NUN**. That's fine with Shelley: "I don't have to go in for fittings."

A Woman of Color and Attitude

A Sephardic Jew, Shelley has no problem being Latina and playing a maid. In fact, she thinks Rosario's willingness to stand up for herself in a traditionally subservient role is one reason she's so popular. Says Shelley: "I was at the market at the checkout stand and an older African-American man said to me, 'I just wanted to thank you for bringing dignity to a woman of color.' And that meant so much to me."

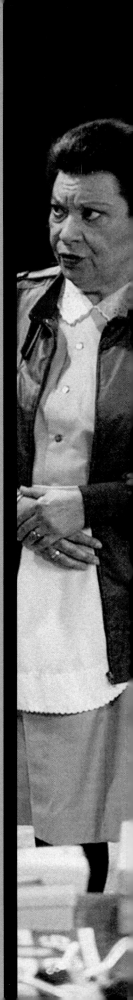

"I WENT IN TO MEET WITH MAX AND DAVID, WHOM I HAD NEVER MET BEFORE, AND WITH JIMMY BURROWS AND THE CASTING DIRECTOR TRACY LILIENFIELD, BOTH OF WHOM I HAD MET WHEN I HAD DONE A PILOT CALLED *NEARLY YOURS.*

WHEN I WALKED IN, THEY WERE GOING TO PULL UP A CHAIR FOR ME, AND I SAID IN MY ROSARIO VOICE, 'NO, I'LL GET IT. IS THIS GOING TO TAKE LONG? I HAVE TO GO HOME AND COOK A CHICKEN.' WHICH WAS TRUE. WHEN I GOT IN MY CAR AS I WAS LEAVING, MY CELL PHONE RANG AND IT WAS MY AGENT. I ASKED, 'HOW'D IT GO?' AND HE SAID, 'YOU START TOMORROW.'"

THE TRUMANS

Blythe Danner *as* Marilyn Truman

Will's mother, Marilyn, keeps an immaculate Connecticut home, a lover on the side, and a blind eye turned to her husband George's infidelity. When Will decides not to play his part in the family charade, Marilyn's carefully ordered world falls apart. A spirit-lifting stay with favorite son Will lasts too long, and parent and child seethe silently until Grace pulls the cork from this bottled-up clan.

TRACY LILIENFIELD, CASTING DIRECTOR:
"Comedy wasn't necessarily Blythe Danner's milieu, and casting her was not a sure thing. But she has really, really gotten it."

Sydney Pollack *as* George Truman

Will's perfect papa hides a host of hurtful secrets that rock his adoring son's world when they come to light. First comes the revelation that George's colleagues think Will is happily married to Grace. Next comes the midlife crisis Ferrari, the midlife crisis mistress, and finally, after forty years of marriage, a separation from Will's mother. Thanksgiving at the Trumans' will never be dull again.

TRACY LILIENFIELD, CASTING DIRECTOR:
"Early on in a show, it's hard to get big stars to appear—you can't just get anybody you want. David Kohan had worked for Sydney Pollack, and we jumped at the chance to use that relationship."

John Slattery *as* Sam Truman

Will's estranged older brother (the two stopped talking after Will objected to Sam's then-fiancée, now ex-wife). While trying to re-unite the brothers, Grace has a fling with Sam.

John Tenney *as* Paul Truman *and* Helen Slater *as* Peggy Truman

Paul, the middle Truman brother, is Will's main rival for their mother's affection. Paul's wife, Peggy, has actually met a Jewish person other than Grace once, at the hairdresser.

Lesley Ann Warren *as* Tina

George Truman's giggly "business associate," Tina, began her affair with George when she catered his company Christmas party.

THE ADLERS

Debbie Reynolds *as* Bobbi Adler

A frustrated, face-lifted chorine who recently celebrated her fiftieth birthday—for the twenty-fifth time—Bobbi Adler is a tough act to follow for her daughter Grace. She always has to be the center of attention. She's prone to belting out a tune. She does an "I Told You So" dance to rub it in when she's right. She's…a helluva lot like her daughter.

Neil Vipond *as* Julius

Bobbi Adler's fey piano accompanist can be counted on to flirt with Will, yet puzzlingly has been married twice.

Sara Rue *as* Joyce Adler

Grace's binge-eating baby sister, who, upon hearing Will was gay, told Grace,"You always ruin everything."

Geena Davis *as* Janet Adler

Grace's free-spirited, irresponsible older sister, who spent most of her adult life living in communes.

THE IN-LAWS

Tom Skerritt *as* Jay Markus *and* Judith Ivey *as* Eleanor Markus

When Grace accompanies Leo to brunch at the Plaza with "friends," she doesn't realize that he's tricked her into meeting his genteel parents from Atlanta, Jay and Eleanor.

SEE P. 100 TO READ ABOUT GRACE'S HUSBAND, LEO MARKUS

THE McFARLANDS

Michael Angarano *as* Elliot

Elliot is Jack's biological son, resulting from a long-ago sperm donation that Elliot's mother, Bonnie, a nurse, swiped from a New York family clinic and used to impregnate herself. Just as Jack despairs at having learned that his own biological father died years ago, Elliot, at age twelve, finds Jack. A teenage girl at heart, Jack makes the perfect guide for his young son through the daily trials (and wardrobe experiments) of the seventh grade.

TRACY LILIENFIELD, CASTING DIRECTOR: "When we were casting Elliot, I hadn't yet heard of Michael Angarano, even though I got the impression that I should have, because he'd already done **ALMOST FAMOUS**. He is really funny, and odd, and quirky, and his hair is cute."

Veronica Carwright *as* Judith McFarland

Judith McFarland is known for her "dry runs," practicing traveling to a place the day before she's due, as she does when she's invited to Will's for Thanksgiving. Like her son, she is fond of doing butt-clenching exercises.

Beau Bridges *as* Daniel McFarland

Daniel was distant and judgmental of his stepson Jack growing up, but now wants to make things right and be a better father figure to Jack's son, Elliot.

Guapo

It's a good thing Jack's pet parrot is the strong, silent type—this bird must know words that would make a pirate blush.

Klaus Von Puppy

Jack takes in this adorable retriever after Will and Grace botch this relationship, too.

THE WALKERS

Suzanne Pleshette *as* Lois Whitley

Karen's mother, Lois, wasn't so much a parent as an accomplice, a con artist who taught her daughter how to leave broken hearts and empty wallets in her wake. After Jack's birthday biography video brings this big, bad mama back into Karen's life, the only thing that can separate them again is a force even mightier than their familial bond: a six-figure payoff.

TRACY LILIENFIELD, CASTING DIRECTOR: "We knew Suzanne Pleshette could be tough and sarcastic, and had some "Karen-isms" in her. And the writers were able to play up the really funny differences in her and Megan's voices. In fact, it worked out so well that Max and David cast her in their next series, **GOOD MORNING, MIAMI.**"

Dan Futterman *as* Barry

Will wants to give Karen's unappealing, fresh-from-the-closet cousin Barry the brush-off, but Jack convinces him to "gay it forward" instead. Under Will and Jack's mentorship, Barry develops an unrealistic body image, chooses fashion over comfort, lives beyond his means, and dumps both his teachers. Ah, the sweet smell of success.

TRACY LILIENFIELD, CASTING DIRECTOR: "We flew Dan Futterman in from New York, which we have never done for someone to read for us before. He had let his beard grow, and came in like that, like the 'bad' Barry."

Minnie Driver *as* Lorraine Finster

Former stripper Lorraine meets Stanley Walker while working in the prison cafeteria. Soon the hermaphroditic hussy has usurped Karen's place in her manse and, worse, in her walk-in closet. Stanley dies on top of her, and leaves her nothing in his will but his affection. She and Karen grudgingly form a bond when her father and Karen fall for each other.

Mason *and* Olivia Walker

Stan's children from a previous marriage. Mason is chubby (and on the swim team) and Olivia is emotionally needy.

SEE P. 100 TO READ ABOUT KAREN'S LATE HUSBAND, STAN, AND HER LATEST HUSBAND, LYLE FINSTER

HUSBANDS

Woody Harrelson *as* Nathan
Grace's neighbor in 12C whom she meets while scolding him for taking her wet laundry out of the washing machine.

Gregory Hines *as* Ben Doucette
Will's boss, whom Grace dates while she's still dating Josh.

Corey Parker *as* Josh
A new age-y man to the point of repulsion, and a bit too fond of the forehead kiss.

Harry Connick, Jr. *as* Dr Marvin "Leo" Markus
Grace's globe-trotting doctor husband.

Tom Verica *as* Danny
The fiancé with whom Grace has lived for one year at the time of the show's pilot, when she breaks off the engagement.

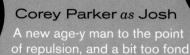
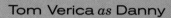

Rip Torn *as* Lionel Banks
A wealthy businessman whom Karen meets in a bar and, unable to resist his charms, she has an affair with him while still married to Stan.

Stan Walker
Her obese billionaire husband whom she met in 1985 while he was married. The two officially hooked up ten years later.

John Cleese *as* Lyle Finster
The father of Stan's mistress, Lorraine Finster, Karen sleeps with him at first just to bother his daughter, but finds herself falling in love, and marries Lyle in a big Season Six finale Vegas wedding.

& LOVERS

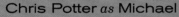

Branden Williams *as* Scott Sender

Twenty-three-year-old video store clerk whom Will decides to give a chance, even though he measures his age in quarter-years.

Patrick Dempsey *as* Matthew

A closeted sportscaster whom Will meets while trying to help Jack impress him at Banana Republic.

Chris Potter *as* Michael

The boyfriend of seven years with whom Will broke up by the time of the pilot.

Bobby Cannavale *as* Police Officer Vince

Will meets Officer Vince when he writes Karen a traffic ticket during a driving lesson, which Will decides to fight. Sparks fly during the ensuing court date, leading to real dates for Will and Vince.

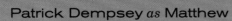

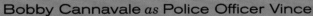

Shelley Morrison *as* Rosario

Jack's thousand-dollar green-card bride.

Dave Foley *as* Stuart LeMarc

Will's client and CEO of Stuff I Invented in My Garage Industries. Will initially paid Jack 74 cents and an old Chap Stick to date Stewart, but Jack found himself falling for him.

MARK
the guy with six toes.

ROB OF ROB AND ELLEN
with whom Grace had sex while Rob and Ellen were broken up.

IAN
a guy Will thinks is like Frankenstein and who turns out to be married.

STANLEY FINK
a mortician who touched dead people and then cooked short ribs for Grace; set up by Grace's mother.

Will's TA in college.

SCOTT BARKY
who had to touch everything ten times and then smell it; set up by Grace's mother.

CAMPBELL
a guy from high school with whom Grace went to see Loverboy, and now meets again at Karen's cabin in Vermont.

NICHOLAS
a cellist with the Boston Symphony with whom Grace had a tempestuous six-week relationship, and who comes back into town with his new girlfriend looking for a three-way.

GLEN GABRIEL
a high school classmate who played in a band and was in a Jewish gang, whom Grace runs into and begins dating.

IRA
a guy who made strange sounds at orgasm (and to whom Grace lost her virginity), and is now a nurse.

ELIZABETH TAYLOR
to whom Karen accidentally got married, becoming husband number eight.

MARTINA NAVRATILOVA
the nine-time Wimbledon singles winner who was straight until she met Karen.

MR. TYLER
Karen's teacher who let her out of doing a term paper, and who is now a state senator.

TEDDY KAZINSKI, THE UNABOMBER.
They lost touch, which is a shame, because he had been such a good letter writer.

Every member of **CROSBY, STILLS, NASH, AND YOUNG.**

THE SULTAN OF BAHRAN, A.K.A. HABIBI SHOSHANI PADOUSH AL-KABIR,
of Fort Lee, New Jersey.

CLAYTON
Who could make love to Karen all night.

MR. STEIN
Will's boss and her fellow member in The Losers Club, founded on anti-love principles.

CANDICE BERGEN
who apparently fooled around with Karen after trying sake for the first time.

FLINGS

MANY TO KEEP TRACK OF...

NEIL
Will's mother's dentist's bridge partner's annoying and overconfident son.

ZACH
the first man Will ever went out with, after Jack secretly paid him forty dollars to do so. He ended up stealing Will's identiy and traveling around Europe on his credit cards.

The cute souvlaki vendor from the corner of 72nd and Central Park West.

CHARLIE
a blind date with a Scottish brogue, set up by Will's boss, Ben Doucette.

STEVEN
a guy at Will's old law firm with whom he had a summer fling while still seeing Michael.

ALEX
who breaks up with Will on his answering machine after Will misses a date with him.

CHRIS
Will's imaginary boyfriend, i.e., a guy he sees all around town but never has the nerve to talk to—until he meets him at the airport.

MITCHELL, A.K.A. CUDDLEBUM
Will's rebound boyfriend after breaking up with Michael.

PAUL BUDNICK
a needy, desperate guy whom Will continues to see only to have access to his loving St. Bernard, Pepper.

SCOTT KELLY
a guy who dumped Will during Grace's junior year in college. Grace wipes out on her moped on her way over to console Will in his dorm.

ROBERT
the ballet dancer who embarrasses Will in public.

WALTER
Jack's ex-boyfriend, whom Will later dated.

CURT
a cute guy Will meets at the gym and goes on one date with, but then who avoids Will's calls and gives him the nickname "The Nibbler."

ROCCO
whose temporary breakup with Jack inspires him to write.

PAUL
Jack and Will both meet him at a party, and then both date him.

MITCH
a guy with whom Jack was caught celebrating their "half-week-a-versary" on top of Stan's Viking oven.

DENNIS
a cute fellow student nurse with whom Jack does some over-the-smock fondling.

STEVE, RAOUL, MIKE, DAN, AND TOM
all of whom dumped Jack.

JOSH
Grace's sensitive boyfriend.

BERTRAM
a miserly 80-year-old millionaire whom Jack picks up at an art opening, hoping to be lavished with gifts.

PAUL
a barista at Jumbo Java on 72nd Street who gives Jack free iced-coffee drinks every hour on the hour.

BJORN STEVENSON
a Swedish ex-boyfriend who is the true inventor of the Subway Tush.

FERNANDO
a hot Latin number with whom Jack has a date instead of going home to his wife, Rosario, on their first anniversary.

CRAIG FISSAY
NBC Executive whose number Jack gets while protesting the cut of the gay kiss on *Along Came You.*

RAMON
from the Dominican Republic.

The cute ugly guy from the Kiehl's counter at Barney's

CAMERON
A wealthy theatre lover who hires Grace to decorate his city and country homes.

CLARK
another date Jack has scheduled for after his date with Fernando on the same night.

The love of Jack's life—some guy from Belize.

DEREK
a fellow student nurse.

A restaurant bartender with whom Jack made out while wearing face glitter and a Barbarella costume.

THE FRIENDS

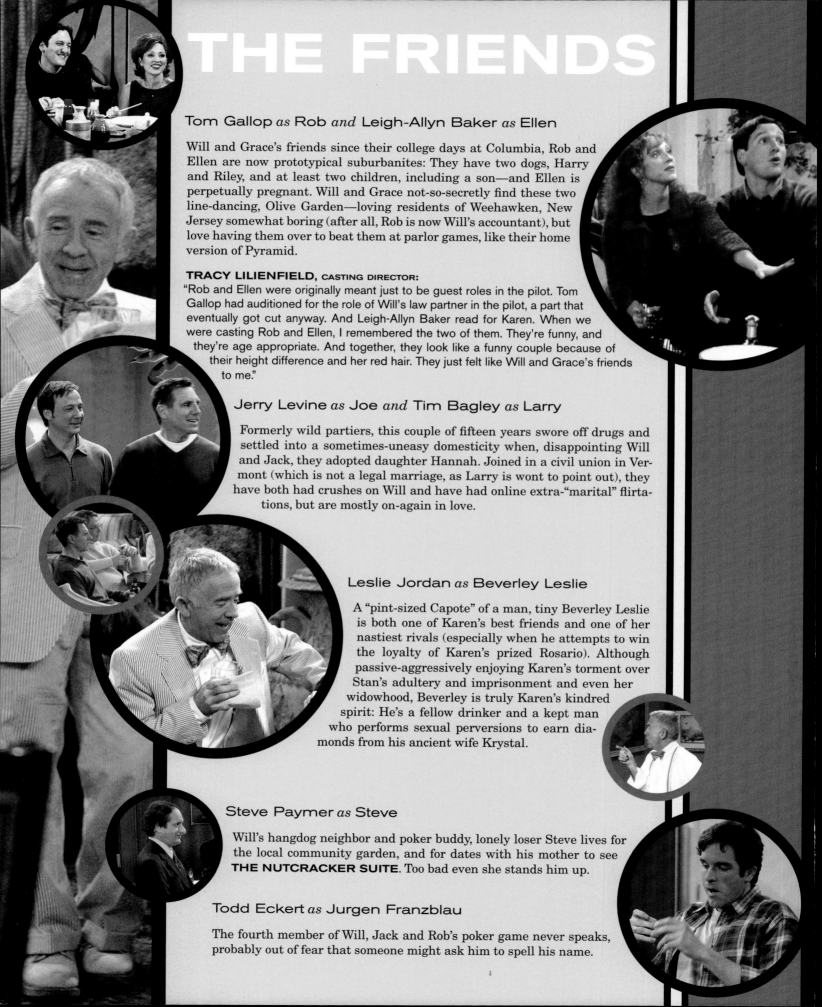

Tom Gallop *as* Rob *and* Leigh-Allyn Baker *as* Ellen

Will and Grace's friends since their college days at Columbia, Rob and Ellen are now prototypical suburbanites: They have two dogs, Harry and Riley, and at least two children, including a son—and Ellen is perpetually pregnant. Will and Grace not-so-secretly find these two line-dancing, Olive Garden—loving residents of Weehawken, New Jersey somewhat boring (after all, Rob is now Will's accountant), but love having them over to beat them at parlor games, like their home version of Pyramid.

TRACY LILIENFIELD, CASTING DIRECTOR:
"Rob and Ellen were originally meant just to be guest roles in the pilot. Tom Gallop had auditioned for the role of Will's law partner in the pilot, a part that eventually got cut anyway. And Leigh-Allyn Baker read for Karen. When we were casting Rob and Ellen, I remembered the two of them. They're funny, and they're age appropriate. And together, they look like a funny couple because of their height difference and her red hair. They just felt like Will and Grace's friends to me."

Jerry Levine *as* Joe *and* Tim Bagley *as* Larry

Formerly wild partiers, this couple of fifteen years swore off drugs and settled into a sometimes-uneasy domesticity when, disappointing Will and Jack, they adopted daughter Hannah. Joined in a civil union in Vermont (which is not a legal marriage, as Larry is wont to point out), they have both had crushes on Will and have had online extra-"marital" flirtations, but are mostly on-again in love.

Leslie Jordan *as* Beverley Leslie

A "pint-sized Capote" of a man, tiny Beverley Leslie is both one of Karen's best friends and one of her nastiest rivals (especially when he attempts to win the loyalty of Karen's prized Rosario). Although passive-aggressively enjoying Karen's torment over Stan's adultery and imprisonment and even her widowhood, Beverley is truly Karen's kindred spirit: He's a fellow drinker and a kept man who performs sexual perversions to earn diamonds from his ancient wife Krystal.

Steve Paymer *as* Steve

Will's hangdog neighbor and poker buddy, lonely loser Steve lives for the local community garden, and for dates with his mother to see **THE NUTCRACKER SUITE**. Too bad even she stands him up.

Todd Eckert *as* Jurgen Franzblau

The fourth member of Will, Jack and Rob's poker game never speaks, probably out of fear that someone might ask him to spell his name.

THE NEIGHBORS

Molly Shannon as Val Bassett

If imitation is the sincerest form of flattery, maybe out and out theft is the highest form of praise. Crazy neighbor Val tries to steal Grace's best friend Will, her customers, and the music box she got on her bat mitzvah. Although we'll miss the catfights, it's probably for the best when Val moves on to healthier pastimes, like stalking Jack.

TRACY LILIENFIELD, CASTING DIRECTOR:
"Molly Shannon is great at being nutty, and Max and David really liked that. She was on **SATURDAY NIGHT LIVE** at the time, and NBC loved that cross-promotion. So they wrote the part specifically for her."

Marshall Manesh as Mr. Zamir

Will's next-door-neighbor in 9B, Mr. Zamir likes to take off his shirt in the laundry room, snoop through other people's things, and steal Grace's newspaper. But that's not the worst of it: he also loves the movie **XANADU**.

Rosanna Arquette as Julie

Grace bonds with her boundary-free Brooklyn neighbor until, during a complimentary massage, Julie's boundary-free fingers perform a service for which one usually expects to pay extra.

THE LABORERS

Laura Kightlinger as Nurse Sheila

Nurse Sheila sure gets around; she pops up wherever our heroes hand in their specimen cups.

Louis Giovanetti as Officer Bob

After Will's sensitivity seminar for New York's Finest, Officer Bob asks Will if his friend with the tight abs and the nice, high ass might be gay. Maybe it's just a coincidence that when Will's laptop is stolen, Officer Bob's first on the scene.

Brent Sexton as Guard

The security guard at the Brooklyn House of Detention for Men has little patience for Karen and Grace's neuroses when they come to visit Stan.

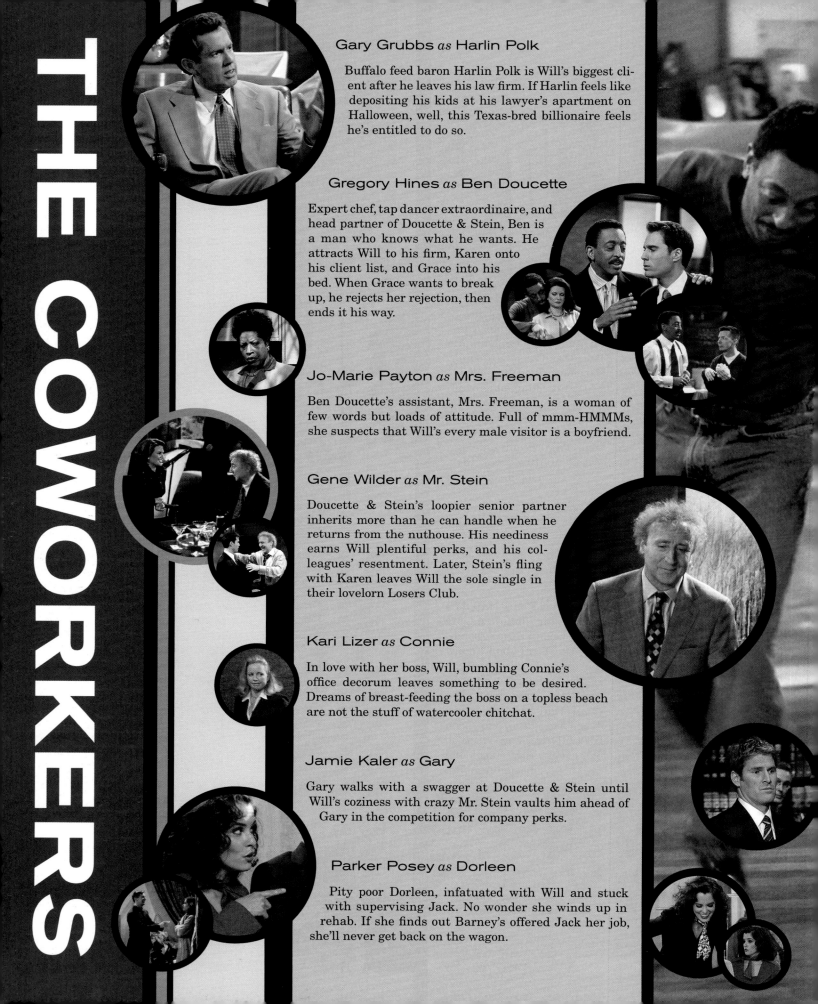

THE COWORKERS

Gary Grubbs *as* Harlin Polk

Buffalo feed baron Harlin Polk is Will's biggest client after he leaves his law firm. If Harlin feels like depositing his kids at his lawyer's apartment on Halloween, well, this Texas-bred billionaire feels he's entitled to do so.

Gregory Hines *as* Ben Doucette

Expert chef, tap dancer extraordinaire, and head partner of Doucette & Stein, Ben is a man who knows what he wants. He attracts Will to his firm, Karen onto his client list, and Grace into his bed. When Grace wants to break up, he rejects her rejection, then ends it his way.

Jo-Marie Payton *as* Mrs. Freeman

Ben Doucette's assistant, Mrs. Freeman, is a woman of few words but loads of attitude. Full of mmm-HMMMs, she suspects that Will's every male visitor is a boyfriend.

Gene Wilder *as* Mr. Stein

Doucette & Stein's loopier senior partner inherits more than he can handle when he returns from the nuthouse. His neediness earns Will plentiful perks, and his colleagues' resentment. Later, Stein's fling with Karen leaves Will the sole single in their lovelorn Losers Club.

Kari Lizer *as* Connie

In love with her boss, Will, bumbling Connie's office decorum leaves something to be desired. Dreams of breast-feeding the boss on a topless beach are not the stuff of watercooler chitchat.

Jamie Kaler *as* Gary

Gary walks with a swagger at Doucette & Stein until Will's coziness with crazy Mr. Stein vaults him ahead of Gary in the competition for company perks.

Parker Posey *as* Dorleen

Pity poor Dorleen, infatuated with Will and stuck with supervising Jack. No wonder she winds up in rehab. If she finds out Barney's offered Jack her job, she'll never get back on the wagon.

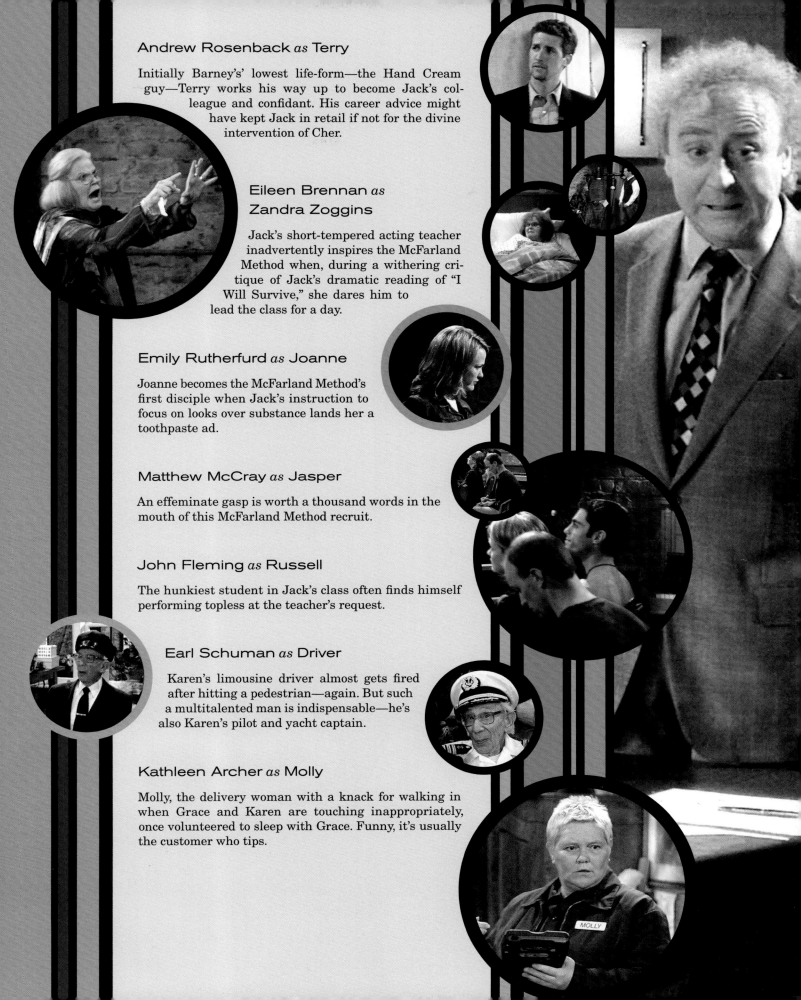

Andrew Rosenback *as* Terry

Initially Barney's' lowest life-form—the Hand Cream guy—Terry works his way up to become Jack's colleague and confidant. His career advice might have kept Jack in retail if not for the divine intervention of Cher.

Eileen Brennan *as* Zandra Zoggins

Jack's short-tempered acting teacher inadvertently inspires the McFarland Method when, during a withering critique of Jack's dramatic reading of "I Will Survive," she dares him to lead the class for a day.

Emily Rutherfurd *as* Joanne

Joanne becomes the McFarland Method's first disciple when Jack's instruction to focus on looks over substance lands her a toothpaste ad.

Matthew McCray *as* Jasper

An effeminate gasp is worth a thousand words in the mouth of this McFarland Method recruit.

John Fleming *as* Russell

The hunkiest student in Jack's class often finds himself performing topless at the teacher's request.

Earl Schuman *as* Driver

Karen's limousine driver almost gets fired after hitting a pedestrian—again. But such a multitalented man is indispensable—he's also Karen's pilot and yacht captain.

Kathleen Archer *as* Molly

Molly, the delivery woman with a knack for walking in when Grace and Karen are touching inappropriately, once volunteered to sleep with Grace. Funny, it's usually the customer who tips.

SEASON

FOUR

AS *WILL & GRACE* CONTINUED TO EVOLVE IN ITS FOURTH SEASON—ADDING
MICHAEL ANGARANO AS ELLIOT AS THE SIXTH REGULAR CAST MEMBER
IN ITS OPENING CREDITS—THE SHOW'S WRITERS CONTINUED TO LOOK FOR
WAYS TO DIG DEEPER INTO THEIR CHARACTERS' EMOTIONAL LIVES.

9/11

"With Karen, we had felt from year to year that 'If it ain't broke, don't fix it,'" Max Mutchnick explains. "Megan always knocked her comedy out of the ballpark, and no one wanted her to do anything but annihilate people around her and then have a sip of vodka."

In fact, the writers had come to rely on her just the way she was. "When we were pitching a scene in the writers' room," Max notes, "we would say what all the other characters were talking about, and wouldn't even mention what Karen was doing in the scene." Their pattern of using Karen as a go-to funny girl was so well recognized that they even developed a shorthand for it. "Then the very last thing we would say about a scene was 'and Megan will say 'ba ba ba.''" It meant that you could just give Megan a funny line to comment on and sum up what's going on," he explains.

But as the show reached its fourth season, the writers, impressed with Megan's ability to juggle both sillier and more heartfelt moments, began to look for ways to give her something more dramatic to play. They opted to do something they had deliberately avoided in the past: experiment with the marriage they considered to be the emotional anchor grounding her otherwise spacey character to earth. And they even toyed with introducing her previously unseen husband, Stan.

"I used to say to Megan that if we ever wrote a scene with her and Stan, she would be the perfect wife. She wouldn't be bitchy, or drinking—she would be Nan Kempner. Actually, that's a bad example," Max remembers. But that scene was not to be, since Max and David maintained that they could envision only one man in the part.

"Karen was married to an offscreen presence," David explains, "and not being able to show Stan made her stories more difficult to do. How do you get at Karen's emotional core without seeing Stan? Yet, who else could live up to the description we'd given of Stan except Marlon Brando?" But after some cursory discussions about casting the infamously unattainable actor, the duo decided that Stan's invisibility was working as it was.

Will & Grace & Baby?

The writers brainstormed ways to alter the marriage in order to bring out the sharp-tongued Karen's loving instinct when it comes to her man. They ruled out making Stan sick; they briefly considered having the couple lose their fortune, but decided that it would change her character too severely. They settled on legal trouble, which was also a good way to get Will involved in the story line.

Other changes were also planned for Will's life: namely, the life-altering decision to have a baby with Grace. David explains that the story line came from a very organic idea: "All the women we knew were beginning to panic and think it was time to have kids."

David himself had made a pact at age sixteen with his then-girlfriend Janet Eisenberg (the inspiration for Grace), that, if neither was married by thirty-five, they would start a family together. And as Will and Grace hit their mid-thirties without prospects of long-term romantic partners, gay or straight, they would naturally come up with a similar idea.

By raising the baby issue with no intention of following through, the writers knew they were committing the sitcom equivalent of an old mystery no-no: pulling out a gun but not firing it. "The problem with the baby story was that it seemed like that's where they would go naturally, even though we all felt like Will and Grace can't really have a baby," David explains. "But the point of the fourth season was to show that they're at the point in life where possibilities are dropping out. They have to look at each other at a certain point and face that they both want families, yet there are things that they want that they're starting to realize they may never get."

THE THIRD WHEEL GETS THE GRACE

Written By: DAVID KOHAN & MAX MUTCHNICK

KAREN:
"I've got drinks piling up on my desk and a stack of pills I haven't even opened yet."

...sperate to spend more time with Grace, Nathan volunteers to [join] her at the big Barneys sale. Too much time shopping convinces [Na]than that some tasks are better left to Will, and he deserts [Gra]ce to go find a sports bar. Karen brings Rosario to the sale to [cele]brate their fifteenth anniversary, but flees after Rosario admits [she]'s stalling in order to spend more time with Karen. Jack tries to [bon]d with Elliot by buying him clothes, and father and son survive [the] revelation that Elliot prefers not to wear leather pants to gym [cla]ss and would rather shop at Target. Will, who has been denying [tha]t his new French jeans are actually women's, finally gives in [and] auctions them to the highest bidder.

RECURRING CHARACTERS
Shelley Morrison *as* Rosario
Michael Angarano *as* Elliot
Woody Harrelson *as* Nathan

WILL:
"Have you seen [Gra]ce around marked-[do]wn cashmere? It's [li]ke the first twenty minutes of Saving Private Ryan."

SHELLEY MORRISON: I loved how it turned out in this episode that even with all the yelling the two of them do at each other, Rosario just wanted to spend more time with Karen. It was very touching.

[MEG]AN HAYES: Meg and I—or, as I call her sometimes, Megalicious—came [up] with the bit with the credit card. I had always wanted to do something [abo]ut a credit card between breasts—just a comedy bit I'd thought of one [day] and filed away in my mind. So I suggested that, and then Megan came [up] with the butt as the last part. We walked off to the side and tried it out, [and] then showed it to the writers, and they loved it.

[?]: Although all the gals at Barneys go crazy for Will's French [wom]en's jeans, in reality, they're from Diesel—women's, but [not] French.

PAST AND PRESENTS

Written By:
JON KINNALLY & TRACY POUST

Grace is furious after Karen trumps Grace's birthday gift to Nathan—the book *Zen and the Art of Motorcycle Maintenance*—with an actual motorcycle. Grace's follow-up effort, an expensive watch, also fails. But the third time's the charm as Grace offers her love, and Nathan pronounces it the best gift he's ever received. Will's childhood nemesis joins the firm and reverts to his bullying ways until Will finally takes a stand.

GRACE:
"Congratulations. I see they're finally giving out medals for evil."

GUEST STAR
Adam Goldberg *(Saving Private Ryan)* as Will's grade-school bully and new coworker Kevin Wolchek

RECURRING CHARACTER
Woody Harrelson *as* Nathan

NATHAN:
"There's nothing like hopping on your hog in the morning and riding her 'til your butt gets tired."

JACK:
"You're preaching to the choir, okay?"

ERIC McCORMACK: In one scene, Adam comes in and I'm putting moisturizer on my hands. I hadn't tried it in rehearsal, but I asked Jimmy if I could slip because my hands are slippery, and he said, "No honey, it'll look like you get hurt." So on the first pass, I said my line, "No, that's not moisturizer," and no major laughs. On the second pass I asked Jimmy to let me try it, and what ended up on television is my favorite physical moment on the show, where I lean on the desk and slide down and hit my face. I love it is because it's really unexpected, particularly for Will, and it was improv.

403 CROUCHING FATHER, HIDDEN HUSBAND
Written By: ADAM BARR

Jack convinces Grace to be Elliot's date to a school dance, but when Elliot wants to ditch Grace in favor of his crush, Nancy, it brings back bad memories of Grace's middle-school years. Grace consoles a pair of young wallflowers, while Jack's floor-clearing *NSYNC routine turns out to be just the hook Elliot needs: Nancy has a gay parent, too. Meanwhile, it's the Karen-who-cried-wolf when one prank too many makes Will clown around and drop his pants in front of FBI agents whom he mistakes for Karen's hired hands.

KAREN:
"Honey, I often ask a lot of people on my staff to do different things. Cook sometimes cleans. Cleaner sometimes cooks. Driver sometimes provides an alibi."

RECURRING CHARACTERS
Michael Angarano *as* Elliot
Landry Allbright *as* Elliot's love interest, Nancy *(first appearance)*
Kari Lizer *(series writer) as* Will's awkward, lustful secretary, Connie *(first appearance)*

ADAM BARR: When we originally conceived of the school dance, it was just a story about Jack and Elliot, not just how the son comes to terms with the fact that his dad is gay, but that he finds pride in it. We fit Grace into it later, after pairing Will and Karen together in the B story. And Grace's lines grew into a really funny part of the show. The original scenes of her bitching and spilling her guts to these girls who just wanted to talk about turtles were much longer, but had to be trimmed down for lack of time.

FYI: Note how the carpet in the hallway between Will's and Jack's apartments has been replaced with a hardwood floor.

JACK:
"No offense, girls. Today's weirdos are tomorrow's talk show hosts and sensitive singer-songwriters."

404 PRISON BLUES
Written By:
ALEX HERSCHLAG

KAREN:
"So honey, if you want to leave, I'm s[ure]
you have things to [do].
After all, there's fas[t]
mistakes to be made[.]
I'm sure it's happ[y]
hour at some
gay bar."

Will freezes in front of a TV camera during the gang's visit to Stan in prison, so Jack persuades him to join his acting class. After a rough start, Will wows cranky and imperious acting teacher Zandra by getting in deep—and embarrassing—touch with his emotions, and is able [to] breeze through his next on-camera interview. After the prison vi[sit,] Karen asks Grace to stay the night. Grace adapts all too readily [to] the leisured life, and Karen and Rosario team up to get rid of he[r.]

RECURRING CHARACTERS
Shelley Morrison *as* Rosario
Eileen Brennan *as* Jack's acting instructor, Zandra *(first appearanc[e])*
Brent Sexton *as* Prison Guard *(first appearance)*

EILEEN BRENNAN: For Zandra, I took what the writers gave me and added parts of acting teachers I've worked with myself, like Stella Adler a[nd] Uta Hagen, and pushed their tough personalities to a comic level. The firs[t] time I appeared, in this episode, I didn't use my cane, but while I was doi[ng] my second episode, Jimmy Burrows saw me with it, so he suggested that I use it. I loved the idea, because props are the greatest thing an actor ca[n] have—that and a scene partner who listens. Sean Hayes is really the reas[on] why Zandra's character works. Acting is reacting, and he's one of those people who gives you great things to play off of and helps you bring out t[he] best parts of your own character.

WILL:
"I haven't done a lot of acting before. Actually, that's not true—for 19 years, I played the role of a heterosexual."

ZANDRA:
"My guess is, not very convincingly."

SHELLEY MORRISON: The bathtub scene in this episode is one of my favorites. Sometimes if an episode has too many sets, they build some off the side, so that the only way the audience can see what's going on wher[e] we're filming is on the monitor. The bathtub scene opened up with Megan in the tub with bubbles and she's talking to somebody, and then the came[ra] panned over and there I am sitting in the tub with her with my sunglasses [on.] The audience laughed so much, they had to stop the take. I'm very modes[t] so I had had them make me a muumuu all the way down, and Megan, who[']s modest too, was wearing a body stocking. I'm a breast-cancer survivor, an[d] had a prosthetic breast on, and I was afraid it was going to pop out—I did[n't] realize they were going to have so much water in the tub. When the scen[e] was over, it took six guys and a crane to lift me out of there.

405 LOOSE LIPS SINK RELATIONSHIPS
Written By: KARI LIZER

...ace and Nathan feel insecure after comparing sexual histories, ...d Karen makes things worse by convincing Grace to give Nathan ...at sex and Nathan to withhold sex entirely. The two are at an ...passe until Will points out the ridiculousness of taking advice ...m Karen. Jack tries to weasel himself a Friday night off from ...rneys by promising supervisor Dorleen a date with Will, and ...d a modeling job from Dorleen. When Jack's ruse is discovered, ...leen busts him down to the lowest form of life at Barneys— ... guy hawking hand cream.

RECURRING CHARACTERS
Woody Harrelson *as* Nathan
...Parker Posey *as* Dorleen, Jack's boss at Barneys *(first appearance)*
Andrew Rosenbach *as* Barneys Hand Cream Guy,
later named Terry *(first appearance)*

...LINDA RITZ: Normally I do every bit of set dressing, but when we ...ted to get involved with stores like Barneys and Banana Republic, they ...d that, in order to use their name, we build the sets to their specs, using ...r crew. With Barneys, part of the arrangement was that I would go to the ...e and pick out merchandise for whatever department we were showing, ...also go through their showcase area where they keep some of their own ...ps for the store. Then, I would add whatever other interior props I needed, ...antiques. On the day of the shoot, two of their best window dressers ...1 Beverly Hills would come in to dress the mannequins and fill the set ... perfectly folded clothes.

> **JACK:**
> *"Thrilled to be here, love you, love everything about you, thinking about being you for Halloween."*

406 THE RULES OF ENGAGEMENT
Written By: JEFF GREENSTEIN

Upset that Nathan proposed to her during sex, Grace turns him down. When Will helps Grace realize that she would have said yes under different circumstances, she decides to arrange a romantic dinner and ask Nathan to marry her. While Grace prepares her special night, Will and Nathan go to a bar and happen to see two men get engaged. Nathan decides that only a proposal without so much effort is one that's meant to be, so when Grace pops the question, he breaks up with her instead.

> **GRACE:**
> *"It's just not how I ever imagined being proposed to, okay? I'm supposed to be holding a bouquet of wildflowers, not my own ankles."*

RECURRING CHARACTER
Woody Harrelson *as* Nathan

MEGAN MULLALLY: When all four characters are talking in the hallway, and Grace asks how she should fix her mistake with Nathan, and Karen and Jack run away, the cartoony way we exit was my idea, and Sean and I worked it out. We did it again that season in *Jingle Balls* when we exit the Barneys window that Jack is decorating. Sean and I can do things in perfect unison because we have this really weird affinity. We've totally freaked each other out by doing the exact same thing, having the exact same instinct, at the same time. Eric and Debra have that, too, and that doesn't happen very often.

> **JACK:**
> *"Grace, I cannot pretend I'm straight! I did that all through preschool—I'm not about to go back."*

JEFF GREENSTEIN: Originally, we had planned for Will, Jack, and Karen to be involved in Grace's story in this episode—her breakup with Nathan. But we soon realized that the three of them didn't have enough to do in the beginning, so we spent a whole day thinking of a B story that would be the right size to fit into the show. It took a full day of work, and finally we came up with a subplot about "tip sliding"—where, as Jack says, you can slide someone else's tip for the bartender over and present it as your own. We wrote a few scenes: at first Will is horrified that Jack and Karen think tip sliding is okay; then Will calls his old law professor who also thinks it's fine; and finally Will, at the gay bar with Nathan at the end, tries it himself and gets into trouble. But after all that, the episode ended up really long, and we had to cut 80 percent of it—now it's just a mention at the start of the show.

(407) BED, BATH, AND BEYOND
Written By: JHONI MARCHINKO

Grace won't get out of bed after her breakup with Nathan, so, one at a time, her friends try to cure her depression. Jack's song medley only makes Grace cry; Karen's role-play of Nathan brings on a hot kiss that drives Karen from the room; Rosario gets engrossed slides from Grace's childhood. The gang finally drags Grace into the shower, but she remains determined to heal in her own time and proceeds to depress everyone else by pointing out their own miseries. Will, Karen, and Jack crawl into bed with Grace, and the next day, she's the first one back on her feet.

a Favorite Episode of...

RECURRING CHARACTER
Shelley Morrison *as* Rosario

JHONI MARCHINKO: The kind of episodes I love to write and love to watch are the ones that have a lot of emotion going on underneath. I love the funny stuff that comes out of those moments, when you're on the verge of tears. Like in the scene where Will and Karen start to get depressed about their own lives and join Grace in bed, it was so emotional—and then Jack comes in and says how Grace had referred to him as an actor-singer when he'd always thought dance was his strong point. The joke was funny and sweet in that moment. And I like when music can be the beat to close an episode. I really had my heart set on using Annie Lennox's song *Seventeen Again,* because I envisioned the ending scene with the sun coming up and it's a new day, and the song lyrics are talking about feeling rejuvenated. But two days before the episode was due, we still hadn't gotten a hold of Annie Lennox for permission.

JEFF GREENSTEIN: In the old days before TiVo, audiences weren't even aware of episode titles, but now we have to think of them. I like the titles *Bed, Bath and Beyond,* and *Lows in the Mid 80s,* which is one of my favorites because it's not a pun—it's a weather term, and it reminds you that it's the flashback show without making a big deal about it.

FYI: The travel agent who calls to confirm Nathan's plans, "Jhoni, from Hoffman Travel," is named for, and voiced by, series executive producer Jhoni Marchinko.

GRACE:
"Baruch atoh adonai, I'm going to die alone."

ROSARIO:
"You better watch it, lady, 'cause the next time you take a bath it'll be 'rub-a-dub-dub, I drop the blender in the tub.'"

FYI: The slides Grace shows Rosario of her as a little girl and at her bat mitzvah are real-life childhood photos of Debra Messing.

(408) STAR-SPANGLED BANTER
Written By:
CYNTHIA MORT

ELLIOT:
"Oh wow, you've got an Xbox!"

KAREN:
"Hey hey hey hey! Just because my husband's in prison does not mean you can talk dirty to me!"

Tensions run high when Will backs a gay man for the city counc[il] election and Grace backs a Jewish woman. When both candidate[s] voice intolerant views during simultaneous fund-raisers at the apartment, Will and Grace swear off politics. Meanwhile, Jack forces Karen and Elliot to learn to get along, and the two bond o[ver] prank phone calls to the ailing Rosario. Sadly, Jack blows his au[di]tion for the part of a corpse on *Six Feet Under* because "one part [of] me refused to play dead."

GUEST STARS
Douglas Sills (Broadway's *Little Shop of Horrors*) *as* city council candidate Ted Bowers
Anne Meara *(Sex and the City) as* neighbor Mrs. Friedman

RECURRING CHARACTERS
Shelley Morrison *as* Rosario
Michael Angarano *as* Elliot
Marshall Manesh *as* Mr. Zamir

WILL:
"Well if I implied that you're anything less than a big Jew, I'm sorry."

ANNE MEARA: You can tell a successful show by the food they put out. *Will & Grace* put out a great spread—they didn't have lox, but they had No[va]. My big line in the episode, to Grace: "There's an old Jewish expression —you're cheap and your husband's gay" was suggested by Max Mutchnick on the set one day. Everyone there had such a seamless way of working together, and they were all so generous—literally, because they let me kee[p] a lovely suede coat I wore. I offered to pay for it—I'm not a shnorrer—but Max said, "No, that's yours." And I've worn that coat for three years now.

LORI ESKOWITZ-CARTER: I love the black sleeveless Cacharel tee tha[t] Grace wears, with the trompe l'oeil pattern of a string of pearls. I like to p[ut] her in anything with a pearl theme, because it's her signature look.

409 STAKIN' CARE OF BUSINESS

Written By: BILL WRUBEL

[Gra]ce turns to Karen when she needs money to expand the busi-
[nes]s, but after demanding a presentation to justify the loan, Karen
[tur]ns her down. When Karen later gets trapped in the office eleva-
[tor,] Grace returns the favor and demands a presentation to justify
[lett]ing her out. At the gym, Will dodges Mitchell, the "rebound guy"
[he] dated after Michael left, and while so doing meets the attractive
[Cu]rt. When Curt dodges Will after their date, Will learns that what
[go]es around goes around: he is Curt's rebound guy. Also at the
[gym], Jack grows indignant when his effort to coin a new workout
[cat]ch phrase, "stake it," succeeds too well.

> **JACK:**
> *"He went off
> the Zone for you?
> Gosh, that line's
> older than 'This is the
> first time I've ever
> done this with
> a man.'"*

[SE]AN HAYES: I went on a trip to Hawaii with some friends, including Max.
[We] were sitting at dinner, and someone was having steak. I asked him to
["st]ake it," meaning my fork, as in "Let me have some of your steak." We loved
[the] phrase, and thought it would make a great thing for Jack on the show.

[FYI]: The non-speaking loan officer at the bank
[is s]eries writer Alex Herschlag.

> **WILL:**
> *"Don't lie.
> Don't do that.
> Not here.
> This is a gym.
> This is gay
> church."*

[DE]BRA MESSING: At the end of this episode,
[Meg]an has a huge monologue in our office scene
[tog]ether, where she tells me why she can't give me a busi-
[nes]s loan. All week, she kept saying, 'I usually get six lines per episode—I'll
[nev]er be able to learn all this.' She got in front of the audience and she just
[cou]ldn't get the whole thing out. She would get five-sixths of it, and then
[wou]ld mess up one word, and the audience would sigh. So I had an idea, to
[I] cut the monologue out of the script and taped it to my forehead. So
[the]y shot her whole speech over my shoulder, so that you couldn't see
[that] I had the script page covering my whole face. And Megan's perform-
[anc]e was perfect, because 99 percent of getting it right is just knowing
[you] have the crutch there if you need it. And it was fun for the two of us,
[con]quering that moment.

410/411 A MOVEABLE FEAST

Written By:
KARI LIZER

On Thanksgiving, the gang decides to fulfill their familial obligations as a group, with each of them allotted one hour in which to
take care of business: Karen visits Stan in prison, where he tells
her to go ahead and sleep with other men; Grace's mom reacts to
her breakup with Nathan with an infuriating "I-told-you-so dance";
Jack's stepfather defies expectation by being nice to Elliot; Will's
mother, asked to choose between his companionship and his brother Paul's, opts for Paul. The wounded friends regroup and decide
to make the family rounds again, this time giving themselves only
two additional minutes each in which to patch things up: Karen
tells Stan that she's angry with him and doesn't want to sleep with
other men; Grace's mom promises never again to do the "I-told-you-
so dance" even as Grace admits that her mom has been right about
many things; Jack gets his stepfather to admit he was a terrible
dad, and the two decide to get to know one another better.

GUEST STARS

Lainie Kazan (*My Big Fat Greek Wedding*) as Grace's Aunt Honey
Jon Tenney (*Brooklyn South*) as Will's brother Paul Truman
Helen Slater (*Supergirl*) as Will's sister-in-law Peggy Truman
Kenneth Mars (the movie *The Producers*) as Grace's Uncle Sid
Nick Offerman (*Megan Mullally's real-life husband*) as
Mrs. Truman's plumber
Beau Bridges (*The Fabulous Baker Boys*) as
Jack's stepfather Daniel McFarland
Clinton Leupp (*better known to drag fans as Miss Coco Peru*) as
Jack's friend Lawrence

RECURRING CHARACTERS

Shelley Morrison as Rosario   Michael Angarano as Elliot
Debbie Reynolds as Bobbi Adler   Neil Vipond as Julius
Blythe Danner as Will's mother, Marilyn Truman (*first appearance*)

MEGAN MULLALLY: It's kind of fitting that the first time my character ever
kissed a guy who wasn't Stan, it was with the plumber—played by my
husband, Nick Offerman.

MAX MUTCHNICK: When you're gay, your definition of family takes on a
whole new meaning. It's not what people traditionally know as Thanksgiving
growing up, where you're sitting down with your mom and your dad. You
create new family, and I think this episode captured that really nicely.

FYI: The episode title refers not only to the Thanksgiving meal, but
is also an an in-joke among the show's writers: "A Moveable Feast"
is the name by which they refer to their file of jokes deleted from
each episode.

412 WHOA, NELLY

Written By:
ADAM BARR

Will and Grace fix up George Truman's mistress, Tina, in the hope that she'll end the affair with Will's dad. Larry is a last-minute substitution for Tina's date, and Tina falls hard for his sensitivity. When Tina disparages Will's father, Will defends his father and inadvertently talks Tina back into loving him. Elsewhere, Karen is horrified to learn that she has purchased a gay horse. She's ready to consign him to the glue factory when he nibbles on a mismatched scarf and Karen decides she can't part with such a fashion-conscious beast.

> **JACK:**
> *"But we love him!"*
> **KAREN:**
> *"Yeah? Well, now a million kindergarten kids with elbow macaroni and glitter can love him, too."*

RECURRING CHARACTERS
Tim Bagley *as* Larry
Lesley Ann Warren *as* Tina

ADAM BARR: Jon Kinnally had a friend who did hair and makeup for show horses. We played with the idea of Jack doing that as a gig, but realized we had to find something more substantial...so that led us naturally to the idea of him taking care of a gay horse. All the big laughs in that episode came to us pretty fast and furious once we had the idea. It was fun having the horse onstage, and it was a fun, silly way to tell a gay pride story sideways.

> **JACK:**
> *"Our horse is gay. He practices the love that dare not speak its neighhhm."*

TIM BAGLEY: I almost never break, but I broke with Debra in our scene out on the patio toward the end of the show. She is someone who can really make me laugh. It was so mean to make Larry try to continue his fake relationship with Lesley Ann Warren, and the way Debra said it was so hysterically hideous that I could not get through it without laughing.

413 JINGLE BALLS

Written By:
LAURA KIGHTLINGER

Will suspects that Grace is judgmental about his ballet dancer b
friend, Robert, and pounces on her every comment as evidence. I
Grace points out that Will himself is embarrassed by Robert and
has been projecting his discomfort onto her. Meanwhile, after Ja
betrays Grace and grabs a Barneys Christmas window decoratic
job for himself, he panics over Dorleen's 24-hour deadline. Altho
at first happy to let Jack go down in flames, Grace overhears his
desperate prayer to Santa and selflessly saves his job with a bea
tiful window display.

GUEST STAR
Larry Sullivan *(The Trip)* as Robert

RECURRING CHARACTER
Parker Posey *as* Dorleen

> **KAREN:**
> *"Grace, it's Christmas, for goodness' sake! Think about the baby Jesus. Up in that tower, letting his hair down so that the three wise men could climb it, spin the dreidel, and see if there's six more weeks of winter."*

MELINDA RITZ: To put together the window that Grace ultimately desig
for Barneys, we were in total coordination with the store, who said they
would like to make it look exactly like a window at Barneys in New York. T
told me I didn't have to do a thing, that they would do it all. At 5 p.m. on th
night of the shoot, one hour before showtime, two tiny boxes arrive from N
York—not nearly enough to fill this entire window. So I had to race to a pro
house and pull a truckload of stuff to be shipped over immediately, and
we had to throw together that window in an hour.

FYI: The young blonde woman doing a split in the background a
dance class is series writer Sally Bradford.

414 DYEING IS EASY, COMEDY IS HARD
Written By: DARLENE HUNT

...ace spoils her ex-fiancé Danny's wedding with an embarrass-...rehearsal dinner toast that scares off the bride. Grace lures ...back with a flattering Danny story, but Grace is left shaken by ...warm memories. Will tells the other guests he's a professional ...nis player to avoid admitting he's a lawyer, and meets an IRS ...nt telling the same lie. Elliot's mother, Bonnie, prohibits Jack ...n seeing Elliot after Jack gets him a "gay haircut." When Karen ...naps Elliot, Jack returns him to Bonnie and accuses her of hat-...him for being gay. That's imposible, Bonnie explains, because ...herself is a lesbian but is waiting to tell Elliot in her own time.

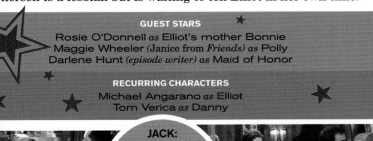

JACK:
"Prove it! Say something lesbionic."

BONNIE:
"Home Depot."

JACK:
"Wow, Elliot has two gay parents. That's, like, every kid's dream!"

...VID KOHAN: Originally, the character of Bonnie, Elliot's mother, was ...written as a lesbian. We figured Rosie wouldn't want to do that—this ...just before she came out publicly. But then Rosie told us that she was ...ppointed, and that she wanted to play a gay character. We loved the idea, ...e it would make the story a little more interesting. There's an element in ...episode that we've hinted at a couple of times, the tensions and resent-...nts between gay men and gay women. I don't know if before this we had ...e the best job of portraying it—there was an episode we had done earlier ...t we're not too proud of, where, because of the way we edited it, Jack ...med to be lesbian bashing. Here, the relationship that Jack develops with ...nnie, and the respect they find for each other, makes for a nicer moment.

...: Darlene Hunt, who wrote and appears in this episode, also ...ote a play, *Platonically Incorrect,* which was adapted into a sit-...n pilot for ABC in 2003. The pilot, which was not picked up as ...eries, centered on a platonic male-female couple and their raun-...er sidekicks (sound familiar?) And, when the play ran as ...off-Broadway workshop production in 2001, Darlene Hunt ...peared opposite Sean Hayes.

415 SOMEONE OLD, SOMEPLACE NEW
Written By: JEFF GREENSTEIN

Will and Grace look for a bigger apartment so each of them can enjoy some privacy. After Sandra Bernhard throws them out of her place—which, thanks to Will and Grace, she still hasn't managed to sell—they fall for an expensive pad, and sublet their own to Rob and Ellen for an outrageous markup. Jack horrifies Karen with a birthday visit from her lowlife mother, whom Karen had always said was dead.

KAREN:
"Sunny's out of bed? Finally! Von Bulow, get your ass in here!"

SHELLEY MORRISON: In the scene where Jack and Rosario find out who Lois really is, they wanted me to faint. And I said, "Look, folks. I'm brittle. I ain't fainting." So then they quickly came up with the idea, which I thought was hysterical, of me saying the line that everyone now remembers, "Santa Maria, it has a mother!" And it worked out so much better.
The only blooper I remember making was in this episode, when they had me change a line I said to Sean and call him "Martin Scorsissy." He didn't know that line was coming, and he turned and gave me such a look, I broke up.

GLENDA ROVELLO: When the broker takes Will and Grace to see two different apartments in this episode, it's actually the same apartment both times. We just moved walls around and added details to the wainscoting to make them look different. For the first apartment, to make it smaller, we covered up the spiral staircase and the kitchen that you see in the second apartment with walls.

FYI: After her appearance here, Suzanne Pleshette would go on to star in the first season of Kohan and Mutchnick's other NBC sit-com, *Good Morning, Miami* as Claire, series star Mark Feuerstein's character's grandmother.

ROSARIO:
"Santa Maria, it has a mother!"

416 SOMETHING BORROWED, SOMEONE'S DUE

Story By: KARI LIZER

Teleplay By: ADAM BARR & BILL WRUBEL

Will and Grace's plot to scare Rob and Ellen out of their sublet of their old apartment stalls when Ellen goes into labor. At the hospital they run into Karen, whose attempted reconciliation with her con artist mother, Lois, has involved her in a scam of a dying man's money. All ends well when Lois can't bring herself to use Karen in her plan (plus, the mark's daughter got wise), and Rob and Ellen decide to move back to New Jersey.

KAREN:
"I want to clean up the fetid reeking aftertouch of the common man."

RECURRING CHARACTERS

Shelley Morrison *as* Rosario
Tom Gallop *as* Rob
Leigh-Allyn Baker *as* Ellen
Suzanne Pleshette *as* Lois Whitley

LEIGH-ALLYN BAKER: In this episode and a few others, I suddenly have short, black hair. I had done it for a pilot that I was hoping would get picked up called *Nobody but You*. When I came in to do *Will & Grace*, Max was not thrilled about the hair. The writers made a joke about it, but they really wanted me to dye my hair back to red.

LOIS:
"I'm your mother. You got everything from me—your looks, your guts, your ambition. The only thing you didn't get from me is that voice. That voice you got from your father."

417 GRACE IN THE HOLE

Written By:
BILL WRUBEL

Grace recognizes one of Stan's fellow prisoners as her old high school crush, Glen, and persuades Will to represent him in court. When Grace finds out she's being two-timed in the visitors' room, she asks Will to drop the case, but he refuses and gets Glen his parole. Rosario gives Karen a taste of prison life by betting that she and Jack can't last three days locked in Rosario's quarters. The stakes? If Rosario loses, Karen gets to hunt her like a fox; if Karen loses, she has to visit Stan every day for a month. But after a few days locked up with Jack, Karen purposely throws the bet when she realizes how much imprisoned Stan must be suffering.

RECURRING CHARACTERS

Shelley Morrison *as* Rosario
Brent Sexton *as* Prison Guard

GRACE:
"He was in a Jewish gang."

WILL:
"What is that, exactly? They drive by and slash your credit rating? Was he a Bloodberg or a Cripstein?"

HE SHOOTS, THEY SNORE

Written By:
SALLY BRADFORD

[Wh]en Grace opens her interior design seminar at the New School [wit]h a history lesson, she bores her class into truancy. She lures [the] class back after Karen, under pressure, promises to let them [tou]r Katie Couric's house. But when Karen turns out to be lying [abo]ut even knowing Katie, the class abandons Grace [for] good. Up in Connecticut, Will fills in for Jack [at] Elliot's basketball tournament and quiets [the] boy's fears after his first kiss. Jack feels [tha]t Will hijacked a precious parental [mo]ment, but when Elliot blows the game, [Jac]k acts like a dad and shares his hard-[wo]n experience with failure.

RECURRING CHARACTERS
Michael Angarano *as* Elliot
Landry Allbright *as* Nancy

A CHORUS LIE

Written By:
JON KINNALLY & TRACY POUST

When Jack suspects that Owen, his competition for a spot in the Manhattan Gay Men's Chorus, is straight, he enlists Grace's help in blowing Owen's cover. After Grace gets a rise out of Owen, Jack outs him to the club, only to lose the spot to him, anyway, because the club has a policy of tolerance (and the choral director wants to share a room with Owen). Meanwhile, Karen passes Will off as a gigolo at her high society Valentine's Day Party, and soon the unsuspecting Will is awash in clients requesting his services. Will storms away when Karen admits her lie, but returns later to do the spotlight dance with her just in time to spare her from a humiliating moment alone.

GUEST STARS
Matt Damon *as* Owen
Patrick Kerr (blind pianist on *Curb Your Enthusiasm*) *as* Choral Director
Gay Men's Chorus of Los Angeles *as* Gay Men's Chorus of New York

RECURRING CHARACTERS
Shelley Morrison *as* Rosario
Leslie Jordan *as* Beverley Leslie

a Favorite Episode of...

TRACY POUST & JON KINNALLY: Of all the episodes we wrote, this is both of our favorites. Matt Damon fit so well into the show, and we loved having him singing.

LESLIE JORDAN: When we shot this episode, there was a scene with Beverley Leslie's wife Krystal. They had hired an actress named Sparkle, who was, I think, 98 years old. They put her in a wheelchair and put a tiara on her. The gag was that I am mean to her, and she never speaks—she just pulls on me. Sparkle was so cute, and it was heartbreaking when they decided to cut the character because they realized they could never show my wife.

JEFF GREENSTEIN: We've done episodes that either have incredibly strong A stories and lesser B stories, or a nominally funny B story and a nice heartwarming A story. But I always think of this episode as the one that had that great A story and a great B story. It had that Shelter Island story that was fantastic and it had Matt Damon.

420 WEDDING BALLS

Written By:
LAURA KIGHTLINGER

When Will's cousin Allison gets sick, Grace steps in to help her fiancé plan the wedding. Grace gets too caught up in the fun of it all, and before long she acts like she's the one about to tie the knot. Elsewhere, Jack feels excluded when Will and Karen bond over a book, so to salvage the peace, Will and Karen stage an argument.

GUEST STARS
Tracy Nelson (*Square Pegs*) as Will's cousin Allison

JACK:
"Someone's got a big vocabulary, and a little dic-tionary."

KAREN:
"A friend is someone you gossip about and make out with when your husband's in the hospital."

KAREN:
"I was going to have my staff read it, but I was worried that knowledge leads to freedom."

421 FAGEL ATTRACTION

Written By:
JENJI KOHAN

After Will's laptop computer is stolen, he agrees to go undercover with Detective Gavin Hatch to bust open a gay laptop theft ring. Jack recognizes Hatch from gay group therapy and warns Will th true to his pathology, Hatch has invented the crime ring in order to start a relationship with him. Jack also gives Will the key to getting rid of Hatch: he is repulsed by the sight of food caught in teeth. Karen restrains Grace from violence when neighbor Val steals her design, her materials, and (almost) her client. But afte explaining that violence doesn't solve anything, Karen comes to Grace's defense with a chop to the neck she learned through tai c

GUEST STARS
Michael Douglas *as* Officer Gavin Hatch
Barry Livingston (*My Three Sons*) as Grace's client Vince

RECURRING CHARACTERS
Molly Shannon *as* Val
Louis Giovanetti *as* a cop

WILL:
"It's been a lon time since I slou danced. With a c Whose gun is pok me in the back …I hope."

FYI: Michael Douglas was nominated for a 2002 Emmy award for "Outstanding Guest Actor in a Comedy Series" for his appearance on this episode. Ironically, his *Fatal Attraction* co-star Glenn Clos was that year's nominee for outstanding guest actress, also for *Will & Grace*.

ERIC McCORMACK: Some of the most satisfying moments I have on the show is when I can get a laugh out of one of my idols. In one take, I tried to break up Michael Douglas. When I came to sit down beside him on the couch, my line was something like, "I have to confess something," and then added, "I used to whack off watching *The Streets of San Francisco*." Micha never breaks, though, so he just leaned back with a big smile. And there wa about thirty seconds of nonstop laughter from the audience, so he was just waiting, looking at me. Finally, the laughter died down, and he turned to me and said, "You liked Karl Malden that much, did you?"

KAREN:
"This woman has more talent in her little-boy breasts than you have in your whole body."

422 CHEATIN' TROUBLE BLUES
Written By: ALEX HERSCHLAG

WILL:
"Fantastic. Everybody's cheating on everybody. Suddenly my parents are Fleetwood Mac."

[Wil]l's parents are so affectionate with each other at their anniver-[sar]y party in the Rainbow Room that Will feels sure his father has [end]ed the affair with Tina. But when each parent surreptitiously [me]ntions wanting to bring "a buddy" along on the cruise Will gives [the]m for their anniversary, Will blows the lid off the family's decep-[tion], and his parents decide to separate. Charged with bringing the [cak]e, Karen and Jack climb a lot of steps when Karen confuses her [own] life with the opening scene from *Speed* and refuses to take the [ele]vator to the Rainbow Room.

RECURRING CHARACTERS
Sydney Pollack *as* George Truman
Blythe Danner *as* Marilyn Truman

[TRIVIA]: The man in the Rockefeller Center elevator when Will and [Gra]ce rush in is David Kohan's comedy writer father, Buz.

[DAV]ID KOHAN: After college, I worked as Sydney [Poll]ack's assistant. It's funny how Will the WASP's [fath]er is Sydney Pollack, and Grace the Jewish [one]'s mother is Debbie Reynolds. But Sydney is [grea]t in the part, and I will say this: he was the only [directo]r of note who was willing to do the show at the [time], and he did it as a favor. Plus, he may be not be [a W]ASP, but he's from South Bend, Indiana, so I thought [that] counted for something.

MARILYN:
"Oh, no, Grace, please? I'm dying to talk to you. I can't talk to my friends. They're so sophisticated and elegant."

423 WENT TO A GARDEN POTTY
Story By: SALLY BRADFORD

Teleplay By: **TRACY POUST & JON KINNALLY**

Will rescues a beloved artifact from his parents' marriage, Squatsie, the garden gnome. After he places it in the community garden, Grace accidentally shatters Squatsie, and pins the blame on the nasty farmer of a neighboring plot. When Will is caught meting out a retaliatory urination on the neighbor's prized lettuce, Grace cops to being the gnome-wrecker, and they all mend fences with a group hug. Meanwhile, Jack quits Karen's TV ad campaign over fears of heterosexual typecasting, but when Zandra pounds some sense into him he begs for his job back.

GUEST STAR
Tom Poston *(Newhart)* as Norman

KAREN:
"Honey, that was really moving. You know, I think I got a little misty… down there."

RECURRING CHARACTERS
Eileen Brennan *as* Zandra
Steve Paymer *as* Steve

GIL SPRAGG: To create an easily breakable Squatsie, we located the correct garden gnome, and then had it cast in plaster so that it became very fragile. We added on fake ears and a nose so that it did not resemble the original product. Then we had the paint department paint it to look like our own design.

TRACY POUST: We knew we wanted to write something set in a community garden. The idea of the garden gnome came from the writers' room. Someone thought it would be funny to have Will attached to this stupid sculpture, and have Grace destroy it. We did have Grace also swat flies in Season Three in *Crazy in Love*, and sometimes we do accidentally repeat ourselves. Swatting flies first came from an Adam Barr bit—he does it in the writers' room, and it's hilarious.

424 HOCUS FOCUS

Written By:
SALLY BRADFORD

Will wins a session with the zany—and almost certainly substance-abusing—celebrity photographer Fannie Lieber, but then he and Grace can't agree on which portrait of themselves is a keeper. Fannie finally shocks the two into a meaningful shot with her unexpectedly powerful suggestion that they have a baby together. Elsewhere, Jack upbraids Karen after she upstages him during their magic act. In retaliation, she wreaks havoc on the act, but reconciles with Jack when she hears him, thinking his magic may have actually turned her into a rabbit, making a soulful apology to the beast. ★

GUEST STAR
Glenn Close *as* Fannie Lieber

KAREN:
"I'll have you know, there are parts of me that were just a twinkle in a scientist's eye three weeks ago."

JACK:
"Now, for my next trick, I will ask my lovely assistant to step inside the magic box."

KAREN:
"Uh-oh, I might be a little rusty. I haven't done that since my junior year at Sarah Lawrence."

FYI: Glenn Close was nominated for a 2002 Emmy Award for "Outstanding Guest Actress in a Comedy Series" for her appearance on this episode. ★

425 A BUNCH OF WHITE CHICKS SITTIN' AROUND TALKIN'

Written By: **DAVID KOHAN & MAX MUTCHNICK**

GRACE:
"I want to travel the world. Anywhere. Everywhere. You know, as long as it's clean, and they speak English, and it's safe."

Over a bottle of wine, the gang vows to make sure they don't die with regrets: for Karen, this means having a long-delayed conjug[al] visit with Stan; for Jack, scoring a Broadway audition; for Grace, running a marathon; and for Will, having a baby with Grace. Tak[en] off-guard by Will's baby-making desire, Grace tells a therapist that she's not ready to fall back on the plan to use Will's "safety sperm," but his description of them as parents wins her over. Kar[en] storms out of her conjugal visit when she learns that Stan has been caught doing insider trading again and will remain in pris[on] much longer. Jack bombs in his Broadway audition and decides to abandon acting for good.

KAREN:
"I've been putting on a brave face for eight months. Well, eight months ago in Brazil I had one put on."

MAX MUTCHNICK: I hate to admit that we've borrowed TV from TV, but [the] idea for this episode came from an episode of *Maude* I remember as a chil[d] where Bea Arthur just spoke to the camera. She was at a shrink's office, and she spoke to the shrink for the entire episode, and I realized that we have the actors to pull off the same concept, so we did it. I was very pleased with how it turned out.

[Wi]ll and Grace try artificial insemination, but when Will's sperm [sa]mple gets switched with Rosario's Mop'n'Glo, they're left with a [mi]ssed opportunity and a sticky floor. They next try to have hotel [roo]m sex, but neither can go through with it, so it's back to the lab. [Wi]ll ends up alone at the clinic after a collision with a lamppost [lea]ves Grace in the care of a man on a white horse. Meanwhile, [Ka]ren is sorely tempted by the romantic overtures of Lionel Banks, [an]d Jack, after a fall transports him to a tête-à-tête with Cher in [he]aven, then quits his new job as assistant floor manager at [Bar]neys to resume his attempts at a career in acting.

GUEST STAR
Cher *as* Herself

RECURRING CHARACTERS
Shelley Morrison *as* Rosario
Michael Angarano *as* Elliot
Laura Kightlinger *as* Nurse Shelia
Andrew Rosenback *as* Terry
Rip Torn *as* Lionel Banks *(first appearance)*

JACK:
"I do ask that after you have completed the act of making sweet, sweet love that you get Will a one-way ticket back to Homoville, before he gets too comfortable in 'gina Heights."

JEFF GREENSTEIN: Will and Grace's physical comedy scene, when they attempt to psyche themselves into having sex in the hotel room, is one of my favorites we've ever done. When you have four physical comedians who are as gifted as these four, you do try to use physical comedy as often as you can. Jimmy helps us so much with that, because we writers work in our heads with words and dialogue, and Jimmy is so good at coming up with a way to physicalize a beat.

LIONEL:
"You don't have sex for money?"

KAREN:
"No, I do not. For jewels, for furs, for mixed securities— like a lady."

[JA]NET EISENBERG: I feel like I should take some responsibility for Cher [bei]ng on the show, because she is the light of my life and always has been. [Ma]x and David wouldn't know a thing about Cher if it weren't for me. I've [lov]ed her since the first or second grade, and to know me has always been [to k]now what's going on with Cher, or any Cher sightings or memorabilia.

JACK:
"You ARE God! Chastity? Elijah? It all makes sense."

DEBRA MESSING: I got hurt really badly filming the lamppost stunt at the very end of this episode. During the week, we were rehearsing that on the stage, but with just a flat wall. I experimented and found out that when I was running towards the wall, I would be okay if I turned my head back at the very last second. The closer I get to the wall and the quicker the turn, the funnier it's going to be. During rehearsal I just did the stunt all-out to show it to the writers, and I waited too long. I turned too late, and when I slammed into the wall, I sprained my neck. And it was excruciating.

OUT OF THE CLOSET:
FABULOUS WARDROBES

As a **BOSTON COMMON** veteran, costume designer Lori Eskowitz-Carter knew she'd have to bring her best game to **WILL & GRACE**. "Max knows a ton about clothes," she says. "Sometimes I think he knows more than me." Creating looks to reflect the personalities of cutting-edge, fashion-conscious New Yorkers proved to be a special challenge, and a special thrill. Unlike the typical sitcom, says Lori, "It's about the clothes here."

Will's conservatism colors his flair for fashion at work and at play. At the office it's a three-button suit with a classic shirt and bold colored "rep" tie (a favorite of Max's, named for its repetitious stripe). Will unwinds—or at least tries to—in top-label casual wear: John Varvatos, Dolce & Gabbana, Armani, Gucci and Prada.

Lori's quick to share credit for Will's killer looks with Eric. "You could throw Will in some Banana Republic stuff and he'd look great" she says. "His physique is like a male model's, and he wears clothes beautifully."

SIGNATURE LOOK

Fashionable restraint in a good suit with a good white shirt with French cuffs and a "rep" tie.

WILL

GRACE

The look of **WILL & GRACE**'s most fashion-forward character is the hardest to define…and the most fun to design. "She wears everything," says Lori. "Anything from a $10 T-shirt to the high, high end that I had to borrow because I couldn't afford it." Like the character who wears them, Grace's clothes are all over the place.

SIGNATURE LOOK

Contemporary Katharine Hepburn in pearls and an open-collared men's tailored shirt over a black Armani suit with wide-legged pants.

Lori and the rest of the creative team took a second look at the flamboyant sweater they'd tied around Jack's neck in the pilot episode and decided to make a change. Lori explains: "If Jack is such a gay and 'out there' character, America can relate to him more if he looks like a 'normal' guy." Now Jack fits right in—in J.Crew, Banana Republic, and Abercrombie & Fitch.

JACK

SIGNATURE LOOK

Subversive Everyman in jeans and a sweater-vest with an Oxford underneath.

Success breeds success, as Karen's evolving look proves. In the early days, Lori's budget didn't allow her to drape Karen in the style to which she should have always been accustomed. My, how things change. "Now, a lot of companies will give us stuff," says Lori. "Designers like to be able to say they've outfitted the **WILL & GRACE** girls." Karen looks right at home in Emporio Armani, Dolce & Gabbana, and Prada.

SIGNATURE LOOK

Like a cool $985 million bucks in a top-label black suit.

YOU'RE WEARING WHAT?!

JACK: *"Nice shirt. Somewhere a ballerina is shivering."*

GRACE: *"I hate myself."*
KAREN: *"Of course you do, honey. How could anybody be happy in bat mitzvah ruffles?"*

WILL: *"Hey, Leather Tuscadero."*

WILL: *"It's unisex."*
GRACE: *"Sweetie, that's wha gay men always say when they wan to wear women's clothing."*

"Hello Sporty Spice!"

Attention Fans:

Grace's pilgrim shoes and Will's womanly sweater were supposed to look bad! Usually though, the costume-related zingers come from the writers' and actors' wicked wits during rehearsal.

GRACE: *"I want to get arrested."*
JACK & KAREN: *"Go outside in that outfit."*

WILL: *"I'm afraid the ragtag bunch of French sailors you stole your outfit from want it back."*

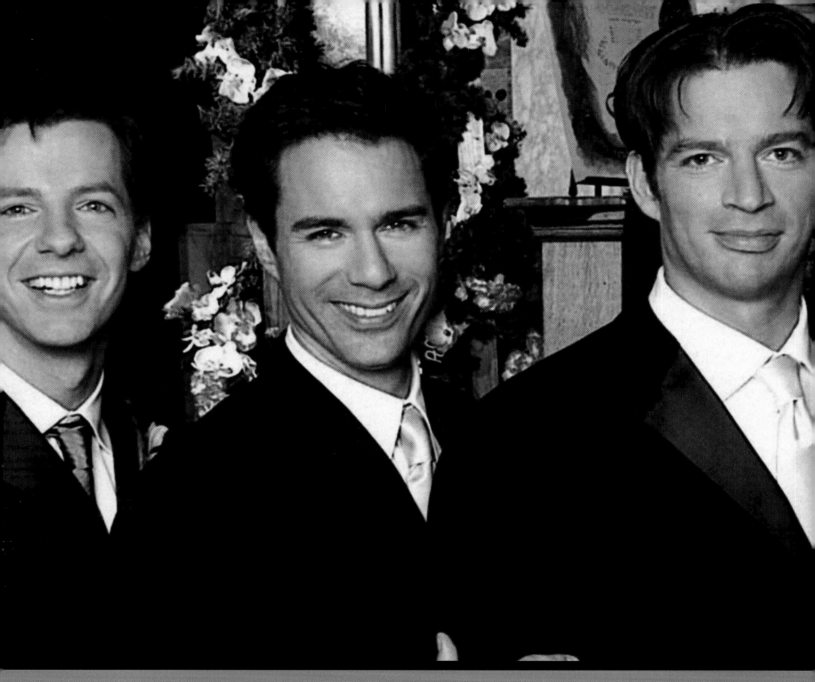

SEASON

FIVE

"In the third season," Jhoni remembers, "Max had come to me and said, 'You're going to take over this show eventually.' I said I wasn't, because I'm not the kind of person ever to stay anywhere for that long. But I just fell in love with the writers and the actors, and here I am, six years later."

The Year Mom & Dad Left

When Jhoni and Jeff convened a week ahead of the rest of the writers in July, they began to lay out their vision for the series' year ahead, which included some big changes. "Season Five was interesting because that was the year Mom and Dad left," Jeff says.

The new showrunners decided to create stories in a different way than before: by creating a more serialized "story arc" for each character, creating mileposts for his or her story line developments throughout the season. Aside from the Season Four story line of Will and Grace considering having a baby—which the writers found themselves having to undo as Season Five started—the show had never been planned quite so far in advance.

"I had never worked on a show that had an arc, but Michael Patrick King told me that on **SEX AND THE CITY**, he started at the beginning of the season and stretched a single story arc out, and then it was so much easier to fill in the gaps."

"In Season Five, the first ten episodes are like a soap opera," Jeff says. "Grace meets Leo. Grace falls in love with Leo. They have their first kiss. It comes to a crisis with Will. She meets his parents. There is an impulsive marriage. It is all very chained together."

Jeff and Jhoni also wanted to change the pattern that they had often found the show reverting to in the past. They vowed to mix it up a little: no more episodes with Will and Grace in a more grounded A story, and Jack and Karen in a zany B story. And to grow the show's characters, they created what Jeff and Jhoni refer to as their "SECRET WEAPONS":

GAYER WILL

"Will is wry, ironic, and acerbic—but what we found as we got to the third or fourth season is that, sometimes, Will is buzzkill. He's the one shaking a finger in other characters' faces, and that's a thankless job. The other three are off-the-wall characters, and we wanted Eric to have more of a chance to be, too. So we "feminized" Will a little bit in Season Five, and made him goofier. Seeing him with his pinky out, drinking from a teacup on the sidelines of a soccer game is funny, and we had earned the right to do that because we already established that Will is a dignified character. His only problem is his lack of romantic fulfillment, so we decided to do the "Fagmalion" arc because we wanted to see him fall in love. We knew he couldn't get the guy, because it's not funny when you do in television comedy. But we wanted to try it."

CENTERED GRACE

"We felt that we had played out every 'hag' story that we could, and Grace's codependency with Will was getting repetitious. But when Grace fell in love, she became less neurotic, less off-the-wall, less jangly, and more of a woman—a Grace we liked a lot better. We wanted Debra Messing to win an Emmy in Season Five, and one of the things that contributed to that was writing her differently: as less of the nincompoop, and more as someone a little more sure of herself. We also vowed to make her stronger by not doing any more of Karen insulting Grace and Grace just taking it. We wanted to change the nature of that relationship."

WISE JACK

"We decided no more Jack the Dummy all the time. We wanted to give him something that he's good at. That led to the acting class, where, in that room, Jack could be a wise man, looking over his glasses. Sean is hysterical doing that stuff. As funny as he is being the dumb guy, Sean as the wise-dumb guy is even funnier."

KAREN UNLEASHED

"We had always insisted that Karen stay with Stan, because her love for him was one of the few things anchoring the character. But in Season Five, we decided to try something new, and started to dissolve her marriage. Once Karen became single, we could show her dating and being sexual—with men and with women. She's got that rockin' bod, and we wanted to free her to hump up against people and go on dates."

Written By: **ADAM BARR**

, the man on the white horse, deposits Grace at the clinic for
deposit from Will. She and Will had agreed not to date while
y try to conceive, but their resolve is tested when Will kisses a
at a club and Grace secretly hangs on to Leo's phone number
r he asks her out. Meanwhile, Karen gives in to her desire for
nel, but their night together is interrupted by Stan's return.

RECURRING CHARACTERS
Rip Torn *as* Lionel Banks
Laura Kightlinger *as* Nurse Sheila
Harry Connick, Jr. *as* Dr. Leo Markus *(first appearance)*

AM BARR: When we wrote the Season 4 cliffhanger, with the guy on the
e with a big hat in silhouette, we knew that when it came time to figure
stories for the next season, we'd have to fill in that character. When we
e back, for a long time the hat threw us. Were we casting Tom Selleck or
Wayne? We spent a long time trying to address the question of why he
on a horse in the middle of Central Park. We had painted ourselves into
rner, knowingly. One of the things I've learned from Jimmy Burrows is that
always play all your cards, go for broke, and you'll always figure a way out.

KAREN:
"I am a married woman. Sure, my husband is an enormous bulldozer of a man who has to be hit with a stun gun before he can be weighed or medicated, but when I said yes to his attorneys, I meant that to be forever."

502 BACON AND EGGS

Written By:
ALEX HERSCHLAG

Grace's pregnancy test is negative, but she and Will resolve to keep
trying. Leo continues to court Grace, and though she insists it's not
a good time for her to begin a relationship, she finally gives him a
call. While stalking Kevin Bacon, Jack accidentally gets hired as
Kevin's personal assistant. His first assignment: tracking down
Kevin's stalker. Caught in the act, Jack fingers Will. But Will has
the last dance; he gets the chance to live Jack's dream of hanging
out with and dancing to *Footloose* with Kevin, who believes that
every star needs a stalker. Elsewhere, guilt-ridden Karen musters
the willpower to end her affair with Lionel in person after her
appointed messenger Rosario ends up sleeping with him herself. ★

KEVIN BACON:
"If I had a dollar for every time my jock strap had been stolen from the gym…"

JACK:
"You'd have one hundred eighty-six dollars."

GUEST STAR
Kevin Bacon *as* Himself

RECURRING CHARACTERS
Shelley Morrison *as* Rosario
Harry Connick, Jr. *as* Leo
Rip Torn *as* Lionel Banks

ALEX HERSCHLAG: Jimmy had run into Kevin Bacon, and asked him to be
on the show. I spoke to him on the phone and told him my concept for the
character, and he had a really good sense of humor about himself and wanted to go for it. I wanted him to play not himself but a character named Kevin
Bacon, who was cheap and needy—I love Jack Benny—so that he would have
his own comic persona, and not just be the person for Jack to be funny off of.
All week in the writers' room, we had vowed that we were NOT going to put
in a *Six Degrees of Kevin Bacon* joke, because it was a cliche. But we found
a good place for it, and we put it in and it worked. Overall, I think that the fact
that Kevin was willing to do the dance made the episode.

BILL WRUBEL: I remember when we were talking about the moment where
Will and Kevin Bacon were to dance the *Footloose* dance together, and I was
thinking to myself, "This will never be as enjoyable as us talking about it right
now." But when we were on the stage that night shooting it, it was huge. ★

503 THE KID STAYS OUT OF THE PICTURE
Written By: JHONI MARCHINKO

Will makes plans for fatherhood, while Grace secretly has the time of her life with Leo. Jack persuades Will to stop pressuring Grace about another insemination, while Karen advises Grace to come clean about Leo. Grace can't bring herself to admit she's broken their no-dating pact, and when Will discovers he's been lied to, he lashes out. He accuses her of flaking out during the most important decision of their lives, and she retorts that he wants her to be even more miserable than he is. Furious, Will throws her out of the apartment.

WILL:
"Go to hell, Grace."

RECURRING CHARACTER
Harry Connick, Jr. *as* Leo

ERIC McCORMACK: The last scene of the episode—the huge argument that we had over the baby—is probably my favorite five minutes of my career. That scene remained basically unchanged from the very first table read, and we didn't rehearse it much. And there was nothing in that episode, or in the history of the show, to let that audience know that something like that was coming. That night, we hit that scene and there were no screw-ups. We played it so real and I felt like Debra and I had never connected better. The line where I say "Go to hell, Grace," which might as well have been "Fuck you," was the parallel of Grace saying, "Go to hell, Will" in the pilot. When we stormed out our separate ways, there was this quiet, and I heard Jimmy softly say, "Beautiful. Cut." And the audience just stood up. You just don't expect you'll ever have that experience on a half-hour show.

DEBRA MESSING: The whole week of working on this episode was exciting, because Will and Grace had never gotten into a rough, raw, really harsh fight before. This was intended to pull the rug out not only from underneath the characters' feet but the audience's. It was really exciting because it felt like all the rules of sitcom storytelling and style were thrown out the window. After we did the scene once, the audience was silent, and I could hear gasps. I remember Eric and I looked at each other and registered that that had never happened before.

KAREN:
"The gays love their presents. Just wave something shiny in front of their faces, you can get whatever you want. That's how we got Manhattan from the gay Indians."

JEFF GREENSTEIN: To me, this is one of the best episodes in the history of the series, with the big blowout between Will and Grace. There is a wonderful line that Jhoni wrote: "I am not going to be miserable for you." That's what the show is all about. Anytime you get to a moment that touches the bedrock of the show, it is always electrifying.

 ## 504 HUMONGOUS GROWTH
Written By:
KARI LIZER

Jack and Karen scheme to make peace between Will and Grace getting them both to a birthday party for Joe and Larry's daughter, Hannah. Will and Grace compete for their friends' affections but in the process they make children cry and topple the birthday cake. It looks like Jack and Karen's plan will fail, until they lock the feuding ex-roommates together in the moonwalk. There, Will confesses that his hurt is made worse by the feeling that Grace his only option for parenthood, and the two reaffirm their love for each other.

RECURRING CHARACTERS
Jerry Levine *as* Joe
Tim Bagley *as* Larry
Mary McDonough *(The Waltons) as* a Mom

a Favorite Episode of...

ADAM BARR: My favorite episodes are this episode and *The Kid Stays Out of the Picture,* because that was the first time in a long time where we had real, gritty emotional territory to play in.

JACK:
"When couples split, one person always gets the good friends. So if you don't kiss up to Joe and Larry first, you'll end up like the ex Mrs. Giuliani. He got the two cool gay guys, and all she got was a part in The Vagina Monologues.*"*

MEGAN MULLALLY: The scene with Jack and Karen talking about the invitation to the child's birthday party is one of my favorites, because it's just a really funny, short moment between the two characters, with great comedy writing.

505 IT'S THE GAY PUMPKIN, CHARLIE BROWN
Written By: GARY JANETTI

organizes a pumpkin-picking bike ride in the Catskill Moun-
[t]ns and brings along Kim, a pint-sized outdoors enthusiast
[wit]h a giant-sized crush on Will—or, in Jack's parlance, a "pocket
[gay]." During the ride, Grace feigns enthusiasm until one mishap
[too] many leads her to admit that she wasn't meant for the great
[out]doors. Love is in the air, though, as Leo answers with a pas-
[sio]nate kiss, and Will is later seen sneaking a certain pint-sized
[ent]husiast into his apartment. Rather too much love is in the air
[at] Walker Inc., where Karen's admission of her affair with Lionel
[is p]reempted by her discovery of Stan in *flagrante* in his office
[wit]h the prison cafeteria lady.

GUEST STARS
James Marsden *(Step by Step)* as Kim, the "Pocket Gay"
Reginald VelJohnson *(Family Matters)* as Dr. Kaplan

RECURRING CHARACTER
Harry Connick, Jr. *as* Leo

> **JACK:**
> *"What you have is a 'pocket gay.' The perfect, travel-sized homosexual. Just pop him in a man purse, a briefcase, and you're good to go. In ten years, they'll be making them all that way."*

[GAR]Y JANETTI: In the gym in the morning, I
[use]d to see these guys who are unique to the
[gay] community: they're muscular but they're
[also] very small. So my friend and I just started
[callin]g them pocket gays. The perfect man,
[exce]pt bizarrely short.

[FYI:] The trick-or-treaters are played by David Kohan's daughter
[Mar]ia and assistant film editor Todd Morris' daughter Bianca.

[GAI]L LERNER: "Café Jacques is my favorite example of where something
[spru]ng from one of our real lives. Alex Herschlag came in one day and
[said] that he and his wife had been looking in a catalog at café tables, and
[woul]dn't it be great if Jack had a café table in the hallway, and that became
[Café] Jacques. And that has since bailed us out of a lot of troubled scenes
[whe]re we didn't have enough room for another set, or needed jokes as
[char]acters crossed from one apartment to another."

---

506 THE NEEDLE AND THE OMELET'S DONE
Written By: JON KINNALLY & TRACY POUST

> **GRACE:**
> *"I've already fooled him into liking me. I don't know if I have the energy to fool two older, wiser people who I can't confuse by having sex with."*

Grace mouths off to Leo's "friends" Eleanor and Jay over brunch
at the Plaza, only to learn that Leo lied—they are actually his
parents. Grace's embarrassment is almost forgotten when she
and Leo use the occasion to say "I love you" for the first time.
Elsewhere, Zandra turns her acting class over to Jack when his
continued ineptitude disgusts her. Jack instructs his classmates
to emphasize style over substance—"acting is attracting"—and
to find gay subtext in everything—"Jack-ting." When Zandra later
throws him out, he starts his own class with a couple of surprise
converts from Zandra's. Will admits he's "Bo-curious," and joins
Karen for a trial Botox injection.

RECURRING CHARACTERS
Harry Connick, Jr. as Leo
Eileen Brennan as Zandra
Judith Ivey as Leo's mother, Eleanor Markus *(first appearance)*
Tom Skerritt as Leo's father, Jay Markus *(first appearance)*
Emily Rutherfurd as Jack's acting student, Joanne *(first appearance)*
John Fleming as Jack's hunky acting student, Russell *(first appearance)*
Matthew McCray as Jack's acting student, Jasper *(first appearance)*

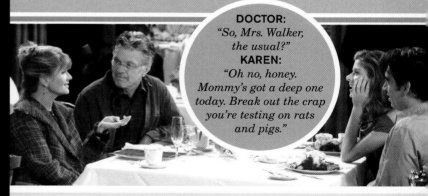

> **DOCTOR:**
> *"So, Mrs. Walker, the usual?"*
> **KAREN:**
> *"Oh no, honey. Mommy's got a deep one today. Break out the crap you're testing on rats and pigs."*

JHONI MARCHINKO: We don't really ever create a character with the
intention of the character recurring. In the case of Jack's acting student
Joanne, we love Emily Rutherfurd, who's fantastic. We just threw her in there
one time and it was such a success that we decided every time we go back
to Jack's class, let's use these same people. The same thing happened when
we brought in Eileen Brennan as Zandra, Jack's acting teacher.

FYI: Now playing Russell, one of Jack's acting students, John
Fleming started working on *Will & Grace* as a non-speaking background actor, but in a television rarity, he was then cast in
this recurring role.

507 BOARDROOM AND PARKED PLACE
Written By: GAIL LERNER

When Stan cuts Karen off from her money, she's reduced to living in her limo with Rosario and paying sneak visits to Will and Grace's shower. Karen's about to swallow her pride and accept her friends' help when Stan loosens the purse strings and she moves into the Palace Hotel. When Will learns that his boss, Mr. Stein, has just returned from the loony bin, Stein showers him with perks to buy his silence. Upset that his good fortune comes at his colleagues' expense, Will rebuilds Stein's confidence until he cuts off the bribes.

RECURRING CHARACTERS
Shelley Morrison *as* Rosario
Kari Lizer *as* Connie
Gene Wilder *as* Will's boss, Mr. Stein *(first appearance)*
Jamie Kaler *as* Will's coworker, Gary *(first appearance)*

> **KAREN:**
> "If I gave in to every persuasive argument, I'd be in some crazy three-way marriage with Maury Povich and Connie Chung."

GAIL LERNER: To come up with some of Mr. Stein's legal jargon for his first intimidating speech, I called a lawyer friend and spent half an hour of her firm's partner's time interviewing him. And of course Gene Wilder came in and he just couldn't remember that line, so he just wound up saying, "Your billing system is lousy!" and it worked. I couldn't exactly say, "But, Mr. Wilder, I did research!"

FYI: In 2003, Gene Wilder won the "Outstanding Guest Actor in a Comedy Series" Emmy Award for his appearance in this episode.

508/509 MARRY ME A LITTLE/ MARRY ME A LITTLE MORE
Written By: JEFF GREENSTEIN & BILL WRUBEL

> **LEO:**
> "Hey, thanks. We're just a bunch of old married folks now, right?"

> **LARRY:**
> "Well, you are. Our marriage isn't recognized by the state of New York. Mazel tov."

In Central Park, Grace and Leo wander into a mass wedding se[] as a stunt for the *Today* show and impulsively marry on the spo[] Will feels excluded, so they make it up to him with a big recepti[] After disastrous toasts from Jack and Karen, touching ones fro[] Will and Leo, and a musical one from Grace that's a little of bot[] guests' questions reveal to Grace how little she knows about he[] new husband. When she finds out she doesn't even know his re[] first name—Marvin—she runs off. Leo's attempt to calm Grace down is foiled by Katie Couric, who tells them that their weddi[] is invalid because their judge wasn't licensed in New York. Leo about to send the guests home when Grace reappears with a de[] ration of love and a determination to marry for real.

GUEST STAR
Katie Couric *as* Herself

RECURRING CHARACTERS
Shelley Morrison *as* Rosario   Harry Connick, Jr. *as* Leo
Tom Gallop *as* Rob   Leigh-Allyn Baker *as* Ellen
Jerry Levine *as* Joe   Tim Bagley *as* Larry
Debbie Reynolds *as* Bobbi Adler   Neil Vipond *as* Julius
Judith Ivey *as* Eleanor Markus   Tom Skerritt *as* Jay Markus

DEBRA MESSING: I loved as Grace getting to go through with her very proper, traditional, beautiful wedding to Leo. In my real life, I had a very low-key wedding in a meadow. So now I feel lucky that I've gotten to have it both ways—I went the simple route in real life, and got to wear the fanta[] $20,000 Vera Wang princess-like gown on TV.

JEFF GREENSTEIN: We wanted a crisis where Will freaks out at the moment where Grace is actually going to get married, but we struggled [] how to do it. We decided that she should take him to the place where th[] actually met, and where she once said "That's the man I am going to spe[] the rest of my life with." That is such a powerful statement because that i[] what he needs to hear at that moment. The interesting thing about that s[] is that we wrote it and re-wrote it and what happens on this show is that jokes get piled on. We shot it single-camera and without an audience, ou[] that rooftop in New York. When we got back, I remember Jhoni saying to [] in the editing room, "Why are all these jokes in here? When you pitched [] scene to begin with, it was moving and now there's too much comedy in [] So we cut them all out.

510 THE HONEYMOON'S OVER
Written By: SALLY BRADFORD

...er the Palace Hotel throws Karen out, she moves in with Will ...l quickly wears out her welcome. When Grace returns from her ...neymoon she takes Karen in, but that situation quickly becomes ...olerable, too. Karen runs away after she overhears Will and ...ace plotting to get rid of her; when they find her at a bus stop, ...e admits her real distress is over Will and Grace's separation, ...l they promise that their feelings for her will never change. ...k scoffs at a former student's threat to send the "gay mafia" ...er him, but changes his tune after his salon's shampoo boy does ...ad job. Will insists there's no such thing as the "gay mafia," ... Elton John begs to differ. ★

ELTON:
"A word of advice, Will—don't dismiss things you know nothing about. And don't walk in ten-inch heels. It's hell on the ankles."

GUEST STAR ★
Elton John *as* Himself

RECURRING CHARACTERS
Shelley Morrison *as* Rosario
Kathleen Archer *as* Molly, the lesbian delivery woman

...IC McCORMACK: Elton's partner, David Furnish, and I went to high ...ool together, where we were both in lots of shows. So Elton's appearance ...he show was because of that connection. After the first season, my wife, ...t, and I were invited to their Oscar party. It was the first time I'd seen ...e in seventeen years, and I met Elton. They hadn't seen the show yet, ...I sent them tapes, and they became the first major British fans of *Will &* ...ce before it was even airing there.

...NI MARCHINKO: All of our actors add so much to these characters, ...once we discover something, we do try to write more of it. In this epi- ...e, when Will yells at Karen for singing loudly along to a Tom Jones song, ...an said the line we'd written, but in a way we loved: "Fine—I'll leave you ...ooooone." We loved the weird voice that she found and started writing it ...ke in the next season, in *The Accidental Tsuris*, when Karen says, "Now ...along, so your daddy and I can make luuuuv." Megan comes up with a ...f voices. Sean, too, started doing that screeching "What?!" that we call ..."howler monkey" voice—now we write it that way into the script. ★

511 ALL ABOUT CHRISTMAS EVE
Written By:
ADAM BARR

When Leo strands Grace with an extra ticket to the Christmas Eve performance of *The Nutcracker Suite,* she lures Will away from a pampered evening with Jack and Karen at the Palace Hotel, only to yank the ticket away again when Leo returns. The process repeats itself again when Leo gets beeped, and Will is left feeling badly used—not just by Grace, but also by Jack and Karen, who force him to recite *'Twas the Night Before Christmas* like a Rockette, and *The Twelve Days of Christmas* like the Count from *Sesame Street.* Will and Grace acknowledge that things have changed now that Grace is married...and then Will and Leo realize that neither of them really wants to see *The Nutcracker.* The whole gang ends up back at Karen's singing carols to the unwilling hotel staff.

RECURRING CHARACTERS
Harry Connick, Jr. *as* Leo
Steve Paymer *as* Steve

KAREN:
"Pleasure us, fast and nasty. And extra points if you can find a way to work in that shoeshine mitt."

WILL:
"You know, this is a lot like the first Christmas. Except we did get a room, none of us are virgins, and instead of the baby Jesus, we have a plate of cheeses."

ADAM BARR: I had originally written a completely different story line for the Christmas episode, where Karen's first husband, a Dennis Hopper type, comes back into town. But that was too big a story to drop in casually, so we completely threw that out, and everyone wrote this new story together.

(512) FIELD OF QUEENS

Written By:
KATIE PALMER

GRACE: *"Listen, Mister. I've kissed Karen more times than I can count, and every single time I've felt something."*

When Jack talks Will into joining a gay soccer league, Will quickly discovers how unathletic he truly is. He is about to quit when Jack persuades him to stick it out, as an example to Elliot, who wants to quit his own soccer team. Will plays in the next game and accidentally scores the winning goal. Karen is lovestruck after Grace pushes her into a date with dashing restaurateur Milo. When Milo fails to call, Grace confronts him at his restaurant and consoles Karen, and the two friends realize that their familiar roles—the single gal and the married lady—have reversed.

GUEST STARS
Andy Garcia *as* restauranteur Milo
Matthew Glave *(The Wedding Singer) as*
gay soccer team captain Kirk

RECURRING CHARACTER
Michael Angarano *as* Elliot

JEFF GREENSTEIN: Our plan to have "Karen unleashed" led to one of the most lovely moments of Season Five: the role reversal at the end of this episode. It is such a powerful moment because they are both such wonderful actors. Grace says this is an interesting role reversal—"Now I am a married person and you are the single girl." Grace says, "I like it," and Karen says, "I hate it." That is what is so remarkable about Megan Mullally. She can be orbiting Pluto one minute, and make you cry the next. She is astounding.

WILL: *"This is gay soccer. We'll probably just run over there and compare Tony predictions."*

(513/514) FAGMALION PART 1 & 2:
GAY IT FORWARD
ATTACK OF THE CLONES

Part 1 *Written By:* JON KINNALLY & TRACY POUST

Will wants nothing to do with Karen's cousin Barry, a shlubby, clueless guy who's just come out and has no idea how to be gay. But Jack reminds Will that it is their obligation as "senior gays" to take Barry under their wing and train him, just as Jack did f Will back in the 80s. Elsewhere, Grace's new massage therapist friend Julie freaks Grace out when her fingers drift unprofessio ally far south.

RECURRING CHARACTERS
Dan Futterman *as* Karen's cousin, Barry *(first appearance)*
Rosanna Arquette *as* Grace's neighbor, Julie *(first appearance)*

JHONI MARCHINKO: The idea from this episode came from Kari Lizer, came into the writers' room one morning and said, "I think I had sex with massage therapist last night." It was just like Grace's story here—her fema massage therapist had rubbed her boobs and gave her a massage that s thought got a little inappropriate.

BARRY: *"This seems so superficial. Are gay guys only about bodies and face*

JACK: *"Absolutely not. They're on about bodies. Faces you c cover up with a cute hat or a leather hood."*

Part 2 *Written By:* GARY JANETTI

It's "Queer Eye for the Queer Guy" as Will and Jack set out to remake Barry into a fine figure of a gay man. Meanwhile, Grace and Leo push each other away after Leo commits to a month abroad with Doctors Without Borders. After a change of heart, Grace hops a flight to join him, only to learn that Leo had returned home to Brooklyn to say good-bye the right way.

GUEST STAR
Gary Janetti *(episode writer) as* Zach, Will's first male date

RECURRING CHARACTERS
Dan Futterman *as* Barry
Harry Connick, Jr. *as* Leo

FYI: The woman sitting next to Grace on the plane is played by
Joan Poust, the mother of series writer Tracy Poust.

(515) HOMOJO

Written By:
BILL WRUBEL

[Wil]l and Grace host a game night to reconnect with each other, [but] discover that they have lost their touch. Their resulting vow [to] remember to share with each other the minutia of their lives [re]kindles their magic, and they proceed to trounce the opposition. [Jac]k meets Stan's mistress, Lorraine, and becomes her best friend. [Wh]en Karen angrily forces him to choose between them, Jack [cho]oses Karen—but barely.

RECURRING CHARACTERS

Tom Gallop *as* Rob
Leigh-Allyn Baker *as* Ellen
Jerry Levine *as* Joe
Tim Bagley *as* Larry
[M]innie Driver *as* Stan's mistress, Lorraine Finster *(first appearance)*

JACK:
"We were both at the bottom and we pulled ourselves up with true grit and other people's money."

[▶]: A special "pop-up" version of this episode, annotated with [Wil]l & Grace trivia, aired on April 10, 2003. The lavender pop-ups [rev]ealed alternate versions of jokes; moments that had to be cut [for] time; and other insider trivia.

[LEI]GH-ALLYN BAKER: In this episode, there's the big game-night scene [in th]e second act, where Rob brags to Ellen about having psyched Grace [out] and says, "See how I got in her head?" and Ellen says, "Well, you've [alre]ady been in her pants." That type of joke had been written for my character [and] then cut about three times between the episode where we first found [out] about Rob sleeping with Grace and this one, where it finally made it [to t]he air. But whether she says it or not, don't be fooled: Ellen has not [com]pletely let that go.

[▶]: Karen's claim that she has a receipt for buying Rosario [fro]m her parents seems to contradict what we saw in *Lows in the* [Mi]*d 80s* when Karen meets Rosario in a nightclub. Although it's [very] unlike Karen to hallucinate the receipt story, in this case, there [is a] solution to the mystery: as the pop-up episode explains, after [Kar]en's line about the receipt, Grace originally had a line that was [cut] for time: "Did you ever think maybe those mariachis you gave [a h]undred bucks to at Benny's Burritos might not have been [your] parents?"

(516) FAGMALION PART 3:
BYE, BYE BEARDY

Written By: **ALEX HERSCHLAG**

The *pièce de résistance* of Barry's reinvention is a fabulous haircut for the Human Rights Campaign gala, an event attended by "all the A-list gays." Grace helps Will realize that he has fallen for the man he has transformed, and Will suddenly can't finish a sentence in Barry's presence. As Will struggles to express his feelings, Karen outbids Beverley Leslie in a silent auction for a romantic dinner for two and gives the prize to Jack. When Jack asks Barry to be his date, Will is devastated.

JACK:
"Every A-list gay will be there. The crème de la crème de la crème de la femme."

GUEST STAR
Barry Karas *(real-life HRC president)* as Himself

RECURRING CHARACTERS
Dan Futterman *as* Barry
Leslie Jordan *as* Beverley Leslie

GARY JANETTI: I loved how the tone of this whole episode was very breezy and stylized, like a 1940s screwball comedy set in old New York, which is how a lot of us see the show when it's at its best. I also really liked the story—the arc of how Dan Futterman's character transformed, and how Will is pining for a guy, which was something we hadn't really seen before, so as a viewer you're really invested. And I love anything that takes place at a gala with fabulous clothes.

GRACE:
"This one's slitty, this one's slutty, this one's titty, this one's butty."

GAIL LERNER: I love episodes like this, with one location and one central story that houses all the characters, where they all weave in and out. This one was also special to me because it featured my dear friend, Rebecca Lowman, who played Pamela, the lesbian who ran the silent auction at the HRC dinner.

WILL:
"Let me tell you a little secret we try to keep within the community: gay movies suck. But we're still obligated to go see them."

517 · WOMEN AND CHILDREN FIRST

Written By: LAURA KIGHTLINGER

GRACE:
"You have things to offer. You would be the first person I'd call if I wanted . . . to hurt an orphan's feelings."

Karen storms out of a girls' night out when Grace asks everyone but her how to handle Leo's announcement that he'll stay in Africa for another month. When Grace learns that the other women have received surprisingly good advice from Karen in the past, she confronts Leo with her true feelings and apologizes to Karen for being afraid of her brutal honesty. Jack meets his old baby-sitter, Sissy, and gives her her old job back. Jack, and later Will, happily revert to infancy under Sissy's care, until Jack learns that Sissy's rate has risen with inflation and fires her.

GUEST STAR
Demi Moore *as* Jack's former baby-sitter, Sissy

RECURRING CHARACTERS
Shelley Morrison *as* Rosario
Leigh-Allyn Baker *as* Ellen
Rosanna Arquette *as* Julie

LEIGH-ALLYN BAKER: Ellen has been pregnant twice. The first one I know was a boy, and I have no idea what the second was, but I know I carried it for about 16 months. I think Ellen has quite a temper, and a lot of repressed anger, and I think that the writers enjoy having her pregnant because it's a way for them to have her let all the bitterness come pouring out.

518 · FAGMALION PART 4: THE GUY WHO LOVED ME

Written By: GAIL LERNER

Will and Jack compete for Barry's affections and finally ask him choose between them. Barry chooses Will, but even after a terrif date and a fence-mending talk with Jack, Will is shattered to lea that Barry wants to play the field and isn't ready for a relationsł To preserve her affair with a gorgeous janitor, Karen pretends t a chambermaid. The affair survives Karen's revelation that she' rich, but not the janitor's revelation that he doesn't drink.

JACK:
"Gasp! You just asked him out on a date while he's on a date with me? Will Truman, that is despicable . . . and totally one of my moves."

GUEST STAR
Bruno Campos *(Jesse) as* Palace Hotel handyman Anton

RECURRING CHARACTER
Shelley Morrison *as* Rosario

KAREN:
"Rosie, I just met the most incredible man!"

ROSARIO:
"Are you sure you didn't just lean into the doorknob again?"

FYI: Art Director Glenda Rovello and Set Decorator Melinda Ritz won a 2003 Emmy award for "Outstanding Art Direction fo a Multi-Camera Series" for their work on this episode.

519 SEX, LOSERS, AND VIDEOTAPE

Written By: STEVE GABRIEL

> **GRACE:**
> *"I think I know how to turn a man on. I certainly didn't pass my driver's test by learning how to parallel park."*

...ll reeling from his ordeal with Barry, Will finds comfort by ...ounding a lonely hearts club with Karen and Mr. Stein—until ...learns that his clubmates are doing it on the sly. Karen and ...in agree to break up to spare Will's feelings, but Will comes to ...senses and gives them his blessing. Grace takes Jack's act-...class after he correctly points out that her sexy video for Leo ...dud. Grace understandably dislikes her experience in Jack's ...rthodox class, and later explodes when she learns that he has ...ed her in the shower—at least until she realizes that his tapes ...exactly what she needs.

RECURRING CHARACTERS

Gene Wilder *as* Mr. Stein
Kari Lizer *as* Connie
Emily Rutherfurd *as* Joanne
John Fleming *as* Russell
Matthew McCray *as* Jasper

> **JACK:**
> *"Grace, whatever you have to say, you can say it in front of my class. We expose ourselves to each other every day. Which reminds me: Russell, take off your shirt."*

520 LEO, UNWRAPPED

Written By:
SONJA WARFIELD

Will arranges for Leo's early return to surprise Grace on her birthday. When Leo and Grace inadvertently see each other before the party, Grace decides, for Will's sake, to play along by acting surprised. Leo spills the beans to Will, who in turn plays along so Grace will think she fooled him. When Jack and Karen learn of the spoiled surprise, they create a new one by kidnapping Leo and ditching him in New Jersey. All is revealed at the party, when Leo fails to appear and the friends, after basking in their shared sensitivity toward one another's feelings, go off in the limo to retrieve Leo from the side of the road.

RECURRING CHARACTERS

Harry Connick, Jr. *as* Leo
Marshall Manesh *as* Mr. Zamir

SEAN HAYES: I absolutely love Café Jacques. I don't know myself whether Jack thinks it's real or not. He must actually make some extra cash—probably from Karen and Will. I actually pitched a story idea for Season Seven that I'd really like to do, where Jack creates some special coffee drink, and it's a huge hit in the building. There would be a line down the hallway, because there's only one table at Jacques. And I would whisper to the next person, "It looks like they're getting ready to settle the check."

> **WILL:**
> *"I just broke my favorite bookmark."*

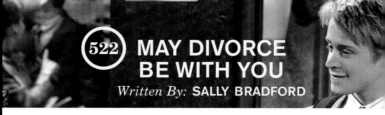

521 DOLLS AND DOLLS

Written By:
KARI LIZER

KAREN:
"God, this is great! Casual sex, mooky bartenders, dirty futons! This is the stuff of life. I'm going to get an STD tonight!"

GUEST STAR
Madonna *as* Karen's roommate, Liz

Karen answers a roommate-wanted ad and moves in with Liz, an office manager and control freak who shares Karen's enthusiasms for booze and boys. After the new friendship collapses in a fight over a guy, Liz's effort to throw Karen out reveals that Karen owns the building and Liz is the one who has to go. Meanwhile, Will falls off his clogs and gets hooked on painkillers. At first, the new happy-slacker Will is a hit, until Grace and Jack discover the reason and stage an intervention to bring back the cranky and critical friend they love.

MEGAN MULLALLY: During the filming of this episode, the audience was really amped up because they knew that they were coming to the Madonna episode. I enjoyed working with her because she worked so hard. She just wanted to rehearse and rehearse and rehearse because she just really wanted it to be good. That's why she's been so successful, because she was so professional. Then, after the show, somebody had instructed the staff photographer to get a picture of Madonna with the four of us in front of a backdrop they set up. But then I felt bad for her, because they had not bothered to mention to her that they also wanted her to take pictures with all the VIPs in the audience. I guess even megastars can be tricked. But she stood there for over an hour taking pictures with people.

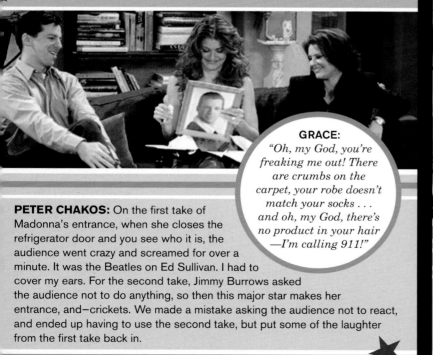

GRACE:
"Oh, my God, you're freaking me out! There are crumbs on the carpet, your robe doesn't match your socks . . . and oh, my God, there's no product in your hair—I'm calling 911!"

PETER CHAKOS: On the first take of Madonna's entrance, when she closes the refrigerator door and you see who it is, the audience went crazy and screamed for over a minute. It was the Beatles on Ed Sullivan. I had to cover my ears. For the second take, Jimmy Burrows asked the audience not to do anything, so then this major star makes her entrance, and—crickets. We made a mistake asking the audience not to react, and ended up having to use the second take, but put some of the laughter from the first take back in.

522 MAY DIVORCE BE WITH YOU

Written By: **SALLY BRADFORD**

Karen is saddled with a seemingly incompetent young lawyer, J. T., when Will is forced to represent Stan in their divorce. Concerned that Karen will lose everything, Will lets slip some information J. T.'s benefit. Karen wants to fire J. T. after she learns he's actua a crafty shark who has tricked Will, but Will reminds her that s will need someone that clever for the difficult proceedings ahead Jack fills in for Karen at Grace Adler Designs and brings in his boyfriend, Cam, as a client. When Cam and Jack split up, he pre sures Grace to turn down the lucrative job Cam has offered. Wh Grace knocks on Jack's door to tell him she has quit in accordan with his wishes, she finds that Jack and Cam are back together— and both friends are relieved that their underhanded, self-inter ested natures are so well matched.

J.T.:
"Get yourself a bikini wax. I like a clean workspace."

GUEST STAR
Macaulay Culkin *as* Karen's divorce lawyer, Jason "J.T." Towne

RECURRING CHARACTER
Shelley Morrison *as* Rosario

a Favorite Episode of...

SALLY BRADFORD: This is my favorite episode I've written. I loved the character we all created in Jason Towne, and thought the episode turned particularly well. It didn't hurt that we had a great actor who brought a lot the role.

523 "23"

Written By: ADAM BARR, SALLY BRADFORD, JEFF GREENSTEIN, ALEX HERSCHLAG, & GARY JANETTI

GRACE:
"I don't know what I'd do if you died. I hope I go first. Then again, you love me so much, that would be unbearable for you. Yeah, you should die first. Definitely you."

LEO:
"Can I go in my sleep, or are you looking for me to suffer?"

...n abruptly dies, and the news that he recently changed his will ...vinces Karen that his mistress, Lorraine, will steal her fortune. ...the memorial service, Karen and Lorraine trade insults while ...k ingratiates himself to both to cover his bases. Amid the trib...s, Leo tells Grace that Doctors Without Borders is sending him ...Guatemala and he wants her to come along. Finally Stan's will ...ead: Rosario gets $10 million—provided she serves Karen for ...ther twenty years; Grace gets Karen's portrait; Will and Jack ...twenty grand for the wedding Stan says is inevitable; Lorraine ...s "nothing but affection"; and Karen gets the rest of the empire.

RECURRING CHARACTERS
Shelley Morrison *as* Rosario
Harry Connick, Jr. *as* Leo
Minnie Driver *as* Lorraine
Jamie Kaler *as* Gary

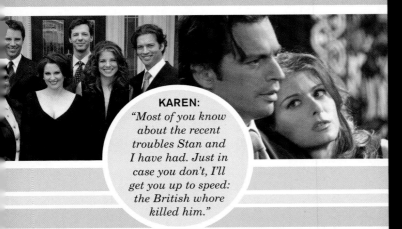

KAREN:
"Most of you know about the recent troubles Stan and I have had. Just in case you don't, I'll get you up to speed: the British whore killed him."

...FF GREENSTEIN: We got to the middle of Season Five and realized that ...n had outlived his usefulness, so we decided to kill him off. That was a big, ...discussion. Max and David didn't love that idea at first. I had also done a ...nplete 180...you get to Season Four or Season Five, and you throw out ...rulebook.

524 "24"

Written By: GAIL LERNER, KARI LIZER, JHONI MARCHINKO, TRACY POUST & JON KINNALLY, BILL WRUBEL

The gang joins Karen on a yacht trip to the Caribbean to scatter Stan's plentiful ashes at sea. Grace, distraught over the prospect of rough living in Guatemala, is touched by Leo's selfless support of her desire to remain in New York—until she learns that Leo's travel buddy, Dr. Morty, is a hot woman. When Grace finally drops the act and admits her concern, Leo reassures her of his love, and they part on good terms. Karen asks to be alone for the scattering of Stan's ashes, and is surprised by stowaway Lorraine, whose love for Stan earns her the right to share in the final good-bye. The solidarity is short-lived, however, as Lorraine tosses Karen overboard during a fight over money, and Rosario plunges in after her. The next morning, Grace finds a letter in which Dr. Morty declares her love for Leo, Will and Jack wake up in bed together; and Karen and Rosario find themselves aboard a Russian freighter loaded, luckily, with 300,000 cases of Stolichnaya.

GUEST STARS
Deborah Harry *as* Herself
Nicollette Sheridan *(Knots Landing)* as Dr. Danielle Morty

RECURRING CHARACTERS
Shelley Morrison *as* Rosario
Harry Connick, Jr. *as* Leo
Minnie Driver *as* Lorraine
Earl Schuman *as* Driver

KAREN:
"You know? For a scheming, husband-stealing, skanky whore, you're good people."

JON KINNALLY: The moments where Karen gets pushed off the yacht by Minnie Driver came up very early in the breaking of this story. I think Alex pitched it, and we all thought it would be funny but worried it would be too big. But we did it, anyway. Our actors are so great with physical comedy that we take advantage of that when we can.

FYI: Art Director Glenda Rovello and Set Decorator Melinda Ritz won a 2003 Emmy Award for "Outstanding Art Direction for a Multi-Camera Series" for their work on this episode.

GAY, SET

& MATCH

A DESIGNER'S DESIGNER

Glenda Rovello sums up in two words what it feels like to hold one of the most demanding design jobs on television: **"pure joy."**

As **WILL & GRACE**'s production designer, Glenda is responsible for the overall look and feel of every single set and location on the show. Week after week, in tandem with set decorator Melinda Ritz and a veteran team of carpenters, painters, and set dressers, she brings **WILL & GRACE**'s world to life. It's hard to imagine a tougher collection of characters to design for—a gay man of extraordinary taste; a talented decorator; a near-billionaire—but Glenda relishes the challenge. "This is what I was meant to do," she says.

In fact, Glenda's eye for environments revealed itself in childhood. "My favorite thing to do was play Barbies," she recalls, "but it was never about the clothes and the pretty hair. I was always building the Barbie houses, building my own furniture. That's how I played." Later came a master's degree in architecture, and eventually a job as assistant to production

A Set Comes Together

designer Bruce Ryan on Max and David's first television series, **BOSTON COMMON**.

When the writers get their "pre-table drafts" to Glenda early, she uses the lead time to "soak it in," or develop ideas in her mind. She has to stay on her toes, though; by the time that writer's draft becomes a pre-table draft, it may change. Or it may change during run-throughs. Jokes might be altered, entire locations scrapped. And sometimes there's simply no time for soaking, such as when a script doesn't come in until just a few days before the shoot!

In every spare moment, Glenda and Melinda hit the books. They scour magazines to keep current and pull ideas for everything from seasonal decoration to carpeting to the set's very walls and windows; for example, the transom windows that admit light into Will's living room from Grace's bedroom were taken from a magazine. Glenda's open mind draws inspiration from a wide variety of styles: "I'm a chameleon," she says.

Oftentimes a design is the product of both research and experience, as in the case of Karen's Vermont cabin in "Secrets & Lays." For that set, Glenda called upon Architectural Digest profiles of Steven Spielberg's and Kevin Costner's rustic cabins, and also her own visits to swanky Aspen retreats.

Glenda knew practically nothing about The Duplex, a Greenwich Village bar/performance space featured in "Grace 0, Jack 2000," when she designed it. "I haven't seen The Duplex to this day," she admits. When it's we-need-it-tomorrow time, research falls by the wayside.

For the noodle shop in "A Gay/December Romance," Glenda's art department assistants visited hundreds of Japanese eateries in search of the right look.

The "Fanilow" script called for Grace to spot her mother in a restaurant with Jack, Glenda decided to make it a kosher establishment, in keeping with the Adler family's holiday spirit.

PUTTIN' ON THE RITZ

Where does set decorator Melinda Ritz find all those beautiful things? Everywhere! "That girl just beats the streets," raves Glenda. What's more, when you've got a hit show on your hands, salespersons can be very accommodating; when they wanted a FrancisFrancis! cappuccino maker, a call to the company yielded three: an orange one for Will, a green one for Jack, and one for Karen.

While most manufacturers would be thrilled by their product's exposure on **WILL & GRACE**, practicality, not to mention federal law, demands that most brand names be masked for the cameras in a process known as "greeking." Sharp-eyed fans may have spotted tape over the names of board games and groceries. If a brand name item must be prominently featured on camera, a graphics department can swing into action and create one from scratch.

"Doing a store is the hardest thing to do," says Glenda. "It just kills Melinda every time." But a cooperative partner can make all the difference; Glenda has nothing but praise for the powers-that-be at Barneys. "That was an amazing collaboration," she enthuses. Barneys shipped all the necessary merchandise to the set…along with the merchandisers to fold it! They sent their store logo, allowed research photos, even lent display artists to dress the mannequins. Similarly, Jack's former employer, Banana Republic, provided merchandise and permitted research photos.

"I don't have an outrageous budget," says Glenda, who confides that in an average week she can spend up to $40,000 for construction without raising flags. That amount doesn't include set decoration, which can cost as much as $20,000 more. Special and double episodes are pricier, and require special approval.

Glenda has developed strategies to tame her bottom line. Among them: a talent for recycling. "I am a great re-user," she boasts. Examples include Grace's sister Janet's apartment in "The Accidental Tsuris," which was a redressed version of ex-boyfriend Nathan's place. Similarly, **WILL & GRACE**'s apartment hunt in "Someone Old, Someplace New" consisted of repeated visits to the same set, its walls and wainscoting altered to create the illusion of different spaces.

These flyers helped hide Debra Messing's pregnancy when she handed them out in the season six episode "A Gay/December Romance."

In "Cheaters," Gil was asked to create a realistic-looking magazine for Jack to pick up at the newsstand, with a centerfold that unfolds again and again.

GIVE HIM HIS PROPS

From his small, overstuffed office on stage 17, a dozen or so yards behind the door to Jack's apartment, Gil Spragg provides **WILL & GRACE** with its props—defined as any object the actors have in their hands during the course of the scene. Along with his son Rusty, "prop master" Gil keeps a small storeroom of items at the ready, in case the actors suddenly come up with a funny bit during rehearsal that requires, say kooky eyeglasses.

Gil's Handbag of Tricks

In addition to files full of Will's and Grace's business cards and stationery and a drawer full of rings, watches, and glasses, Gil keeps an assortment of other items on hand to let the actors do their thing more naturally. Megan Mullally often chooses one of the magazines Gil creates (with, for legal reasons, fake front and back covers) to leaf through at Karen's desk. And Gil presides over another innovation to make the actors' jobs easier: at director Jimmy Burrows's request, all the phones on the **WILL & GRACE** set actually work. This way, "The talent can talk to each other as if they were actually on the phone. They don't have to listen really hard for each other's lines from across the stage."

With the help of the graphics department, Gil created Jack's "Just Jack" flyers, and the campaign buttons Will and Grace use in the season 4 episode "Star Spangled Banter."

Glenda imagines the terrace glassed in like a terrarium. Not even the wind disturbs Will's perfect coif.

THE SET'S ODDEST INHABITANT: (Eric, in *Entertainment Weekly,* dubbed it "Mao Tse-tung having his way with a trout") came from Melinda's personal collection back in the shoestring budget days. It's Melinda's nod to a Mao statue in Max's home.

Confused viewers may have thought they glimpsed this backside in Will's bedroom; actually, he owns two different prints from the same set.

STRICT PARENT: General Electric, Will & Grace's corporate parent, required that the kitchen be designed around their appliances. Their mighty fine appliances.

Melinda keeps cabinets and drawers well stocked so the actors can feel like they're in a real kitchen. Watch what you eat, though: perishable goods are fakes.

THE DOG THAT WILL DOESN'T HAVE Evidently not everyone's an animal lover: this ceramic pooch has been broken.

STEPS TO SUCCESS: director James Burrows insisted that the kitchen be elevated so that it would be a more viable playing area on camera.

Does this chair make my butt look fat? If so, it's because James Burrows asked for extra-padded seats to lift the cast for camera.

COLD LEFT-OVERS: the stove isn't "practical," the TV term for functional in real life.

NIGHTS OF THE ROUND TABLE: no corners means friendlier camera angles when it's time to shoot.

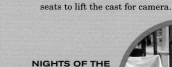

This door, which in real life leads nowhere, supposedly opens into the service stairwell. It's been used only once: during Jack's retreat from a stimulating stripper in "An Affair To Forget."

Will likes 'em hard and well muscled…statues, of course. This Atlas can be found at New York's Rockefeller Center.

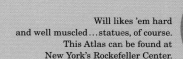

MIRROR, MIRROR ON THE WALL . . .
the side wall, of course, because from the rear wall it would reflect the audience. Another reason not to move it: there's a hidden camera port back there.

WILL'S APARTMENT

Glenda uses primary, monochromatic paint colors to suit Will's disposition, while Melinda communicates his strong innate sense of style by mixing different designers and styles that go well together.

Will favors what Glenda calls "very male oriented images." Melinda elaborates: "If it's not a picture of a man, it's significant in the male, uh, yeah." Phallic plants, phallic sconces, and a phallic soap dispenser drive the point home.

Everywhere viewers see evidence of a man with a refined upscale sensibility and a salary with which to indulge it. Melinda has given Will an antique Biedermeyer secretary, Jasper stones, Blossfeldt prints, Jonathan Adler vases and pillows, even a pricey **SOME LIKE IT HOT** coffee table book. All that good taste is enough to make straight male viewers reach for an application to **QUEER EYE**.

These transom windows admit light into Will's windowless living room from Grace's bedroom. Or, behind the scenes, from studio lights.

An antique Biedermeier secretary has replaced this bookcase, but the jasper stones can still be found on top.

This piece of set dressing gets more viewer mail than any other, most of it asking whether the portrait is of Will or Desi Arnaz. It's actually an anonymous figure from a private collection

A TIP "TRADING SPACES" NEVER TOLD YOU:
phallic fixtures enliven any room.

This Blossfeldt print sports tall, firm towers: Will's favorite architecture

Will's working fireplace was a bone of contention in "Election," but in real life it's a nonfunctional dud. Sort of like Grace after her break up with Nathan.

There wasn't a dry eye in NBC's accounting department when Max backed Melinda's purchase of this $2,800 beauty from Los Angeles's Brenda Antin Antiques. Max nixed a Pottery Barn imitation.

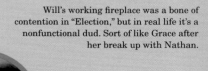

Could these be examples of what Glenda calls "male oriented images"?

Let the sunshine in…or not, if there's a wall right behind these drapes. On some shoot days, Grace's office becomes a room-with-a-half-a-view.

Soho's Puck Building was chosen for its Palladian windows; the production was thrilled to get permission to use this well known New York landmark.

The eternal sunshine of the spotless mind is nowhere in evidence. Viewers learn lots about Grace's character from this creative, cluttered, colorful mess. Not to mention an assistant who's as much of a mess as the desk.

GE OR NOT GE, IS THE QUES
corporate parent G
Electric isn't bossy
which brands are us
small appli

Outstanding penmanship won art department assistant Tim the job of chalking these ever-changing reminders and inspirationals. Tim's attendance is also exemplary, and he plays well with others.

SWEATING THE SMALL STUFF:
Melinda purchased entire decorators' libraries and hand picked the books she wanted on Grace's shelves.

Look back by the curtains for this chair inspired by the style of designer Barbara Barry, whose clients have included Michael Ovitz, The Savoy Hotel, and the Brooks Brothers flagship store on Manhattan's Madison Avenue.

This character-defining chair, usually piled with junk, has sat unfinished for years; Melinda calls it "the project Grace can't finish."

A decorator herself, Melinda stocked Grace's space with fabrics from companies she favors.

Debra loves to toy with Grace's work stools, which raise or lower with a whirl of the seat. She told Entertainment Weekly "it reminds me of one of those Sit 'n' Spins!" Maybe Grace is too dizzy to tidy up.

GRACE'S OFFICE

Feminine pastels and violets differentiate Grace Adler Designs from Will's and Leo's more masculine palette. Grace's desk is intentionally chaotic. "She can do for others, but can never get her own act together," says Glenda. The two unfinished chairs that have stood by Grace's design table since Season One underscore the point. And then there's the Karen factor: Glenda and Melinda know that Grace's "assistant" would never lift a finger to help straighten up.

All that glitters is from Melinda's personal collection.

This column was borrowed from the defunct sitcom **CAROLINE IN THE CITY**. Good thing they didn't borrow its ratings.

s low hanging, pendulous, an-blown globe would fit right ith Will's décor. Actually, it's a ce Adler trademark.

These two works of art hail from Melinda's personal collection. At least no one in these prints is having his way with a trout.

Karen and Grace each spent time locked in the elevator in "Stakin' Care Of Business." To make it seem to operate, the cast crouches, then stands when Jimmy calls "action."

KAREN'S TOOLS OF THE TRADE: cosmetics and pharmaceuticals. Honey, looking that good is work. After an outraged viewer wrote to complain that Karen would never use Pond's hand cream, the staff made sure that Karen's supplies have been kept upscale ever since.

BACK OFF, PETA: no zebras were harmed during the making of this carpet: it's a fake.

LOOKS AREN'T EVERYTHING: the main reason this seagrass carpet is here is to quiet footfalls on the floor.

Tiffany boxes announce that Grace Adler Designs gets even the little things right.

GRACE & LEO'S APARTMENT

When the time came to design Leo's apartment, Glenda knew little about him except that he's a surgeon and "he's not a dope...he picked Grace!" Determined to create a great space for Grace's great catch, she started with rich, vibrant colors to reflect a masculine presence, and with Melinda established a "black leather and Craftsman look" that could evolve very quickly after Grace moved in. And so it did, with new furniture, paint, and artwork.

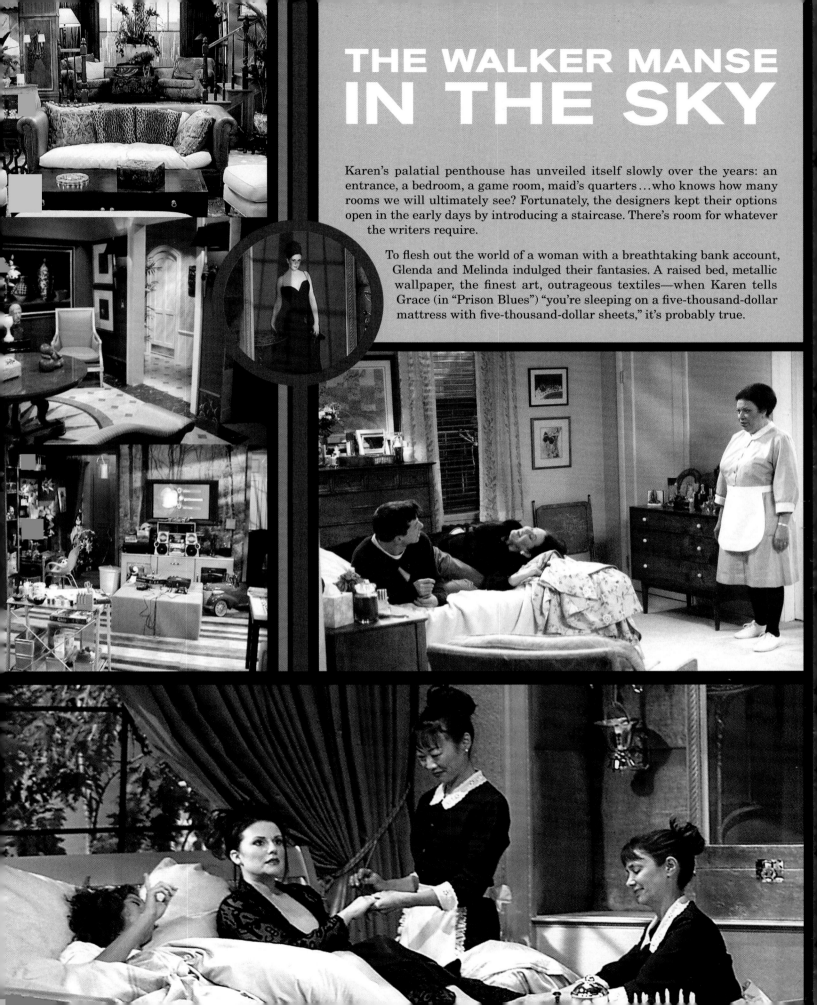

THE WALKER MANSE IN THE SKY

Karen's palatial penthouse has unveiled itself slowly over the years: an entrance, a bedroom, a game room, maid's quarters...who knows how many rooms we will ultimately see? Fortunately, the designers kept their options open in the early days by introducing a staircase. There's room for whatever the writers require.

To flesh out the world of a woman with a breathtaking bank account, Glenda and Melinda indulged their fantasies. A raised bed, metallic wallpaper, the finest art, outrageous textiles—when Karen tells Grace (in "Prison Blues") "you're sleeping on a five-thousand-dollar mattress with five-thousand-dollar sheets," it's probably true.

SEASON

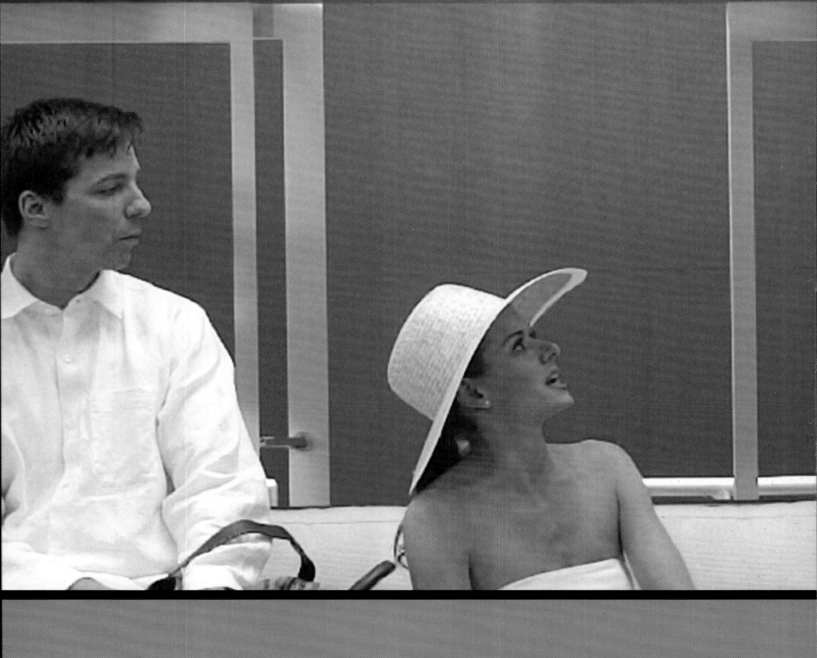

SIX

"We had to do a lot of fancy footwork," Jeff explains. With Debra obeying doctor's orders to rest for a few weeks, and Harry Connick about to leave to tour with his band, traveling to New York was now out of the question. "We suddenly found ourselves with three episodes that were dependent on the story arcs we had planned, so we had to hastily piece together some scripts."

And tonight's guest star is...

They had initially planned to begin the process of uncoupling Grace and Leo. In the beginning, there would be a crisis, and Leo would commit to staying at home with Grace. The marriage would work well for a few more episodes, but then some cracks would start to show. Their problems would finally surface during the hour-long tenth episode, to be shot in New York in October: Leo would impulsively buy a house as an anniversary present for Grace, leading her to realize that he is overcompensating for how miserable he is, having stayed. Ultimately, Grace would encourage Leo to go and get his wanderlust out of his system, explaining his continued absence. By the time of the one-hour season finale, Grace and Leo would be ready for a divorce. It was all mapped out perfectly.

But when Debra was forced to forego appearing in the episode "Heart Like a Wheelchair" due to her pregnancy, the writers explained her absence by giving Grace food poisoning, then sending her off to Cambodia with Leo. Even after Debra returned to the show, her condition required some changes. One example: they had planned a story late in the season where the still-married Grace gets attention from another man. Now, to avoid having to film those scenes with Debra at her most pregnant, they moved that story into the earlier episode "Strangers with Candice."

By December, the show was back on track, and ready to proceed with its plans: Will dates an Italian cop from Brooklyn; Will and Grace go into business together, "flipping" apartments; Karen dates Lyle Finster to spite his daughter Lorraine, and then, truly in love, proceeds down the aisle; Jack becomes a Student Nurse.

Jhoni explains that the endings to these story lines were left open, so that the writers could assess how they were working before making any final decisions. Karen's romance was always due to conclude with a twist; at one point, one potential ending was for Karen impulsively to marry Beverley Leslie after Lyle leaves her at the altar. With Jack, "We didn't have as much fun with him in nursing school as we thought we would," Jhoni says, adding that the writers discussed several potential ending beats, including Jack getting "discovered" at nursing school graduation and getting back into acting.

And as for Will's romance with Vince the cop, Jhoni explains that the show decided to try something new. In the past, whenever Will or Grace had begun a new relationship, "We always had a plan for the whole thing, that it would start and finish within three or so episodes," she says. "With Vince, we decided that if we found an actor who really clicks with Will, we'd keep going with it and see where it takes us."

Just when it seemed that Season Six was settled, it was announced in March that Debra Messing would miss the last four shows of the season, and the question of how-long-should-they-stay-married was birthed anew. Executive producer Tim Kaiser explains that despite the original plan for divorce in the season finale, "ultimately we couldn't do Grace and Leo's story justice without both of them on the screen," and so, the union survived. But Jhoni notes that in Season Seven, the marriage will ultimately be doomed—if only because Harry Connick needs to return to his full-time music career.

601 DAMES AT SEA
Written By:
ADAM BARR

...er waking up naked in bed together, Will and Jack ridicule the ...a that they might have had a drunken fling, while privately, ...ch makes plans to let the other down easy. Back in New York, ...t when they are about to examine their innermost feelings, ...ren—who returned to her yacht with Rosario on a Jet Ski stolen ...m the Russian freighter—says her surveillance video proves ...thing happened between them. Leo returns home for his forgot-...a bag, and Grace confronts him about Dr. Morty's letter. Leo ...presses his love and upon his departure gives Grace another ...ter, this one saying that he's remaining with her in New York. ...ren weighs her obligation to Rosario as the two take turns ...ving each other's lives.

RECURRING CHARACTERS
Shelley Morrison *as* Rosario
Harry Connick, Jr. *as* Leo

JACK
"Well, this is just great. When we get to St. Bart's, I'm buying myself an EPT, and so help me, if that stick is blue...! I am not going through this alone—not again."

...IC McCORMACK This episode had one of ...rare occasions where I suggested a joke—...ing Grace if her rock-covered purse was ...m the Betty Rubble collection"—and it went ...he show.

...ELLEY MORRISON In the scene where Rosario is choking, I wanted ...do it very subtly, and not gasp broadly—it's not funny if you think, "Oh, my ...d, she's really choking!" And when Karen saves me, I'm supposed to spit ...a piece of biscotti. So I experimented until I found out just what size bite ...take so that it would really fly.

...FF GREENSTEIN The scene where Will and Jack wake up in bed ...gether touches on the great well of affection that we've established ...tween the two of them—and maybe there is more of it from Jack to Will ...n there is from Will to Jack, or at least that Will is willing to let on. In my ...ginal draft of "Lows in the Mid 80s," the moment in the supermarket where ...k declares his love for Will was not there. But Max said, "I think this scene ...eds to be about the fact that Jack loves Will." It was great because it has ...t a depth to that story and to that relationship. Just as Will and Grace have ...lassic romantic-comedy relationship, Jack and Will do, too: they are some-...es adversarial, they depend on each other, and they love each other.

602 LAST EX TO BROOKLYN
Written By:
ALEX HERSCHLAG

Grace keeps her cool when Leo invites ex-girlfriend Diane to a dinner party, but blows her stack when she learns it's the same Diane—the one Will once slept with the one time he tried sex with a woman. While Leo stews over the fact that Grace is jealous about Diane's one night with Will but not about her past relationship with him, Diane breaks down over Will's revelation that their evening meant nothing to him. Karen finds a silver lining when she unloads Lorraine's unappealing dog Chompers on Diane.

GUEST STAR
Mira Sorvino *as* Leo's ex-girlfriend Diane
RECURRING CHARACTER
Harry Connick, Jr. *as* Leo

ALEX HERSCHLAG: Originally we set out to do a story about Grace having to deal with Leo's ex at a dinner party. But then we came up with the idea that it was somebody Will had slept with also. Once the idea of Diane was introduced, everything clicked together.

DIANE
"It's so nice to be around people who eat food. When somebody has a birthday at Vogue, they put a candle in a lifesaver and then argue about who gets the smallest piece."

FYI: Although the seed for this story line was planted in the Season Three episode *Lows in the Mid 80s,* Diane is played here by Mira Sorvino. We had only gotten only a quick glimpse of writers' assistant Lisa Borgnes playing the part in the earlier episode.

JEFF GREENSTEIN: Episodes where all the characters are together in one room with one problem always turn out the best, but they're the hardest to pull off. I love when Mira Sorvino's character recites the lyrics from *You Spin Me Right Round.* To me, that's such a great reference because everyone knows that song at some level in their psyche. It made her breakdown when she was saying the lyrics particularly funny.

603 HOME COURT DISADVANTAGE

Written By: JHONI MARCHINKO

Will and Jack's plan to cheer up Will's mom, Marilyn, with tickets to *Mamma Mia* goes awry when Jack invites her to stay with Will in his apartment. Will wants to revoke the invitation, but Marilyn's newfound happiness makes him relent. After Karen batters Leo with a barrage of tennis balls during a doubles match with Grace and Beverley Leslie, she reveals that it is because she simply doesn't like him. At first, Leo takes the high road, but eventually he realizes that he cannot stand not being liked. Grace finally persuades Karen to keep the peace by pretending to like Leo just as she does with Will.

RECURRING CHARACTERS
Blythe Danner *as* Marilyn Truman
Leslie Jordan *as* Beverley Leslie

GRACE:
"I might be a little rusty. Last time I played was at Camp Hashomer Hatzaire. I won the singles title and got to try ham."

KAREN:
"Yeah, honey, feel free to keep the Jew talk down to a whisper."

LESLIE JORDAN: One of the big laughs in this episode was when Karen and I are playing tennis and are about to serve, and she criticizes the way I keep grunting, like Monica Seles. So I go over to her and say, "I'll have you know, people at the club talk about my serve." And Jim Burrows told me, "When you walk away, do that sort of Daisy Duke thing," meaning like fixing a wedgie in my shorts, because I'm wearing such tight little tennis pants.

604 ME AND MR. JONES

Written By:
GARY JANETTI

JAMES EARL JONES:
"Like I need this crap at my age. I've got Darth Vader money!"

Grace talks Will and Marilyn into admitting that they're sick of each other's company. Marilyn is on her way out the door—literally—when she breaks her ankle and is forced to settle in for a longer stay. Meanwhile, James Earl Jones enrolls in Jack's acting class after a director compares his performance unfavorably with Jack's. Though Jack pronounces him untrainable, "J.Jo" triumphs onstage and credits Jack's ineptitude for his breakthrough. At the gym, Grace shadows another woman's trainer to get free sessions until she learns the workouts are designed to reduce the breasts and enlarge the butt. ★

GUEST STAR
James Earl Jones *as* Himself

RECURRING CHARACTERS
Blythe Danner *as* Marilyn Truman
Emily Rutherfurd *as* Joanne
John Fleming *as* Russell

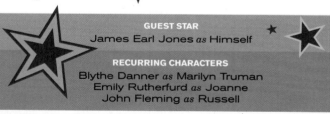

GLENDA ROVELLO: Whenever we used to show Will at the gym, we wou show him at Crunch, which is a real gym. When we were putting together t episode, we started out using Crunch again, but then there was some kind rights issue, so we had to change it at the last minute to a new, unspecifie gym. The set was already standing, so I disguised it with huge posters that I designed with pictures of body parts, and hung them to cover the Crunch graphics on the walls.

605 HEART LIKE A WHEELCHAIR

Written By: JON KINNALLY & TRACY POUST

...l forces Marilyn to stay in her wheelchair so he can hit on Tom, ...unky guy he meets in the park who lives to care for his own ...cient mother. Will finally lures Tom out for dinner, but the date ...ds in disaster when they return home to find that Tom's mom ...s broken her wrist popping Jiffy Pop in Tom's absence. Mean- ...ile, Karen's search for Lorraine leads instead to Lorraine's ...her, Lyle, a charming scoundrel who tricks her into kissing him. ★

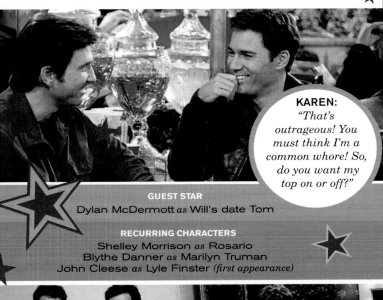

KAREN:
"That's outrageous! You must think I'm a common whore! So, do you want my top on or off?"

GUEST STAR
Dylan McDermott *as* Will's date Tom

RECURRING CHARACTERS
Shelley Morrison *as* Rosario
Blythe Danner *as* Marilyn Truman
John Cleese *as* Lyle Finster *(first appearance)*

TOM:
"Our mothers gave us life. They nourished us. They were our dates to the prom."

...EX HERSCHLAG: I saw a gay man I know pushing his mother in a ...eelchair at the Virgin Megastore, and he told me that taking care of his ...m was one of the great blessings of his life. And a day or so later, I saw ...icago and I held the door open for another man. He never said he was gay, ...he was talking about how he loved Gwen Verdon—and he was wheeling ...mother in a wheelchair, and I thought that might be a good story for Will. ...d then Jon and Tracy wrote this hilarious episode.

...I: This is the first of five episodes that Debra Messing missed due to ...pregnancy.

---

606 NICE IN WHITE SATIN

Written By:
BILL WRUBEL

Grace phones Will from a Cambodian KFC to report that she is suffering nobly. Will's own problems include accompanying a doctor-phobic Karen to a physical with an unprofessional MD; and helping Karen get their money back after Jack quits the nursing classes he has persuaded them to bankroll. When Will and Karen learn Jack was a star student, they get him to confess that he is afraid of success. Jack's ability to get Karen to down the pills she has so far refused to swallow makes him realize that he has found his calling.

GUEST STARS
Jack Black *as* Dr. Isaac Hershberg
Stephanie Faracy *as* Desk Nurse Eva

RECURRING CHARACTER
Laura Kightlinger *as* Nurse Sheila

JEFF GREENSTEIN: We had written a story about Grace wrecking Leo's Doors cover band, which was set up in "Marry Me a Little." That story had to be thrown out completely because with Debra's pregnancy, she was unavailable for a while, and we also didn't have Harry. But we had already shot the other half of that, which was Jack becoming a student nurse. So in deciding how we could piece together an episode, we came up with seeing Karen's visit to the doctor. Fortuitously, Jack Black signed on, and we were able to fashion this episode out of the two story halves.

MEGAN MULLALLY: Originally, it was written for me to spit a pill out just once, but then Jimmy suggested dribbling the pills out two more times. Three times is always best with that kind of stuff, for some reason. I did try to make each time sort of different, and it was hard to keep a straight face when we shot it, because the audience was laughing so hard.

WILL:
"You have to prove you're in good health—or at least, the black market organs that make you up are in good health."

FYI: Series writer Laura Kightlinger, as Nurse Sheila, flirts with Jack Black, her real-life boyfriend—even though it turns out Nurse Sheila is Dr. Hershberg's sister. ★

607 STRANGERS WITH CANDICE

Written By: **SALLY BRADFORD**

Will's date stands him up, and Grace's husband is in Cambodia, so when the gang goes to dinner, each seeks inappropriate comfort: Grace with a former random romantic partner and Will with a woman. Their "dates" leave together after they learn that Will is gay and Grace is married, and both Will and Grace admit their loneliness. When Candice Bergen comes into the restaurant, she and Karen renew their long-running prank war, and Jack becomes its latest casualty.

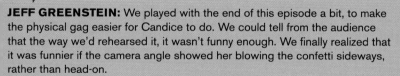

GUEST STARS
Tom Everett Scott *as* Alex
Kali Rocha *(Buffy the Vampire Slayer) as* Stephanie
Candice Bergen *as* Herself,
Karen's "archenemy-slash-best-friend"

JEFF GREENSTEIN: We played with the end of this episode a bit, to make the physical gag easier for Candice to do. We could tell from the audience that the way we'd rehearsed it, it wasn't funny enough. We finally realized that it was funnier if the camera angle showed her blowing the confetti sideways, rather than head-on.

KAREN:
"Honey, you're such a big shot. You're giving me lady wood."

ERIC McCORMACK: There had been a joke in this episode that didn't make it that I loved. The girl at the bar said to Will, "Oh, so you read and you have those arms?" And I said, "Well, I read in the gym." The show was too long, so they cut it.

KAREN:
"I've been thinking about us."
CANDICE:
"Karen, that was a one-time thing. I'd never had sake before."

LORI ESKOWITZ-CARTER: It was hard for me to put Will in a vest, just for them to be able to make fun of him. I fought it for three days, and then gave in and made him one that wasn't totally offensive.

608 A-STORY, BEE-STORY

Written By:
GAIL LERNER

Karen cannot believe that Jack can win a gay spelling bee without cheating, but when she is thrown out for feeding him clues, h[e] gets the chance to prove her wrong. Leo is depressed about turni[ng] down an assignment from Doctors Without Borders, so Will trie[s] to lighten his mood with "Will Truman's New York"—a fussy afternoon of high tea and shoe shopping. When even a Ranger game doesn't do the trick, Leo decides he has to take the job. Will teaches him how to break the news to Grace, but then falls apart when, unexpectedly, Grace decides to go with him.

WILL:
*"What happe[ns]
to the polic[y]
'Don't Ask,
Don't Spell[?]"*

LEO:
"Grace, you want me to be happy, don't you?"
GRACE:
"Not if it affects me negatively in any way."

RECURRING CHARACTER
Harry Connick, Jr. *as* Leo

GLENDA ROVELLO: For this episode, to build the set for "Club Foot," where the spelling bee was being held, I wanted to know what a seedier bar looked like. I wanted to know what the signage was like, and the textures and colors, and to keep up with what's current. For "Club Foot," I sent Tim and Gary [assistants] to the Viper Room on the Sunset Strip.

FYI: To accommodate Debra Messing's pregnancy, Grace appears in only two scenes, in bed, which were actually filmed in Debra Messing's house, allowing her to have bedrest.

FYI: Jack's line about winning the spelling bee—"The other guy couldn't get 'erect,' but I could"—was changed after the NBC cens[or] objected to Jack's original line: "The other guy choked on 'penis.'"

609 THE ACCIDENTAL TSURIS
Written By: JEFF GREENSTEIN

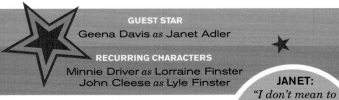

...ace tries tough love on her free-spirited, irresponsible older ...ter, Janet, but when Janet appears to transform into a self-suf...ent corporate employee, Grace is left pining for her old place in ... dysfunctional family dynamic. Karen fends off Lyle's marriage ...posals until Lorraine's outrage at Karen's relationship with her ...her changes her mind.

GUEST STAR
Geena Davis *as* Janet Adler

RECURRING CHARACTERS
Minnie Driver *as* Lorraine Finster
John Cleese *as* Lyle Finster

> **JANET:**
> "I don't mean to toot my own horn, but how many 44-year-olds do you know who have their own apartment and a job?"

...MY BURROWS: After Megan tore a ligament ...ing the week of rehearsals and was confined to ...tches, we had to think about how to restage her ...enes. In most of the scenes, we could have her ...tionary. But the last scene, she needed to come to ...n Cleese's hotel room to say that his daughter was right ...d she was just seeing him to stick it to her. I had an idea, and ...ought Jeff and Jhoni down and said, "Look, what happens if she comes in, ...e has one high heel on one foot and the other high heel broken in her hand, ...d she says something like, 'I ran over here. I slipped in the mud but I had ...ell you something.' Now, she can cross in and then back out, and what's ...at is, that last cross out is so pathetic, that it makes it funnier."

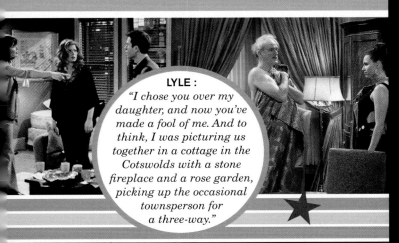

> **LYLE :**
> "I chose you over my daughter, and now you've made a fool of me. And to think, I was picturing us together in a cottage in the Cotswolds with a stone fireplace and a rose garden, picking up the occasional townsperson for a three-way."

...: The Karen-Lyle plot in this episode was originally written as ...t of a planned hour-long show to have been shot in New York ...y; when that plan was scrapped due to Debra Messing's preg-...cy, this story line was combined with the new plot featuring ...et Adler to create this episode.

610 SWIMMING FROM CAMBODIA
Written By: SONJA WARFIELD

Jack complains that his new teacher, Nurse Carver, is a bully, so Karen threatens to kidnap the woman's dogs and makes her promise Jack an A, with no attendance required for the rest of the semester. When Jack misses his classmates' camaraderie, however, he decides to rejoin them. Grace returns from Cambodia for the 25th anniversary of her mother's 50th birthday party, and Will does all he can to prolong her visit. Eventually, he discovers that Grace never booked a return ticket, and when she confesses that she and Leo have decided to separate until his return from Cambodia in the spring, he asks her to move back into his apartment.

> **KAREN:**
> "I once got a rub-on at the airport. Or did I give a skycap a handie? All I know is, I made twenty bucks."

GUEST STAR
Lea DeLaria *as* Nurse Carver

LORI ESKOWITZ-CARTER: Will says it's not, but I actually did put him in a women's sweater for when he comes home from the Barneys sale without Grace's help. This was one rare case where the type of sweater, a tight V-neck, was specifically written into the script

FYI: This episode shows how the writers have chosen to deal with Debra Messing's pregnancy—with fat jokes. Here, Will says he's pretending not to notice the pounds Grace has put on. In a later episode, "A Gay/December Romance," the script called for Karen to call Grace "Rubenesque—and I mean Ruben from *American Idol*," but the line was cut for time.

> **GRACE:**
> "I hate shlepping those bags around. That's one good thing about Cambodia. Those orphans are little, but they can carry a buttload."

611 FANILOW
Written By:
KARI LIZER

Will makes up an excuse to miss Grace's holiday party so he can be first on line for a Barry Manilow concert. After his weak bladder forces him out of line, Will trades his sexual services to an unappealing roadie in exchange for the chance to meet his musical idol. Meanwhile, Grace is hurt when she learns that her mother has lied to her about not being in town for their traditional—and dreaded—Hanukkah shopping. When it appears that Bobbi has chosen Jack's company over hers, Grace is forced to reexamine her mother's importance in her life. ★

JACK:
"What are we in line for? God, from the looks of this crowd, I hope it's birth control."

GUEST STARS
Barry Manilow *as* Himself
Sara Gilbert *(Roseanne) as* the #1 "Fanilow,"
Cheryl, a.k.a. "Copacafana82"
Chris Penn *as* Rudy

a Favorite Episode of…

RECURRING CHARACTER
Debbie Reynolds *as* Bobbi Adler

DEBRA MESSING: *Fanilow* was my favorite episode in Season Six. Since I was very pregnant at that point, it was a challenge for the writers to find new things, more verbal ways for me to be funny. I never realized how physical Grace was until I couldn't do those things anymore. When they had me sitting down in the line for the Manilow tickets, I got to be very sassy. They found a sassiness in Grace that really worked. Also, they wrote one of my favorite moments on the show, when I got to badly sing "Oh Mommy," to the tune of "Mandy" to Debbie Reynolds—I am particularly proud of that performance. ★

ERIC McCORMACK: I make no secret of my love for Barry Manilow. I'm out and proud. When he came on the show, we'd already met a few times and I had already revealed myself a Fanilow. I asked him geeky questions all about the various band members from the live album in 1977. "Where's Keith Loving now? Where's Lee Gurst?" And after his initial amazement over my knowing all these names, he started giving me detailed answers about who had ended up where. He's an interesting guy and has huge fans, but for some reason he's like Rodney Dangerfield—no respect. So I was so happy that this episode was a tribute to him.

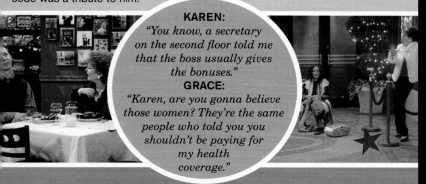

KAREN:
"You know, a secretary on the second floor told me that the boss usually gives the bonuses."
GRACE:
"Karen, are you gonna believe those women? They're the same people who told you you shouldn't be paying for my health coverage."

612 A GAY/DECEMBER ROMANCE
Written By: **JON KINNALLY & TRACY POUST**

JACK:
"This is so unfa[ir]. I would do a sug[ar] daddy for a hor[se]. Hell, I'd do a ho[rse] for a sugar daddy!"

Will revels in the luxuries provided by the plastic surgeon he me[t] at a gallery opening, until his friends point out that he now has his very own sugar daddy. Elsewhere, when the owner of a new neighborhood restaurant Happy Noodle refuses to replace a stea[m]ing hot take-out order that Grace drops on the floor, she calls for a boycott, which Jack and Karen—and eventually Grace herself have a tough time honoring.

GUEST STAR
Hal Linden *(Barney Miller) as* Alan Mills

BILL WRUBEL: When I was living in New York, a noodle shop had just opened up in my apartment building, and I just knew I was going to give th[em] so much business. And like with Grace, the same thing happened. They wanted to charge me for another order of noodles after I dropped mi[ne] and I said I will NOT be coming back in here again! And, I got two of my friends to agree that we'd never go there, and then two days later I saw th[em] eating right in the window. But the place has since gone out of business, so I effectively took them down, albeit about seven years later.

FYI: The two gallery scenes in this episode take place at the "Zelman" and "Offerman" galleries, named for the husbands of Debra Messing and Megan Mullally.

JON KINNALLY: In order to do a story of Will discovering he is a trophy boy, we had to believe he would allow himself to be taken care of. And we decided that, even though Will is well off, and really doesn't need anyone [to] buy him things, he is always the caretaker, and might enjoy, however brief[ly] the role of being cared for. To illustrate this idea, there was a scene at the beginning where Will was making everyone dinner and had been doing so every Friday night for weeks. He was doing all the cooking and cleaning, while the others just complained and barked orders at him. Ultimately this was too much story, and we got rid of it.

(613) ICE CREAM BALLS

Written By:
LAURA KIGHTLINGER

[Wi]ll's shrewd career move to set Jack up with his new client, geeky [ent]repreneur Stuart, backfires when the two hit it off and Jack [be]gins interfering in the deal Will is structuring to sell Stuart's [com]pany. When Will blurts out that he actually bribed Jack with [50] cents and an old Chap Stick to date Stuart in the first place, [Stu]art dumps the truly heartbroken Jack, who has to fight to win [bac]k his new beau. In Vermont, Grace worries about secrets in her [ma]rriage when she and Karen find a secret cache of cash under [th]e mattress in Leo's cabin. But she's relieved for the sake of her [rel]ationship when she learns, at riflepoint, that she and Karen are [in] the wrong cabin and have merely spent the entire nest egg of [Leo]'s next-door neighbors.

GUEST STARS
Kathryn Joosten *(The West Wing)* and Kenneth Tigar *as*
Leo's upstate neighbors Felicia and John

RECURRING CHARACTERS
Kari Lizer *as* Connie
[Da]ve Foley *as* Jack's new boyfriend, Stuart Lamarck *(first appearance)*

> **WILL:**
> *"I need to score points with the firm. I've been trying to make up for mismanaging the office potluck. Like I don't hate myself enough for having two ambrosia salads."*

[JEF]F GREENSTEIN: We had written an episode earlier where Karen had [a g]un, and when we actually got on the stage to rehearse it and had Karen [hol]ding a weapon at a shooting range, it wasn't funny. We killed the episode, [but] we had always talked about Karen and her gun, and we finally do see the [gun] in this episode. The joke about Karen going out to rob the rib joint where [some]body was covering the register turned out, I think, very funny. Maybe it's the [diffe]rence between Karen holding a gun and aiming it at the camera. There [was] a bit in that original episode that I loved. Rosario is at the shooting range, [too,] and one of the writers pitched having her say in voice-over, as she stands [next] to Karen, "All I have to do is turn to the right, pull the trigger, and Mr. [Clea]n will be mine."

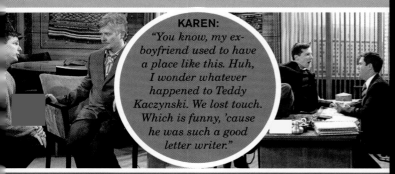

> **KAREN:**
> *"You know, my ex-boyfriend used to have a place like this. Huh, I wonder whatever happened to Teddy Kaczynski. We lost touch. Which is funny, 'cause he was such a good letter writer."*

(614) LOOKING FOR MR. GOOD ENOUGH

Written By: GARY JANETTI

Will takes a cooking class for gay men but, surrounded by Jack and Larry and new lovebirds Jack and Stuart, soon finds himself a sad single in a class full of couples. When a tall, blond newcomer, the one other single man in the room, takes an interest in him, Will is at first delighted—until he suspects the guy may have been hired to do so, and chases him off. Karen's mother, Lois, returns to town, uncharacteristically on the up-and-up. Surprising Karen, Lois recruits Grace to decorate her new place on her meager-but-honest budget and is thrilled with the results—especially when an impressed neighbor offers her a tidy profit, enabling Lois to leave once more to fulfill her dream of owning a McDonald's in Tokyo. ★

GUEST STAR
Tracey Ullman *as* Ann, the instructor of
"Stews and Soups for Gay Men"

RECURRING CHARACTERS
Shelley Morrison *as* Rosario
Jerry Levine *as* Joe
Tim Bagley *as* Larry
Dave Foley *as* Stuart Lamarck
Suzanne Pleshette *as* Lois Whitley

JEFF GREENSTEIN: When we shot this episode, we were thirteen minutes long, but we thought it was fine, because this was supposed to be a super-sized episode. But then NBC juggled the schedule to fit in *The Apprentice*, and we had to cut it back to a half-hour, and cut an enormous amount of material. I still think the episode worked, but we had to cut great jokes. The part of the cooking instructor was not originally written for Tracey Ullman. Once we knew Tracey was going to do the part, we put in the prosthetic finger thing and her weirdness.

> **WILL:**
> *"Let me tell you something. Will Truman doesn't have to pay for it. Will Truman just goes months and months without it, and then just pours all of his sexual energy into his embroidery."*

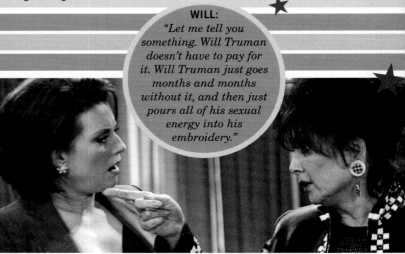

615/616 FLIP FLOP
PARTS 1 & 2
Written By: ADAM BARR & ALEX HERSCHLAG

Will and Grace start a new business venture, buying, refinishing, and then "flipping" apartments, while making a nice profit. When Jack's former mentor Zandra mentions looking to sell her place, the new firm of Will-and-Grace decides that it has found its first project—and, in Jack and Stuart, its first buyers. Meanwhile, Karen's romance with Lyle is going swimmingly, until unwanted houseguest Lorraine guilts Daddy into letting her move into Karen's manse. After selling Zandra's apartment to Jack and Stuart, Will and Grace receive a much higher offer and try to get the apartment back by taking advantage of Jack's cold feet and splitting up the happy couple. But when the guilty "flippers who care" confess their evil plan, they find out that Jack and Stuart have changed their minds about buying the place, anyway. Meanwhile, Karen demands that Lyle discipline his overgrown brat of a daughter, but this time, when faced with an ultimatum, he doesn't choose Karen. Ultimately, it's up to Lorraine to be the bigger woman and reunite her dad with the woman who, as she accepts Lyle's marriage proposal, will become her wicked stepmum.

RECURRING CHARACTERS
Shelley Morrison *as* Rosario
Minnie Driver *as* Lorraine
John Cleese *as* Lyle Finster
Eileen Brennan *as* Zandra
Dave Foley *as* Stuart Lamarck

LYLE:
"Karen, before God, before these toothless whores and aging alcoholics, before my daughter, I proclaim my love. Will you marry me?"

KAREN:
"Of course I will, Lyle. That is how you pronounce it, right?"

JIMMY BURROWS: These *Flip Flop* episodes were originally filmed to air as one hourlong show, but when the network shuffled the Thursday schedule, we had to break it into two halves. It's a problem, because nothing of consequence happens in the first of the two half-hours—it's all meant to set up the second half-hour, which is hysterical.

JEFF GREENSTEIN: Adam Barr had written the first draft of this story, about the first time Will and Grace flip a property, and had written it with a new character as the owner of the apartment. Then we thought, in terms of the shorthand that you inevitably have to resort to in situation comedy to introduce a character quickly, wouldn't it be better if the apartment belonged to Zandra, Jack's old acting teacher? Not only is Eileen Brennan kick-ass funny, but on top of that, we've already established her relationship with Jack, so we saved a lot of time.

JACK:
"Thanks for walking me, Stuart. The streets are really tough out there for a boy alone. Ironically, they're tougher for two boys together."

617 EAST SIDE STORY
Written By:
GAIL LERNER

WILL:
"That apartment belongs to us. I'm not going to let a couple of Ellen-loving, Jenny Shimizu calendar-buying, Uggs-in-the-summertime-wearing lady lovers scare us off."

High on the prospect of their new real-estate venture, Will and Grace decide to flip her Aunt Honey's east side condo, invoking t[he] ire of the reigning lesbian real estate queens, "the Flipping Dyke[s]." After each couple fails in their attempts to divide and conquer through sloppy seduction, Will and Grace agree to keep their bu[si]ness restricted to the west side. Meanwhile, Karen seeks the hel[p] of psychic John Edward in order to gain her late husband's appr[ov]al of her recent engagement. But when the medium isn't availab[le] for a reading, it's the housekeeper to the rescue: turns out, Rosa[rio] does an excellent impression of a heavenly Stan.

GUEST STARS:
Edie Falco *(The Sopranos)* as Deirdre
Chloe Sevigny *(Boys Don't Cry)* as Monet
"the Flipping Dykes"
John Edward as Himself

RECURRING CHARACTER
Shelley Morrison *as* Rosario

EDIE FALCO: The show had called me before, and I was so excited to appear, but I wasn't able to work it out, schedule-wise. That was for the pa[rt] of the cooking instructor, which Tracey Ullman ultimately played. I asked th[em] to keep me in mind for the future, and they called a week later, and I was thrilled. I am so in awe of those four actors. The stuff that they do is really incredible, and really is an art form unto itself. I was impressed with the co[l]laborative nature of the whole thing, and how there were no egos involved[.] They are all so completely involved in the process of making the show, sug[g]esting "You know, it would be funny if I did this." My brain wasn't working as quickly—I was more concerned with getting the blocking right. I was qu[ite] intimidated at first, but all they kept saying was, "It's so easy. It's so much [fun]." I just kept watching them, and I did have fun.

KAREN:
"I just wish it wasn't so big. I'm afraid it's going to leave a mark on Rosario's cheek when I smack her for no particular reason."

FYI: As both Jack and John Edward point out in the episode, Karen's engagement ring comes from "Martin Katz, Jeweler to t[he] Stars," who lends wardrobe supervisor Lori Eskowitz-Carter the pricey pieces seen on the show.

618 COURTING DISASTER

Written By:
SALLY BRADFORD

...ile at the movies with Grace, Jack causes a scene when he spots ...boyfriend, Stuart, and a mystery man at the matinee. Later, ...art explains that, due to an experimentation with heterosexu-...y in college, the younger man is in fact his son, which reminds ...k to reveal that he has a son, too. Meanwhile, Will attempts to ...ch Karen how to drive, but after a run-in with the law, they end ...fighting the ticket in traffic court only to learn that the cop who ...l pulled them over, Vince, is the man with whom Joe and Larry ...l always been trying to set Will up. In the end, it's Karen who ...otiates the plea: she drops her opposition to Vince's ticket in ...hange for a date for Will.

RECURRING CHARACTERS
Dave Foley *as* Stuart Lamarck
Bobby Cannavale *as* police officer *(first appearance)*

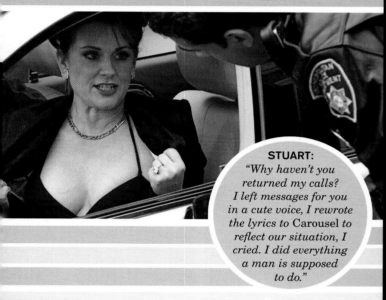

STUART:
"Why haven't you returned my calls? I left messages for you in a cute voice, I rewrote the lyrics to Carousel *to reflect our situation, I cried. I did everything a man is supposed to do."*

3RA MESSING: I love it when they make fun of how badly Grace sings, ...what's even funnier to me is how Grace actually thinks she's a good ...er. In this episode, I was originally supposed to be singing a Mariah Carey ...g, but they said it still sounded too good. So they came up with me sing-...Outkast, but really operatically and nerdy. I love anything about Grace that ...es her imperfect, and not that "leading lady" type who can do anything.

619 NO SEX 'N THE CITY

Written By: STEVE GABRIEL

Will mistakenly takes Grace's advice to play hard to get with his new police officer boyfriend, Vince. But when his game-playing causes a rift in the romance, Will questions Grace's wisdom in matters of the heart, just in time to rescue the relationship. Meanwhile, Jack and Karen are so distraught when they realize that their three favorite television shows—*Sex and the City, Friends* and *Frasier*—are going off the air that they accost Bebe Neuwirth, *Frasier*'s Lilith, when she happens into their coffee-shop hangout.

GUEST STARS
Bebe Neuwirth *as* Herself
Sharon Osborne *as* bartender Nonny

RECURRING CHARACTER
Bobby Cannavale *as* Vince

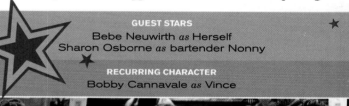

BEBE:
"It's always nice to meet fans. Especially in a public place with lots of witnesses and clearly marked exits."

FYI: Sharon Osborne won her role in the episode at a December 2003 charity auction for the Trevor Project, a foundation to help gay teenagers that many of the *Will & Grace* writers and performers support.

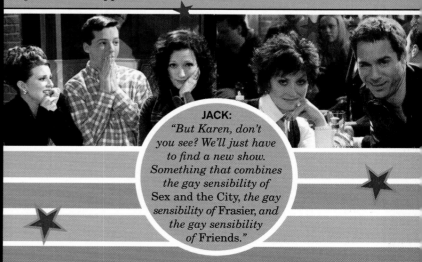

JACK:
"But Karen, don't you see? We'll just have to find a new show. Something that combines the gay sensibility of Sex and the City, *the gay sensibility of* Frasier, *and the gay sensibility of* Friends."

620 FRED ASTAIRE AND GINGER CHICKEN
Written By: AIN GORDON

Will puts his new relationship with Vince to the ultimate test: introducing him to the overly critical Grace. But when Grace abruptly leaves before their scheduled dinner, Will is convinced that she disapproves, and begins to question his own feelings. When he finally confronts Grace about her behavior, she admits that seeing Will and Vince so happy together has upset her in its stark contrast to her messy marriage to Leo. Meanwhile, Karen drops a bombshell on Jack, telling him that, after her upcoming wedding, their friendship as they know it will be over. But when Jack starts to audition for a replacement best friend, a jealous Karen ushers away the finalist candidates, vowing to remain close to the gay man in her life.

RECURRING CHARACTER
Bobby Cannavale *as* Vince

KAREN:
"Just the thought of another woman spanking your fruity booty in a platonic fashion sickens me! That heinie's miney!"

FYI: Vince's reference to the no-food-combining diet proposed by "the redhead from *Taxi*" Marilu Henner is an inside joke: *Will & Grace* director Jimmy Burrows also directed *Taxi*.

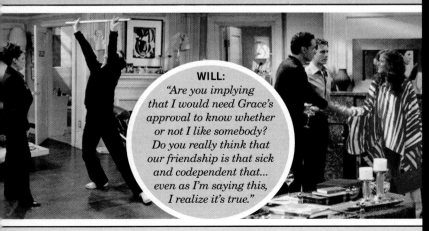

WILL:
"Are you implying that I would need Grace's approval to know whether or not I like somebody? Do you really think that our friendship is that sick and codependent that... even as I'm saying this, I realize it's true."

FYI: The woman on the right, sitting at Café Jacques waiting for her audition to become Jack's new best friend, is series producer Tracy Poust.

621 I NEVER CHEERED FOR MY FATHER
Written By: KARI LIZER

To appease his father's mistress-turned-girlfriend Tina, Will attempts to discover whether there is a new woman in his dad's life. However, when he discovers that the mystery woman is actually his mother, Will must find a way to break the shocking truth to Tina and referee an accidental meeting between the two women. Meanwhile, when Elliot decides to try out for high school cheerleading, Jack is determined to uphold the McFarlan family pom-pom-shaking tradition by coaching his son on how to nab a spot on the squad.

RECURRING CHARACTERS
Michael Angarano *as* Elliot
Blythe Danner *as* Marilyn Truman
Lesley Ann Warren *as* Tina

KAREN: *"So, Elliot, queerleading tryouts, huh?"*
ELLIOT: *"Cheerleading."*
KAREN: *"Yeah, well, we'll see what the kids are calling you when they're stuffing you in your locker on Monday."*

FYI: This episode was originally titled *The Father, The Son, an Holy Crap!*

FYI: On doctor's orders for strict bedrest, Debra Messing does r appear in this episode, nor in any of the remaining episodes of Season Six.

622 SPEECHLESS

Written By:
SALLY BRADFORD

the day of his nursing school graduation, a nervous Jack, ed "Most Popular" in his class, turns to Will for help writing his mmencement address. Reconnecting with his past playwriting eams, Will overanalyzes the speech, searching for—and embel- ning—any life experience that inspired Jack to go to nursing ool. But while delivering the florid address, Jack ultimately alizes that his true dream is still to perform, leading him to nounce from the podium his intention to resume his "career" entertainment.

KAREN:
"Let me get you up to speed. I own you, and what we do is none of your business."
ROSARIO:
"Lady, don't be surprised if your martinis smell of Clorox tonight."

RECURRING CHARACTERS
Shelley Morrison *as* Rosario
Laura Kightlinger *as* Nurse Sheila

: The nurse singing John Mellencamp's "Hurts So Good" at the duation podium is played by Amy Crofoot, Debra Messing's nd-in.

JACK:
"I'm not like you. You've always wanted to be a lawyer. Ever since you were an angry, argumentative baby in pinstriped diapers."

623/624 I DO/OH NO, YOU DI-INT

Part One By: **JEFF GREENSTEIN & JHONI MARCHINKO**
Part Two By: **KARI LIZER & SONJA WARFIELD**

J-LO:
"And just remember, the secret to a happy marriage is... oh, who am I kidding?"

JACK:
"It's so romantic, taking your sacred vows in the city of water slides and titty bars."

Opting to forego, at fiancé Lyle's urging, a grand-society fall wedding and instead to elope to Las Vegas, Karen charters a plane to Sin City with Will and Jack on board. Even Leo returns from Cambodia to meet up with Grace at the wedding, but their reunion is ruined at first by a freak design injury that keeps Grace in New York, then by Leo's confession that he slept with another woman. More drama unfolds when Karen realizes that her new, unbending husband has already begun forcing her to give up her own identity, and she announces at her reception her intention to divorce. But Jack is the most dismayed when he realizes that, with everyone wrapped up in their own lives, no one cares that he just booked a gig as a backup dancer with Jennifer Lopez, an old dancing buddy of Rosario's from the Bronx who has performed at Karen's reception.

GUEST STARS
Jennifer Lopez *as* Herself
Tim Curry *as* Lyle's brother, Marion Finster

RECURRING CHARACTERS
Shelley Morrison *as* Rosario
Harry Connick, Jr. *as* Leo
John Cleese *as* Lyle
Leslie Jordan *as* Beverley Leslie

ROSARIO:
"You said I was your bridesmaid."
KAREN:
"No, I said you're the bride's maid. Now get!"

TIM KAISER: Most actors prefer to play roles rather than [play] themselves, but Jennifer Lopez was happy to get the chance to play herself as a much more down-to-earth person than the tabloid "J.Lo." It wasn't a long, drawn-out process to recruit her, because she loves the show and agreed right away. So we met with her to get a good idea of who she really is, and to write scenes accordingly. We didn't want to show her as some party girl, as she has been portrayed, and didn't want to resort to just a bunch of Ben-bashing, rear-end jokes, which is the typical place most sitcoms would go.

LET'S PLAY PYRAMID

WILL: "YOU GIVE, AND I'LL RECIEVE."

GRACE: "JUST AS GOD INTENDED IT."

WILL: "THE POSTCARD I SENT YOU FROM ITALY. 'EVERYBODY HURTS' BY R.E.M."

GRACE: "THINGS THAT MAKE YOU CRY!"

GRACE: "OK, SHE'S A LAWYER, AND SHE PEES WITH MEN."

WILL: "ALLY McBEAL."

WILL: "MY ONE NIGHT STAND ON FIRE ISLAND."

GRACE: "LATIN THINGS!"

GRACE: "FEMALE SINGER—REALLY, REALLY SKINNY...IF SHE MISSES HER NEXT MEAL, HER HEART WON'T GO ON."

WILL: "CELINE DION!"

WILL: "PROFESSOR GOPNICK'S TEETH—"

GRACE: "THINGS THAT ARE YELLOW."

GRACE: "THINGS THAT ARE DEAD."

WILL: "DRIFTWOOD. JOHN WAYNE. YOUR PARENTS' MARRIAGE."

GRACE: "THINGS THAT YOU LEAN ON."

WILL: "A CANE. A RAILING... EACH OTHER."

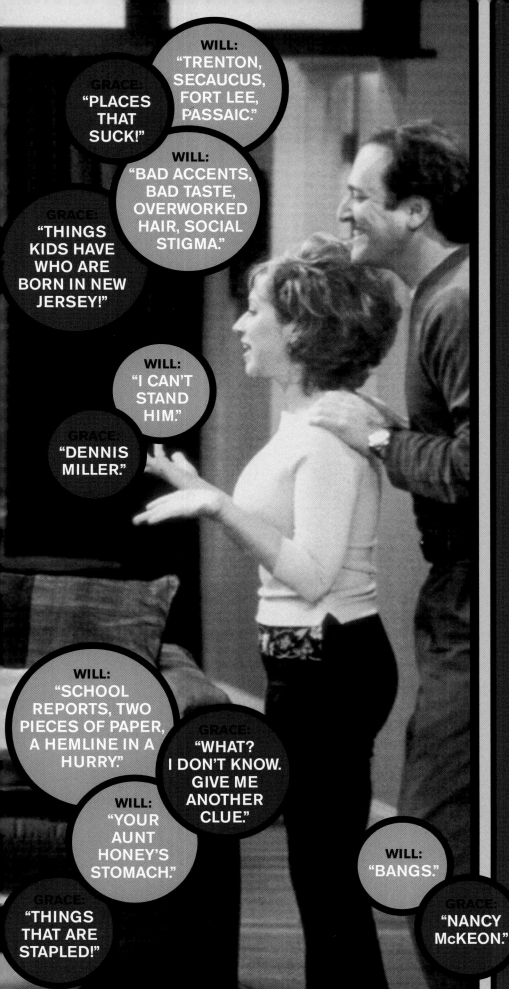

GRACE: "PLACES THAT SUCK!"

WILL: "TRENTON, SECAUCUS, FORT LEE, PASSAIC."

WILL: "BAD ACCENTS, BAD TASTE, OVERWORKED HAIR, SOCIAL STIGMA."

GRACE: "THINGS KIDS HAVE WHO ARE BORN IN NEW JERSEY!"

WILL: "I CAN'T STAND HIM."

GRACE: "DENNIS MILLER."

WILL: "SCHOOL REPORTS, TWO PIECES OF PAPER, A HEMLINE IN A HURRY."

GRACE: "WHAT? I DON'T KNOW. GIVE ME ANOTHER CLUE."

WILL: "YOUR AUNT HONEY'S STOMACH."

WILL: "BANGS."

GRACE: "THINGS THAT ARE STAPLED!"

GRACE: "NANCY McKEON."

NAME GAME

WILL & GRACE
As a philosophy major at Wesleyan University, David Kohan studied the works of twentieth century Jewish theologian Martin Buber. In his book **I AND THOU**, Buber describes two complementary elements of Faith. "The two elements are basically two sides of a relationship," David explains. "You need the *will* to pursue a relationship with God, and the *grace* to receive it. From the time I read that, I always thought that if we ever wrote a love story with two complementary people, those would be great names."

TRUMAN
Will's last name is simply a pun. He's Grace's "true man." In early drafts of the **WILL & GRACE** pilot, Will's last name was, even more precisely, Herman, or "her man"—but the name did not "clear" when it was determined that there were potentially real-life Will Hermans in New York City who might object.

ADLER
Grace's last name was one of the few names not borne of Max and David's real life. "We just liked the sound of it," David explains. "But also," Max adds, "it was specifically a Jewish name, and we wanted Grace to be Jewish."

ROB AND ELLEN
Will and Grace's college friends are named for occasional series writers Rob Lotterstein and Ellen Idelson, whom Max and David met while writing for the HBO series **DREAM ON**. "We have used their names in practically everything we've ever written," Max explains.

THE BOOK OF KAREN

"MILK, MILK, LEMONADE... AROUND THE CORNER, FUDGE IS MADE."

"I FELT BAD BECAUSE I HAD NO SHOES, BUT THEN I MET SOMEONE WHO HAD REALLY BAD SHOES."

"IF YOU WANT PEOPLE TO LIKE YOU, YOU HAVE TO BUY THEM THINGS."

"DID YOU THINK YOU COULD GET INTO HEAVEN WEARING BODY GLITTER? WELL, YOU CAN'T."

"CHRISTMAS CELEBRATES THE BIRTH OF OUR LORD, CARTIER."

"HONEY, I OFTEN ASK PEOPLE ON MY STAFF TO DO DIFFERENT THINGS. COOK SOMETIMES CLEANS. CLEANER SOMETIMES COOKS. DRIVER SOMETIMES PROVIDES AN ALIBI."

"THE BEST WAY TO MAKE YOU FEEL GOOD IS TO MAKE SOMEONE ELSE LOOK BAD."

"WHEN YOU'VE GOT THE BEAU, WHO NEEDS THE 'MO?"

NAME GAME

JACK

When creating the character of Will's best friend, Max and David combined attributes from several of the more outrageous people in their own lives. "He's a composite," Max explains, noting that Jack, as we now know him, was assembled from traits from his former boyfriend, Paul Rowan (who had a predilection for bumping stomachs with hot girls); from a campy, Steve-and-Eydie loving friend named Tom Campbell; and infamously, from a friend named Jack Deamer (who later sued the creative duo for compensation for the portrayal in 2001).

The choice of Jack's last name was inspired by Dave McFarland, who once worked with Max Mutchnick's brother. As a child, he had told Max, he was cruelly nicknamed "McFairyland"—and the show's creators had kept this obvious opportunity for joke-writing in mind.

KAREN

The character of Grace's super-wealthy assistant was based on a woman also named Karen, a college classmate of Max's who is the heiress to the Fisher Construction Company empire in Manhattan. "The inspiration really came from only one thing about her," Max remembers, "which was that she used to take a limousine to work. She kept a day job because she wanted to feel real."

Karen was given the last name "Walker" for the sake of irony; with a limousine and elderly Driver at her disposal, Karen doesn't have to walk anywhere.

ROSARIO

When Max and David needed a first name for Karen's right-hand maid, they needed look no further than to Max's own household help. The real-life Rosario now tends not only to Max Mutchnick's house, but to Sean Hayes' as well.

MASON AND OLIVIA

Karen's unseen stepchildren were named for David Kohan's daughter Olivia and Max's nephew Mason. "I caused an enormous rift in my family when we started writing about how fat 'Mason' was," Max admits. "My Mason is a little heavy, so that wasn't a good thing."

QUIZ

WHICH OF THE FOLLOWING CREATURES WAS NOT A CHILDHOOD PET?

(A) *Klaus von Puppy*

(B) *Daisy*

(C) *Tokie*

(D) *ShuShu*

Answer: A) Klaus Von Puppy is the name of Jack's current dog, originally adopted by Will and Grace. Alas, Daisy, Tokie and ShuShu are now just childhood memories for Will, Grace and Karen, respectively—even if Karen may not really remember what species of pet ShuShu was.

WHICH OF THE FOLLOWING FOODS DOES GRACE ACTUALLY NOT LIKE?

(A) *Carrot cake*

(B) *Individually wrapped processed cheese singles*

(C) *Lox*

(D) *Shrimp*

Answer: A) There aren't many foods that don't appeal to Grace—she maps out her visit to a brunch buffet around the expensive items she eats them, and is willing to keep eating food-poisoning tainted like lox, loves the feel of cheese singles against her face before shrimp. But carrot cake? It's reason enough to make her skip a party, like the one years ago for Will's law school graduation.

WHERE DOES CRAZY NEIGHBOR VAL BASSETT NOT CLAIM TO HAVE LIVED?

(A) *Apartment 15F*

(B) *Apartment 12E*

(C) *Apartment 9C*

(D) *Her storage unit*

Answer: C) Unhinged as she is, Val has never claimed to cohabitate with Will in 9C. She has lived in 12E, and in her storage unit during the Y2K scare. But perhaps strangest of all is her claim when she first meets Will, that she lives in apartment 15F. Will should have known right away that she's crazy—it's only a twelve story building.

WHICH OF THE FOLLOWING IS NOT AN UPDATE OF THE WORLD-RE-NOWNED CABARET ACT, "JUST JACK?"

(A) *Jack 2000*

(B) *Solamente Jack*

(C) *Jack 2001*

(D) *Jack, My World*

Answer: D) Never one to let his act grow stale, Jack adapted his "Just Jack" concept into new editions for 2000 and 2001, and even a Spanish-language version, after a suggestion from then-wife, Rosario. We have yet to see "Jack, My World," but stay tuned—his career ain't over yet.

WHICH OF THE FOLLOWING IS NOT AMONG WILL'S REPERTOIRE OF IMPRESSIONS?

(A) *Valerie Harper in* Rhoda

(B) *Eva Gabor in* Green Acres

(C) *Gene Rayburn, host of* The Match Game

(D) *Regis Philbin*

Answer: B) Will entertains Grace with his Regis, annoys her by finding any excuse to do his Rhoda, and occasionally slips a Match Game "blank" into his conversation. But so far, we've never heard him say that he "gets allergic smelling hay."

WHICH OF THE FOLLOWING MOVIE TITLES WAS NOT PARODIED AS AN EPISODE TITLE FOR WILL & GRACE?

(A) *The Unsinkable Molly Brown*

(B) *The Accidental Tourist*

(C) *Bedknobs and Broomsticks*

(D) *Alice Doesn't Live Here Anymore*

Answer: C) While the show has titled episodes The Unsinkable Mommy Adler, The Accidental Tsuris and Alice Doesn't Lisp Here Anymore, there has not yet been a spoof on the title of the 1971 children's film (but don't several dirty possibilities come to mind?)

WHICH OF THE FOLLOWING FINE RETAIL ESTABLISHMENTS HAS NEVER EMPLOYED JACK MCFARLAND?

(A) *Abercrombie & Fitch*

(B) *Starbucks*

(C) *Barneys*

(D) *Banana Republic*

Answer: A) While Jack has been a barista and was briefly at Barneys and the Banana, he has surprisingly never been employed by Abercrombie & Fitch—but he undoubtedly hoards old copies of their catalog.

WHICH OF THE FOLLOWING WOMEN IS NOT A RIVAL OF KAREN'S?

(A) *Marlo Thomas*

(B) *Katie Couric*

(C) *Candy Pruitt*

(D) *Candice Bergen*

Answer: B) Karen enjoys trading barbs with the Candys, and keeps voodoo dolls of Marlo in her trunk. But she doesn't even know Katie—much to Grace's dismay after she promises access to Katie's apartment as a field trip for Grace's design class.

WHICH OF THE FOLLOWING CELEBRITIES HAS NOT OBTAINED A RESTRAINING ORDER AGAINST JACK?

(A) *Justin Timberlake*

(B) *Kevin Bacon*

(C) *Ricky Martin*

(D) *The U.S. Gymnastics Team*

Answer: C) As far as we know, Ricky Martin has never taken any precautions against "professional crazed fan" Jack McFarland—although he probably should.

WHICH OF THE FOLLOWING IS NOT ONE OF KAREN WALKER'S ALIASES?

(A) *Anastasia Beaverhausen*

(B) *Pilar Palabunda*

(C) *All Beef Patty*

(D) *Butt Masterson*

Answer: D) Fashionably equipped with the proper alias for any occasion—Anastasia for going downscale incognito, Pilar for beating up businessmen in Chinatown and Patty for attending lesbian group therapy—Karen has never gone by the handle "Butt Masterson," which is actually one of Jack's naughty internet screen names.

WHICH OF THE FOLLOWING IS NOT A SEXUAL NICKNAME GIVEN TO WILL?

(A) *The BJ Kid*

(B) *Clammy Hands*

(C) *The Nibbler*

(D) *Big Foot*

Answer: D) Although Will still claims that his shipmates on that gay cruise dubbed him "The BJ Kid" because of his skills at blackjack, the correct answer is "Big Foot," which is one of the cruel childhood nicknames Grace had to endure.

WHICH OF THE FOLLOWING IS NOT A ROOM IN THE WALKER PARK AVENUE MANSE IN THE SKY?

(A) *Kids' playroom*

(B) *Gift wrapping room*

(C) *Billiard Room*

(D) *Kitchen*

Answer: B) Karen doesn't seem to have her own Aaron and Candy Spelling-esque gift-wrapping room yet, but now that Mason and Olivia have gone to live with their mother, their old playroom may just be ripe for a conversion.

WHICH OF THE FOLLOWING IS NOT ONE OF THE CHILDHOOD GAMES WILL PLAYED WITH HIS MOTHER?

(A) *Dry Run with Casserole Dish*

(B) *The Vacuum Game*

(C) *Find the Crust on the Tea Sandwiches at Bergdorf's*

(D) *Pick Out Today's Bra*

Answer: A) Will's rather close early relationship with his mother Marilyn did include some strange games which, like the Vacuum Game and its fudge brownie reward, often involved food. But the Dry Run is actually a trademark of Jack's mother Judith McFarland, who when invited to Thanksgiving timed how long it would take to get to Will's front door while carrying her casserole.

WHICH OF THE FOLLOWING IS NOT ONE OF THE NAMES GRACE HAS PICKED OUT FOR HER FUTURE DAUGHTERS?

(A) *Lilly*

(B) *Ursula*

(C) *Ariel*

(D) *Sheila*

Answer: D) Grace has always wanted to name her first daughter after her great grandmother Lilly, and tells Will when they consider having a baby together that she likes Ursula and Ariel—in fact, quite a few names from *The Little Mermaid*. But Sheila, as she tactlessly tells Nurse Sheila while waiting to get inseminated, is a whore's name.

WHICH OF THE FOLLOWING IS NOT ONE OF GRACE'S MANY RELATIVES?

(A) *Uncle Winnie*

(B) *Uncle Funny*

(C) *Aunt Pesha*

(D) *Aunt Honey*

Answer: A) Grace's family does include phlebitis sufferer Funny, clairvoyant Pesha, and tacky Honey, but elderly Uncle Winnie, who is on such strong medication he mistakes people for balloons, belongs to Will.

IN WHICH OF THE FOLLOWING SPORTS DOES JACK'S SON ELLIOT NOT PARTICIPATE?

(A) *Basketball*

(B) *Soccer*

(C) *Wrestling*

(D) *Cheerleading*

Answer: C) Elliot plays basketball and suffers through soccer, despite his lack of fancy footwork. Jack is happier to see him pick up the pom-poms: turns out, Elliot comes from four generations of male McFarland cheerleaders, including great grandpappy Liam, who continued to cheer after losing an arm in Okinawa. But so far, Elliot has not gone out for wrestling—although unlike with basketball, Jack would probably be happy to attend those matches.

WHICH OF THE FOLLOWING WEDDING CEREMONIES DID GRACE'S BEHAVIOR NOT NEARLY RUIN?

(A) *Jack and Rosario*

(B) *Joe and Larry*

(C) *Karen and Lyle*

(D) *Danny and Sarah*

Answer: C) Both Will and Grace could hardly be described as the ideal wedding guests—they bickered their way through both the Jack/Rosario and Joe/Larry weddings, and Grace's jokes about Danny nearly scared his fiancée Sarah into leaving him at the altar. But Grace can't be blamed for the failure of Karen and Lyle's marriage; after injuring her back installing a sex room for one of the women of The View, she was unable to fly to Las Vegas to attend.

WHICH OF THE FOLLOWING IS NOT ON KAREN'S PAYROLL?

(A) *Pharmacist*

(B) *Backup Pharmacist*

(C) *Physical Trainer*

(D) *Plastic Surgeon*

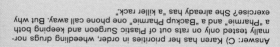

Answer: C) Karen has her priorities in order, wheedling drugs normally tested only on rats out of Plastic Surgeon and keeping both a "Pharmie" and a "Backup Pharmie" one phone call away. But why exercise? She already has "a killer rack."

WHICH OF THE FOLLOWING DOES KAREN NOT CLAIM TO HAVE BEEN ONE OF ROSARIO'S PASTIMES IN HER HOMELAND OF EL SALVADOR?

(A) *Boxing donkeys for cash*

(B) *Playing "Spook the Horse" with her car horn*

(C) *Scooping ceviche out of a bucket on a dirty soccer field*

(D) *Hunting in packs and burying food*

Answer: B) Although Rosario explains that she was an educated schoolteacher in her homeland, Karen insists that she was engaged in some rather unsavory activities. But not "Spook the Horse," which is one of Karen's own favorite games as she's being chauffeured through the countryside.

WHICH OF THE FOLLOWING TV SHOWS IS NOT ONE OF JACK'S FAVORITES?

(A) *Along Came You*

(B) *Rumpole of the Bailey*

(C) *Friends*

(D) *Sex and the City*

Answer: B) Jack and Karen are traumatized by the loss of *Friends* and *Sex and the City,* and Jack is a fan of fictional sitcom *Along Came You*—well, at least he was until they chickened out of showing a gay kiss. But the British comedy *Rumpole of the Bailey*—which Jack calls Bunghole Up my Mainly—is a favorite of Will's.

WHICH ACTING GIG IS NOT ON KAREN'S RESUME?

(A) *The Captain Lenny Show*

(B) *Dynasty*

(C) *Mama's Family*

(D) *Fetish video Next to Godliness*

Answer: A) Karen's eclectic career has included appearances on '80s primetime shows *Dynasty* and *Mama's Family,* although her lines in the latter ended up on the cutting room floor. And she is surprisingly embarrassed by her long-ago role in the fetish video. But Karen has never shared the screen with Will's childhood idol and local kiddie TV host Captain Lenny, which is a shame—with that voice, she'd be perfect for cartoons.

WHICH OF THE FOLLOWING IS NOT A STRICTLY UNSEEN CHARACTER ON WILL & GRACE?

(A) *Grace's father Martin Adler*

(B) *Karen's stepson Mason Walker*

(C) *Will's ex-boyfriend Michael*

(D) *Jack's good friend Rory*

Answer: C) After many mentions of his name, Michael briefly and suddenly reappeared in Will's life in the show's second season, hiring Grace to decorate the New York townhouse he now shares with his new boyfriend. But Martin Adler, Mason Walker and Rory remain men of mystery.

WHICH OF THE FOLLOWING NICE JEWISH BOYS IS NOT ONE OF THE DATES WITH WHOM GRACE'S MOTHER HAS TRIED TO SET HER UP?

(A) *Stanley Fink,* the mortician

(B) *Scott Barky,* who had an obsessive need to touch everything ten times

(C) *Andy Felner,* a former campmate at *Camp Ramah* who played Woodchuck #2 in the Noah's Ark production

(D) A guy from *nicejewishchiropractors.com*

Answer: C) While Bobbi did pick all four potential mates, she is branching out beyond Grace with her matchmaking efforts: she brings Andy Felner to town as a date for Will.

WHICH OF THE FOLLOWING IS NOT A ROLE IN AN ÜBERFEMINIST LOCAL THEATER PRODUCTION FOR WHICH BOBBI ADLER HAS AUDITIONED?

(A) *Millie Loman* in Death of a Salesperson

(B) *Prof. Carol Hill* in The Music Person

(C) *Kim* in Ms. Saigon

(D) *Title role* in Queen Lear

Answer: C) Bobbi won the roles of Millie Loman and Carol Hill, and lost out on playing *Queen Lear.* But so far, the Schenectady Women's Center has not mounted Ms. Saigon.

WHICH OF THE FOLLOWING TWOSOMES DID NOT MEET EACH OTHER IN THE 1980's?

(A) *Joe and Larry*

(B) *Stan and Lorraine*

(C) *Rob and Ellen*

(D) *Karen and Rosario*

Answer: B) Rob and Ellen met at Columbia University in 1985, while at the same time Karen met Rosario in a nightclub. And in 2004, Joe and Larry mentioned recently celebrating their fifteenth anniversary. But Karen's late ex-husband Stan did not meet his mistress Lorraine Finster until his stint in prison in the late 1990's.

WHICH OF THE FOLLOWING FAMOUS FIGURES HAS NOT SLEPT WITH KAREN?

(A) *Martina Navratilova*

(B) *Teddy Kaczinski, the Unabomber*

(C) *James Earl Jones*

(D) *Every member of Crosby, Stills, Nash & Young*

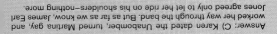

Answer: C) Karen dated the Unabomber, turned Martina gay, and worked her way through the band. But as far as we know, James Earl Jones agreed only to let her ride on his shoulders—nothing more.

WHICH OF THE FOLLOWING CHARACTERS IS NOT A PARENT?

(A) *Janet Adler*

(B) *Larry*

(C) *Jack*

(D) *Stuart Lamarck*

Answer: A) Jack and Stuart bond when they realize that each accidentally fathered a son, while another gay man, Larry, adopted daughter Hannah with his partner, Joe. But Grace's burned-out older sister Janet luckily does not have any children.

WHICH OF THE FOLLOWING AREAS WAS NOT THE SETTING FOR ONE OF LEO'S ASSIGNMENTS FROM DOCTORS WITHOUT BORDERS?

(A) *Africa*

(B) *Thailand*

(C) *Guatemala*

(D) *Cambodia*

Answer: B) Much to Grace's dismay, Leo has accepted assignments in Africa, Guatemala and Cambodia. If only he had been sent to Thailand, perhaps Grace would have stayed with him, for the peanut sauce alone.

WHICH OF THE FOLLOWING IS NOT THE NAME OF A GAY BAR FREQUENTED BY WILL AND JACK?

(A) *Crisco Disco*

(B) *The Tight End*

(C) *The Rainbow Room*

(D) *Boy Bar*

Answer: C) Will and Jack have partied at all of the above establishments, including the famous Rainbow Room atop Rockefeller Center, where Will's parents had their anniversary party and Grace and Leo got married. But even with their presence, the Rainbow Room could hardly be counted as a gay bar.

WHICH OF THE FOLLOWING CHARACTERS HAS NOT APPEARED MORE THAN ONCE ON WILL & GRACE?

(A) *Will's father's mistress Tina*

(B) *Jack's mother, Judith McFarland*

(C) *Grace's ex-fiance, Danny*

(D) *Karen's rival, Beverley Leslie*

Answer: B) Jack's mother Judith has appeared only once, attending Thanksgiving dinner at Will's apartment, where she dropped the bomb that Jack's father was a man in a Nixon mask with whom she had anonymous sex at a pool party in 1968. After that, Jack's "coming-out" news seemed not so earth-shattering.

WHICH OF THE FOLLOWING CELEBRITIES HAS NOT APPEARED ON WILL & GRACE?

(A) *Madonna*

(B) *Elton John*

(C) *Michael Douglas*

(D) *Elizabeth Taylor*

Answer: D) Although Grace was given her middle name after Elizabeth Taylor, an idol of her mother Bobbi's, the legendary actress has so far not appeared on the show.

WHICH OF THE FOLLOWING IS NOT ONE OF STANLEY WALKER'S MANY ASSETS?

(A) *A yacht, the All You Can Eat*

(B) *The retail chain "Senor Mattress"*

(C) *A Krispy Kreme franchise*

(D) *A sweat-shop factory in Asia paying children eleven cents an hour to produce tube socks*

Answer: C) Although Stan's high-volume patronage undoubtedly has kept the donut chain afloat, he has never been said to own any share in the Krispy Kreme company.

YOUR SCORE

0-8

As Karen might say, "What are you, headless?"

9-16

That's okay. Jack is pretty sure that all the questions you did get right were the ones about him anyway. He says to tell you, "Love you, love everything about you, thinking about being you for Halloween."

17-24

Grace knew you wouldn't know them all. She's singing and dancing right now: "I told you so! I told you so!"

25-32

You know waaayyy too much about a TV show. As Will would note, "No wonder you're alone."

ABS-AND-PECSOLUTELY

\abs and peks•oh•'loot•lee\ *(adv)*: without a gay doubt.

ANGRY ARMS

\'an•gry arms\ *(n)*: the gesture Will makes when reprimanding Jack.

BELGIAN WAX, A

\'bel•jun waks\ *(n)*: a regular waxing job, but it hurts so much that you treat yourself to a waffle afterwards.

BIG GIRL UPSTAIRS, THE

\big gurl up•'stehrs\ *(n)*: God

BO-CURIOUS

\bo•'kur•ee•us\ *(adj)*: the state of being potentially interested in getting Botox injections, but unable to admit said interest.

BRUSBAND

\'brus•band\ *(n)*: derived from both the words "husband" and "bride," one of the grooms at a gay wedding, fulfilling the roles of both husband and bride.

CARPOUCHE

\car•'pooch\ *(n)*: a stickler or a grouch; one who will not allow invented words while playing Scrabble.

COMING OUT-FIT

\'kum•ing 'out•fit\ *(n)*: the apparel one wears for the meal at which he comes out to his mother.

DANSKIN [ON] YOUR MANSKIN

\'dan•skin on yer 'man•skin\ *(n)*: skin-tight clothing on a gay man.

DOMO ARIGATOS, MR. TOMATOES

\do•mo ah•ree•'gah•toes mis•ter to•'may•toes\ *(n)*: male genitals (see also "James and the Giant Peaches")

DON QUEERLEONE

\dahn kweer•lee•'oh•nee\ *(n)*: the head of the fabled gay mafia.

FANILOW

\'fan•eh•low\ *(n)*: a Barry Manilow fan so obsessed that he or she would hang out in internet fan rooms and even possibly make his or her own Barry bobble-head.

FLAMING SCHNAPPS ACT OF 1987

\fla•ming shnahps akt\ *(n)*: the legislation which gave homosexuals the right to drink whatever they want.

FREAK BENCH

\freek bench\ *(n)*: the bleacher seating on the sidelines where the ungainly and socially awkward are banished from the seventh grade dance.

GAY CHURCH

\gay cherch\ *(n)*: a gym.

GAY HIGH HOLY DAY, THE

\gay hi hoe•lee day\ *(n)*: aka Halloween.

GAY IT FORWARD, TO

\gay it for•werd\ *(vi)*: the act of a more experienced gay man coaching a man who is just coming out of the closet, just as he himself was coached.

GAY JEAN, THE

\gay jeen\ *(n)*: French, low-cut women's jeans when worn accidentally by a gay man.

GEISHA HAND

\\'gay•shuh hand\\ *(n)*: the mannerism of holding one's hand near one's mouth to cover a flaw, for instance a sore from having had a mole zapped at the dermatologist.

HANDS OF JUDGMENT

\\hands uv 'juj•ment\\ *(n)*: gestures made while criticizing someone's taste, clothing, friends or apartment.

HOMOJO

\\'ho•mo•jo\\ *(n)*: the ability to maintain a deep friendship and connection between a gay man and his hag.

HOMO NOSTRA, THE

\\ho•mo•'no•strah\\ *(n)*: another name for the feared gay mafia.

JACKINESE

\\jak•i•'neez\\ *(n)*: the language one speaks when discussing dating boys.

JACKTING

\\'jak•ting\\ *(n)*: the art of staging a classic play but changing it to include a desired, yet wholly imaginary, homosexual subtext.

JACK-U-CCINO

\jak•u•'chee•no\ *(n)*: the coffee drink speciality of the house at New York's Café Jacques.

JAMES GIRL JONES

\jay•mz gurl jonze\ *(n)*: the inner, loosened-up, apparently gay self that is believed to live inside James Earl Jones, and would lead to him becoming a better actor.

JOCK BLOCK, THE

\jahk blahk\ *(n)*: the maneuver of cutting a friend off from picking up a guy in order to pursue said guy oneself. (Spanish: *El Jocko Blocko.*)

MACHO GASPACHO

\mah•cho ga•spah•cho\ *(n)*: a donation of sperm, subsequently kept cold.

MANOREXIC

\man•or•eks•ik\ *(n)*: the condition when one cannot bear to eat, due to depression over losing a man.

Mc FARLAND METHOD, THE

\mik•'fahr•land 'meh•thud\ *(n)*: a new school of acting, named for its founder, which has already helped countless aspiring actors, actresses, and act-transgendered individuals.

MISTER SISTER

\\'mih•stah 'sih•stah\\ *(n)*: either a drag queen, or the real Cher, who can be mistaken for one.

MOOD STABILIZER PARTY MIX

\\mood steh•bil•i•zer pahr•tee miks\\ *(n)*: a party food favored by rich socialites consisting of uppers, downers, and candy corn, and costing $3000 per batch.

MULTIPLE SARCASM

\\mull•tih•pull sahr•kaz•um\\ *(n)*: a series of bitchy jokes made in a row.

NAG HAG

\\nag hag\\ *(n)*: the female owner of a gay horse.

OLIVER WENDELL HOMO

\\'ah•lih•ver 'wen•dul 'ho•mo\\ *(n)*: a gay litigation attorney.

PENELOPE CRUZ, TO

\\puh•'nel•oh•pee krooz\\ *(n)*: to insinuate one's way into a closed, elite group by starting a relationship with one of its members.

POCKET GAY

\pah•kit gay\ *(n)*: a diminutive gay man, of a perfect, portable size.

POOP 'N' CRUISE

\'poop en krooz\ *(n)*: walking one's dog in order to pick up men.

POOR PEOPLE'S JEWELRY

\poor 'pee•pulz 'joo•el•ree\ *(n)*: a gift of flowers.

PSYCHO CHIC

\'sy•koh sheek\ *(adj)*: a depressed woman's hairstyle after several consecutive days in bed, mourning for her relationship with an ex-boyfriend. Also, the same look Anne Heche had when they picked her up in Fresno.

SAFETY SPERM

\safe•tee sperm\ *(n)*: a best male friend's reproductive fluid, to be used only as a fallback position by a single woman who never meets Mr. Right. *Origin:* "safety school," a college into which one knows one can gain admission, to be used as a last resort.

SCS

\ess see ess\ *(n)*: Scaredy Cat Syndrome. a strain of the Fraidy Cat virus, it is marked by characteristic cowardice and the unwillingness to stand up to a childhood bully now working at your law firm.

SPRAMP

\\'spramp\\ *(vt)*: to spray, foam or bubble, as does a liquid.

STAKE IT

\\'stak it\\ *(vi)*: a workout catch phrase which is both a motivational tool and a stylistic flourish to set one apart.

SUCK PILE, THE

\\suk pile\\ *(n)*: the area of the presents table where bad gifts go—usually includes savings bonds and homemade cards—and may be the appropriate place for the certificate for an adopted panda.

WILLFLOWER

\\'wil•flau•er\\ *(n)*: a gay man who stands in the corner of a bar and observes; a gay wallflower.

YENTL BREAKDOWN, A

\\'yen•tul 'brak•daun\\ *(n)*: a fit of nervousness brought on by the prospect of a homosexual male meeting his father for the first time, culminating in the frenzied singing of Barbra Streisand's *Papa Can You Hear Me?*

ZSA ZSA, TO

\\'zhah zhah\\ *(vt)*: to slap a metermaid.

Thanks

MAX MUTCHNICK, DAVID KOHAN, JAMES BURROWS AND THE WRITERS, CREW AND "FAB FOUR" CAST OF THEIR CREATION WILL & GRACE FOR THEIR INCREDIBLE OPENNESS AND COOPERATION.

To my interviewees Tim Bagley, Leigh-Allyn Baker, Eileen Brennan, Dan Bucatinsky, Edie Falco, Tom Gallop, Leslie Jordan, Rob Lotterstein, Anne Meara, Camryn Manheim, Shelley Morrison, Peter Paige, Kali Rocha, and Scott Seomin at GLAAD.

Kim Niemi, April Brock, Jamie French and Ken Samuel at NBC
Michele Teper at Joan Pearce Research
Ajay Dass at Central Casting
warmup comic Roger Lundblade
Leigh Wetzel, web designer for justjack.com, for her time and generosity

My agent Deborah Warren, and on the publishing end, Julie Merberg, Michael Robin and Richard Fraiman

Mary Kate, Angelo, Tom, Joe and Alison Colucci
Martin Colucci & John Volland
Sally Starin & June Ploch
My hosts in Los Angeles: Beverly D'Angelo, Willie Garson, Tom Jacobson & Ramone Muniz,
James Sie & Doug Wood, and Marc Wolf
Bonnie Datt & Chris Lowe
Frank DeCaro, Sr.
Jay Kogen
Karen, Rick, Jake & Lissy Langberg
Cathryn Michon
Rich Sands, Lois Draegin, Rochell Thomas, Greg Evans, Robert Rorke,
Ari Karpel and the editors and staff at TV Guide
My agents, Ryan Saul and Melissa Read at the Jim Preminger Agency
Patricia Altomare, Louisa Dette, Rosalina Primiano and Judy Bradley

To Frank DeCaro, without whose constant encouragement and support
this book would not have been possible.

To Number Seventeen: Andrew James Capelli, Nomi Joy, Emily Oberman, Bonnie Siegler,
Buster Owen August Scher, and Denise Sommer.

NBC would like to thank the following people who worked day to day to bring this project to fruition:

April Brock, Kim Niemi, Jamie French, Tim Kaiser, Steve Sandoval, Amanda Kowalsky, Shannon Dixon,
Jim Colucci, Deborah Warren, Julie Merberg, Bonnie Siegler, Emily Oberman, Andrew James Capelli,
Sara Newberry, Victoria Alfonso, and Richard Fraiman

MAX MUTCHNICK & DAVID KOHAN FOR SHARING THEIR VISION AND THE PROCESS INVOLVED IN
CREATING A HIT TELEVISION SERIES.

A VERY SPECIAL THANK YOU TO DEBRA MESSING, ERIC MCCORMACK, SEAN HAYES, AND
MEGAN MULLALY FOR THEIR CONTRIBUTIONS TO THIS BOOK AND FOR BRINGING WILL, GRACE,
JACK & KAREN TO LIFE EVERY WEEK ON THE SCREEN.

THE AMAZING WRITING TEAM AT WILL & GRACE

THE CREW AND CREATIVE TEAM AT WILL & GRACE, WHO GAVE SO GENEROUSLY OF THEIR
TIME TO MAKE SURE THE INFORMATION IN THIS BOOK IS ACCURATE

We would be remiss not to mention the following people who contributed their time and efforts as well:

Lorna Bitensky, Jenness Brewer, BJ Carretta, Damian Clinton, Lawnie Grant, Kevin Holden,
Jon Hookstratten, Frederick Huntsberry, Stacey Irvin, Loretta Kraft, John Lavet, Lauren McCollester,
Nancy McDyer, John Miller, George Nunes, David Pai-Ritchie, Jerry Petry, Alan Seiffert,
Eric van der Werff, Ed Wilson, Bob Wright, and Jeff Zucker